THE
NEW RADICALISM
IN AMERICA

[1889-1963]

The Intellectual as a
Social Type

THE NEW RADICALISM* IN AMERICA

[1889-1963]

The Intellectual as a Social Type

CHRISTOPHER LASCH

* The assumption that cultural reform can be accomplished through political action.

Vintage Books
A Division of Random House
New York

VINTAGE BOOKS
are published by
Alfred A. Knopf, Inc. and *Random House, Inc.*

FOR

NELL

ACKNOWLEDGMENTS

I AM GRATEFUL TO RICHARD HOFSTADTER, HAROLD STRAUSS, AND William R. Taylor for reading the manuscript and giving me their encouragement and advice. They have not, of course, always agreed with me. I should also like to thank Alfred A. Knopf for his reading of the manuscript, his generous interest in the work, and his advice on many points.

The Social Science Research Council gave me a grant of money which, supplemented by a grant from the State University of Iowa, freed me from academic obligations in order that I might write this book. The librarians of the State University of Iowa helped me by mailing books to England, where I did most of the writing, and by uncovering a collection of Jane Addams letters, unknown to me, in the library of the University of Kansas. I am greatly indebted to these organizations.

I should like to thank the publishers of the following books for permission to quote from them.

Prentice-Hall, Inc.: *Drift and Mastery* by Walter Lippmann, copyright © 1961.

The Viking Press, Inc.: *Untimely Papers* by Randolph Bourne, copyright 1919.

The Macmillan Company: *Democracy and Education* by John Dewey, copyright 1944; *Social Control* by Edward A. Ross, copyright 1901; and *Twenty Years at Hull-House* by Jane Addams, copyright 1938.

Farrar, Straus & Company: *Memoirs of a Revolutionist* by Dwight Macdonald, copyright © 1957.

G. P. Putnam's Sons: *Advertisements for Myself,* copyright © 1959, and *The Presidential Papers,* copyright © 1960, 1961, 1962, 1963 by Norman Mailer.

Harcourt, Brace & World Inc.: *Intimate Memories* by Mabel Dodge Luhan, copyright 1933, 1935, 1936, 1937; *The Letters of Lincoln Steffens,* edited by Ella Winter and Granville Hicks, copyright 1938; and *The Autobiography of Lincoln Steffens,* copyright 1931, 1937.

Holt, Rinehart and Winston, Inc.: *Characters and Events* by John Dewey, copyright 1929.

Hill and Wang, Inc.: *The World of Lincoln Steffens* by Herbert Shapiro, copyright © 1962.

Appleton-Century: *Seventy Years of It* by Edward A. Ross, copyright 1936.

Houghton Mifflin Company: *Youth and Life* by Randolph Bourne, copyright 1913.

For permission to quote from *Lorenzo in Taos* by Mabel Dodge Luhan, I am grateful to John G. Evans.

Excerpts from the following manuscript collections are quoted with the permission of the following individuals and institutions, to whom I gratefully acknowledge my debt.

Brooks Colcord: the Papers of Lincoln Colcord.

Yale University Library: the Papers of Edward M. House.

Columbia University Library: the Papers of Randolph Bourne.

The Board of Directors of Hull-House Association: the Papers of Jane Addams.

INTRODUCTION

THE MAIN ARGUMENT OF THIS BOOK IS THAT MODERN radicalism or liberalism can best be understood as a phase of the social history of the intellectuals. In the United States, to which this study is confined, the connection is particularly clear. There, the rise of the new radicalism coincided with the emergence of the intellectual as a distinctive social type.

The intellectual may be defined, broadly, as a person for whom thinking fulfills at once the function of work and play; more specifically, as a person whose relationship to society is defined, both in his eyes and in the eyes of the society, principally by his presumed capacity to comment upon it with greater detachment than those more directly caught up in the practical business of production and power. Because his vocation is to be a critic of society, in the most general sense, and because the value of his criticism is presumed to rest on a measure of detachment from the current scene, the intellectual's relation to the rest of society is never entirely comfortable; but it has not always been as uncomfortable as it is today in the United States. "Anti-intellectualism" offers only a partial explanation of the present tension between intellectuals and American society.

The rest of the explanation lies in the increased sensitivity of intellectuals to attacks on themselves as a group. It lies in the intellectuals' own sense of themselves, not simply as individuals involved in a common undertaking, the somewhat hazardous business of criticism, but as members of a beleaguered minority. The tension is a function, in other words, of the class-consciousness of the intellectuals themselves.

Intellectuals have existed in all literate societies, but they have only recently come to constitute a kind of subculture. In fact, the word "intellectual" does not seem to have found its way into American usage much before the turn of the century. Before that, most intellectuals belonged to the middle class, and though they may sometimes have felt themselves at odds with the rest of the community, they did not yet conceive of themselves as a class apart. The modern intellectual, even when he chooses to throw himself into the service of his country or attempts to embrace the common life about him, gives himself away by the very self-consciousness of his gestures. He agonizes endlessly over the "role of the intellectuals." A hundred years ago these discussions, and the passion with which they are conducted, would have been incomprehensible.

The growth of a class (or more accurately, a "status group") of intellectuals[1] is part of a much more general development: the decline of the sense of community, the tendency of the mass society to break down into its component parts, each having its own autonomous culture and maintaining only the most tenuous connections with the general life of the society—which as a consequence has almost ceased to exist. The most obvious victims of this process in our own time are adolescents, who

1. For the distinction between classes and status groups (subcultures?), see Max Weber: "Class, Status, Party," in H. H. Gerth and C. Wright Mills, eds.: *From Max Weber: Essays in Sociology* (New York: Oxford University Press; 1958), pp. 180–94.

live increasingly in a world all their own. The emergence of
the intellectual class in the first couple of decades of the present
century reveals the workings of the same process at a somewhat earlier period in time.

The intellectual class, then, is a distinctively modern phenomenon, the product of the cultural fragmentation that seems
to characterize industrial and postindustrial societies. It is
true that in the United States the agencies of social cohesion
(church, state, family, class) were never very strong in the
first place. Nevertheless, there existed during the first two and a
half centuries of American history a sort of cultural consensus
at the heart of which was a common stake in capitalism and a
common tradition of patriarchal authority. There were social
classes but, compared to Europe or even to American society
during the colonial period, remarkably little class-consciousness;
and whatever the real opportunities for social advancement,
the myth of equal opportunity was sufficiently strong to minimize the tensions and resentments which later came to
characterize American society. "The whole society," wrote
Tocqueville in 1831, "seems to have melted into a middle class.
. . . All the Americans whom we have encountered up to now,
even to the simplest *shop salesman,* seem to have received, or
wish to appear to have received, a good education. Their manners are grave, deliberate, reserved, and they all wear the same
clothes. All the customs of life show this mingling of the two
classes which in Europe take so much trouble to keep apart."[2]
Divisive influences tended to be local and regional rather than
social; and the very intensity of local and regional rivalries
enhanced the social solidarity of each particular part of the
country, so that Southerners, for instance, found what seemed
to be a common interest in resisting the encroachments of the

2. George W. Pierson: *Tocqueville and Beaumont in America* (New York:
Oxford University Press; 1938), pp. 69–70.

Yankee. Under these conditions men of intellectual inclination had very little sense of themselves as a class. The South—the preindustrial society par excellence—offers a particularly striking example of the degree to which such men shared the general aspirations of the *bourgeoisie,* the highest form of which, as is customary in bourgeois societies, was to set up as country gentlemen on lordly estates.[3]

It was only in the North that writers and thinkers began to acquire a sense of being at odds with the rest of society. The transcendentalists and reformers of the 1830's and 1840's, in their protest against the materialism of a society dominated by the Cotton Whigs, in some respects anticipated the attacks of modern intellectuals on the middle class. But the truth of the matter is suggested by the ease with which the reforming impulse after the Civil War was reabsorbed into the stream of genteel culture. The war itself had a unifying effect on New England, as on the South.[4] Abolitionism petered out in mugwumpery, a form of extreme sectional particularism. Indeed, the whole New England tradition—with which American reform until the twentieth century was so completely bound up—precisely embodied everything against which later intellectuals were in rebellion, everything associated with the cultural ascendancy of the middle class.

The term "middle class" seems nowadays to encounter as much resistance, among historians at least, as the term "intellectual." I have been told by historians that the term means nothing, that indeed the "middle class" is a myth. It is true that the term has often been loosely used. But I do not under-

3. See William R. Taylor: *Cavalier and Yankee* (New York: George Braziller; 1961), especially the chapter on William Wirt, pp. 67–94.

4. Antislavery politics, wrote Henry Adams (*The Education of Henry Adams* [New York: Modern Library; 1931], p. 26), represented a "violent reaction" which swept New England "back into Puritanism with a violence as great as that of a religious war."

stand why that should prevent its being used quite precisely. I have used it here simply as a synonym for *bourgeoisie,* to describe a class of people which derives its income from the ownership of property and in particular from trade and commerce—a definition, when applied to American society in the nineteenth century, which includes most of the farming population as well as the bulk of those who lived in towns. It does not include the salaried employees (clerks, salesmen, managers, professionals), whom C. Wright Mills has called the "new" middle class—itself a creation of the twentieth century. The cultural style of the old as distinguished from the new middle class was characterized by that combination of patriarchal authority and the sentimental veneration of women which is the essence of the genteel tradition. Everything I mean to catch up in the phrase "middle-class culture" seems to me ultimately to derive from these characteristic familial arrangements. It is no wonder that the revolt of the intellectuals so often took the form of a rebellion against the conventional family. The family was the agency which transmitted from generation to generation—and not only transmitted but embodied down to the last detail of domestic architecture—the enormous weight of respectable culture; as its defenders would have said, of civilization itself.

Everyone who has studied the history of American reform agrees that the reform tradition underwent a fundamental change around 1900. Some people identify the change with a changing attitude toward government, a new readiness to use government (particularly the federal government) as an instrument of popular control. Others associate it with an abandonment of the old populistic distrust of large-scale institutions, like corporations, and an acceptance of the inevitability of the concentration of wealth and power. Still others define the change as a movement away from the dogma of natural rights toward a relativistic, environmentalist, and pragmatic view of the world.[5] All of these developments, in truth, were going on at the same time, and all of them contributed to the emergence of the new radicalism. Equally important was a tendency to see cultural issues as inseparable from political ones; so that "education," conceived very broadly, came to be seen not merely as a means of raising up an enlightened electorate but as an instrument of social change in its own right. Conversely, the new radicals understood the end of social and political reform to be the improvement of the quality of American culture as a whole, rather than simply a way of equalizing the opportunities for economic self-advancement. It is precisely this confusion of politics and culture, so essential to the new radicalism, that seems to me to betray its origins in the rise of the intellectual class; for such a program, with its suggestion that men of learning occupy or ought to occupy the strategic loci of social control, has an obvious appeal to intellectuals, and particularly to intellectuals newly conscious of their own common ties and common interests.

What I have called the new radicalism was not the same thing as the so-called progressive movement, though it took shape during the "progressive era." Progressivism was influenced by the new radicalism, but it was more deeply indebted to the populism of the nineteenth century. It was for the most part a purely political movement, whereas the new radicals were more interested in the reform of education, cul-

5. See, for instance, Daniel Aaron: *Men of Good Hope* (New York: Oxford University Press; 1951); Charles Forcey: *The Crossroads of Liberalism* (New York: Oxford University Press; 1961); Eric Goldman: *Rendezvous with Destiny* (New York: Alfred A. Knopf; 1952); Morton G. White: *Social Thought in America: The Revolt against Formalism* (New York: Viking Press; 1949); John Braeman: "Seven Progressives," *Business History Review,* XXXV (winter, 1961), pp. 581–92.

CULTURAL RADICALS

ture, and sexual relations than they were in political issues in the strict sense. Many of them, in fact, rejected progressivism; they saw in "uplift" only another manifestation of middle-class morality. Even those like Jane Addams who did not embrace socialism, and whose political position therefore has to be described, for lack of a better word, as "progressive" (or "liberal"), had more in common with socialists than with the kind of progressives one associates with the initiative and referendum, the campaign against the trusts, and the crusade for "good government." What distinguished her from them was not only her insistence on the preeminence of "education" but her sense of kinship with the "other half" of humanity. The intellectual in his estrangement from the middle class identified himself with other outcasts and tried to look at the world from their point of view. This radical reversal of perspective was still another distinguishing feature of the new radicalism, socialist or progressive. The particular political labels are of little importance. What matters is the point of view such people deliberately cultivated.

That point of view—the effort to see society from the bottom up, or at least from the outside in—seems to me to account for much of what was valuable and creative in the new radicalism. On the other hand, the very circumstance which made this feat possible—the estrangement of intellectuals, as a class, from the dominant values of American culture—also accounted for what seems to me the chief weakness of the new radicalism, its distrust not only of middle-class culture but of intellect itself. Detachment carried with it a certain defensiveness about the position of intellect (and intellectuals) in American life; and it was this defensiveness, I think, which sometimes prompted intellectuals to forsake the role of criticism and to identify themselves with what they imagined to be the laws of historical necessity and the working out of the popular will. At certain points in the history of the twentieth century, notably during the First World War, American intellectuals seemed too eager to participate in national crusades, too little inclined to wonder precisely how such crusades would serve the values they professed to cherish; and such episodes, together with the more recent appearance of a cold-war liberalism determined not to be outdone in its devotion to the "national purpose," have left me somewhat skeptical of "pragmatic liberalism" in its more militant and affirmative moods. I have not attempted to disguise my skepticism, or for that matter my admiration for whatever was negative and critical in the new radicalism; but I have not wished to write a tract, another *Trahison des Clercs,*[6] and I state my own prejudices here only in order to make it clear what they are, not because this book is intended to document them.

I am much less interested, in short, in praising or condemning the new radicalism than in understanding where it came from. Even the effort to understand where it came from, unfortunately, will strike some readers as an insidious attempt to discredit the ideas of radicals and reformers by "psychologizing" them away. For some people, it is enough to say that the reformers were moved by the spectacle of human injustice; to say anything more is to deny the fact of injustice. I am unable to understand this argument, nor do I know quite how to meet it (since I cannot understand it), except to say that the reformers themselves did not share this reluctance of their admirers to examine their own motives. They wrote about their motives with all the enthusiasm, and all the honesty, with which they wrote about social injustice, and I have relied very heavily on what they wrote. Of course it would be possible to ignore what they wrote about themselves, and to write instead

6. Julien Benda: *The Betrayal of the Intellectuals* (Boston: Beacon Press; 1959 [Paris, 1927]).

about the evils of capitalism. But that is not the book I have chosen to write. I have written instead about some of the critics of capitalism, in the hope that their history would tell something, if not specifically about capitalism, about the peculiarly fragmented character of modern society, and beyond that, about what it means to pursue the life of reason in a world in which the irrational has come to appear not the exception but the rule.

Not only the scope and design of this study but its method needs a word of explanation. I have chosen to approach the new radicalism chiefly by means of a series of biographical essays, although I know that for a social historian to proceed in this way is almost to invite misunderstanding. The connection between biography and history is never altogether clear, and it is especially obscure in the case of social history. The political historian can justify the study of notable men by reference to their influence on events, the literary historian by reference to the intrinsic value of their works. For the social historian such considerations are ruled out from the start. His subject is the social structure, the people he writes about are often anonymous, and if he ventures on biography at all, it must be—so it would seem—with the excuse that his subjects are "representative men." By taking this position, however, he lays himself open to the objection that a representative man is a contradiction in terms; for is not a human being, by reason of all that makes him human, something unique?

The subjects of this book were chosen in deliberate violation of the notion that a social historian ought to write about people "typical of their times." One of them was a hunchbacked dwarf, another an extremely neurotic woman with an irregular emotional history, another a counselor to Presidents. All of them were extremely articulate people—a fact which further sets them off from the run of humankind. But it is this very fact, though it further distinguishes them, which makes up their value to the study of the history of American society. They articulated experiences which, whether or not they were representative experiences in the sense of being widely shared by others, were nevertheless representative in another sense: they could only have happened at a particular place at a particular time. Some experiences are archetypal: men undergo them simply because they are human, the experiences are inherent in the human condition. But others are closely rooted in a social context, and by listening carefully to what people say about them, one can sometimes learn more about a given society than by more formal sociological analysis.

CONTENTS

THE
NEW RADICALISM
IN AMERICA

[1889–1963]

The Intellectual as a
Social Type

1 / Jane Addams:
The College Woman and
the Family Claim

[I]

AS RECENTLY AS A HUNDRED YEARS AGO, IN THE MORE SPARSELY
settled parts of the world, life still seemed to hang by the
most tenuous of threads. Science and social security had
not yet dissipated the terror and uncertainty of existence. Few
were the families that had not known at first hand the equal
outrages of premature death and a too long-drawn-out old age.
The miniature tombstones in the village cemetery, the elders
rocking, rocking on the porch, gave testimony, impossible to
ignore, of the arbitrariness of the natural order of things.
Madness too, if not more common then than now, seems
somehow to have been more immediate and palpable. In family
histories one reads of the uncle or sister or brother gone suddenly crazy. One senses the bafflement and helplessness of those
still sane in the face of this grimmest of witnesses to the inscrutable sadness of life.

No wonder, then, that the religious habit of mind persisted
long after dogma itself had ceased to be a matter of great concern. It was not only that religion held out the promise of an
eventual deliverance from this vale of tears. Piety was not only
consolation but self-control. It was a way of restraining the

destructive despair that people sensed in themselves. The precariousness of life gave rise to a secret rebellion, a wish not merely to curse one's fate but to revenge oneself upon it, to indulge to the full one's grief and resentment. The violence without corresponded to a violence within.

Founded on a psychological rather than an intellectual imperative, the religious impulse might withstand the onslaught of rationalism, it might survive the passing of the traditional forms of worship. But the disintegration of dogma, though it did not weaken the religious impulse, deprived it of intellectual context. Theology as an intellectual discipline fell into disuse, and the ministry ceased to be the most learned of professions. Formal religious affiliation came to seem entirely arbitrary; a man such as Jane Addams's father might call himself a Quaker, yet go to a different church every Sunday. John Addams would not discuss his religious beliefs. "I am a Quaker," he would say, and, when pressed, "I am a Hicksite Quaker"; "and not another word on the weighty subject," says his daughter, "could I induce him to utter."[1] Religion was no longer a set of postulates, to be examined and argued, but an ideal of personal conduct.

That, indeed, had all along been the unmistakable tendency of American sectarianism, of Quakerism especially. It was not strange, therefore, that John Addams, standing at the end of a long tradition, should have passed along to his daughter an ideal of religious conduct almost stoic in its insistence on absolute self-dependence. "You must always be honest with yourself inside," he told her once, "whatever happened."[2] As late as 1910 she still considered her father's advice, or thought she considered it, "perhaps on the whole as valuable a lesson

1. Jane Addams: *Twenty Years at Hull-House* (New York: Macmillan; 1910), p. 16.
2. Ibid., p. 15.

as the shorter catechism itself contains."[3] (But "what unconscious echo," writes Margaret Tims, "was evoked in her adult observation of the 'unlovely result' when 'the entire moral energy of an individual goes into the cultivation of personal integrity'?"[4]) Certainly it stood her in good stead during her struggle against later efforts to enlist her in more conventional forms of piety. At that time, she says, when she was trying to resist the pleas of her teachers at Rockford Seminary that she become a missionary, she came once again to her father for help. In her memory the two conversations, the one during childhood, the other during adolescence, merged into one. "Once again I heard his testimony in favor of 'mental integrity above everything else.' "[5]

John Addams's public life, like his religion, was already, in the mid-nineteenth century, an atavism, a throwback to the early republic. Migrating to northern Illinois from Pennsylvania in the 1840's, he settled on the Cedar River near Freeport (where Jane Addams was born in 1860), built a mill, prospered beyond all his expectations, acquired a bank, went to the state senate, died a leading citizen of the state. He helped found the Republican Party in Illinois. Mazzini and Lincoln were his political idols. The combination of keen entrepreneurial appetite and republican zeal, like everything else about him, smacked of an earlier time. In his own day the newly rich cultivated aristocratic leisure, yearned after all that money was said to be unable to buy, and sent their daughters to Europe in search of advantages that a colonial culture seemed no longer able to provide. The Addams family itself mirrored the change in microcosm. John Addams's first wife Sarah, who died when

3. Ibid.
4. Margaret Tims: *Jane Addams of Hull-House* (London: Allen & Unwin; 1961), p. 19. She refers to a passage in Miss Addams's *Democracy and Social Ethics* (New York: Macmillan; 1902), p. 274.
5. *Twenty Years at Hull-House*, p. 15.

Jane Addams was only two, belonged in spirit to the world of her husband. The following incident evokes her perfectly. Though she had repeatedly warned her children not to play beside the millrace, lest they be swept under the wheel, they persisted in doing so.

One day Sarah, looking from the back door, saw the two children at their perilous frolic. Fear for them stiffened her courage. With resolute strides she walked across the yard. In their absorption, Weber and Alice did not hear her. With quick, unhesitating strength she pushed the little boy—whom she regarded as the leader—into the water. Alice gazed horror-stricken as her brother struggled helplessly, while their mother ran to the curve of the stream by the bridge. As her son was borne to that spot, Sarah reached out a sure arm and drew him to the bank. . . . There was no more careless playing by the mill-race.[6]

John Addams's second wife, by contrast—Ann Haldeman, the handsome widow of one of the prominent men of Freeport —sought to impose on her family all the tastes and manners of a more affluent generation. "A bay window was added to the downstairs living room, letting in more sunlight—and the piano took its rightful place there, often flooding the room with music. . . . The frocks of the Addams girls . . . had new tastefulness in color and line. The dining table . . . that Ann brought . . . became a gracious spot at which the children exchanged their village ways for new amenities."[7] But she did not become Jane Addams's mother until the girl was eight. By that time Jane Addams had upon her the stamp of her father's stoicism.

Raised in a pious household, under the authority of a some-

6. Marcet Haldeman-Julius: "The Two Mothers of Jane Addams," type-script in Jane Addams MSS, Swarthmore College Library. The author of this account was the daughter of Alice Addams Haldeman, one of the elder sisters of Jane Addams.

7. Ibid.

what stern, remote, and even forbidding man, Jane Addams nevertheless underwent nothing, as a girl, that could be called a religious education. She went to Sunday school, she prayed, she longed with all her heart to be worthy of her virtuous parent. But that religion was also a field of speculation—something her ancestors could easily have told her—seems never to have occurred to her. The letters of St. Paul, which she was required to read in Rockford Seminary, repelled her, though the gospels, which an indulgent tutor allowed her very freely to translate from the Greek, impressed her with the beauty of their language. (Those were "the only moments," she later confessed, "in which I seem to have approximated in my own experience to a faint realization of the 'beauty of holiness.' "[8]) The purely aesthetic appeal, however, was not enough for one brought up on Quaker piety. If she ever considered religion as a calling, something to which she might devote her life, it was as a field of missionary work. The Rockford Seminary, to which she was sent at seventeen for the equivalent of a college education, specialized in training girls for service in foreign missions, and powerful efforts were made to attract Jane Addams to the cause. She was not much tempted, although, as I have said, she had to call upon her father in her struggle to stand up to her teachers. A girl of keen mind, with a taste for philosophy, could no more be content with mere good works, devoid of intellectual excitement, than the daughter of John Addams could accept a religion of beauty detached from rigorous standards of personal conduct.

It was in the latter respect that she was to prove so different from her friend Ellen Gates Starr (later the co-founder of Hull-House), whom she met at the seminary as a freshman and with whom she maintained a life-long association. Ellen Starr eventually resolved the contradiction with which as

8. *Twenty Years at Hull-House*, p. 51.

schoolgirls they grappled in common by embracing the Cath-
olic Church. She was attracted to the Church, like so many
intellectuals, by the beauty of its elaborate ritual. Her conversion, however, came late in her life. As a girl she found the
subject of religion as baffling and yet as unavoidable as Jane
Addams did, and together—first in conversations at the seminary, then, after Miss Starr went off to teach in Chicago, in
a long correspondence—they strove to reduce their doubts and
confusions to order.

They were about equally ignorant of theology. At the same
time they agreed that religion was vitally important; one could
not get along without it. But they were unable to allay each
other's misgivings, even as they cautioned each other about the
danger of entertaining them. Thus one finds Jane Addams
holding up to her friend the advice of their classmate Sarah
Anderson: "I do not think we are put into the world to be religious, we have a certain work to do, and to do that is the main
thing." But at the same time she was convinced that the success
of the work "in a large degree depends upon our religion."
Sometimes—"I suppose when I am wrought up"—it seemed
to her that she could go no further in life until she had "settled"
the question of religion. "Could I but determine *that* and have
it for a sure basis, with time and space to work in I could train
my powers to anything, it would only remain to choose what."[9]

That theology had ceased to have much intellectual appeal
to pious young women is suggested by Jane Addams's having
to rely, in matters of faith, on the wisdom of her contemporaries, or on the writings of secular authors: Tennyson,
Browning, Macaulay. When Ellen confesses that she can't
believe in the divinity of Christ—"the reality is about like that
of certain characters in fiction, Dicken's [sic] especially"—Jane

9. Jane Addams to Ellen Starr, Nov. 22, 1879, Ellen Gates Starr MSS,
Smith College Library.

urges her to read Tennyson's "In Memoriam," which puts the matter in its proper perspective. "Don't you see that you are all right. . . . If you realize God through Christ, it don't make any difference whether you realize Christ or not, that is not the point. If God has become nearer to you, more of a reality through him, then you are a Christian, Christ's mission to you has been fulfilled. Don't you see what I mean. If you have a God you are a Deist, if you more clearly comprehend that God through Christ then you are a Christian." But, Jane confesses, "Christ don't help me in the least. . . . I feel a little as I do when I hear very fine music—that I am incapable of understanding."[1]

So much speculation on this subject finally leaves her merely impatient. Her father's daughter, she can only wave it aside: "Every time I talk about religion, I vow a great vow never to do it again." Her creed "is ever *be sincere* & don't fuss."[2]

Six months later, in spite of her vow, she is going over the same ground again: she cannot do her "work" unless she first settles the question. "If I could fix myself with my relations to God & the universe, & so be in perfect harmony with nature & deity, I could use my faculties and energy so much better & could do almost anything." But she seems no nearer than before to a resolution of her perplexity. The doctrine of the incarnation seems more than ever to elude her. "I don't think God embodied himself in Christ to *reveal* himself, but that he did it considering the weakness of man; that while man might occasionaly [sic] comprehend an abstract deity he couldn't live by it."[3]

In this letter, written when Jane was in her third year at

1. Ellen Starr to Jane Addams, July 27, 1879, Addams MSS; Jane Addams to Ellen Starr, Aug. 11, 1879, Starr MSS.
2. Ibid.
3. Jane Addams to Ellen Starr, Jan. 29, 1880, Starr MSS.

the seminary, she confesses to having embarked on "an awful experiment." For three months she has not prayed. The worst of it is that she feels "no worse for it" at all. "I feel happy and unconcerned and not in the least morbid." Ellen advises her to desist. "I did the same thing once, for longer than you say— very much longer. But not as an experiment. I did it because prayer, the form of prayer, was a mockery to me then, & I was too sincere to use a lifeless form." But no good can come of such experiments, "& harm *might*."[4]

A few weeks later Jane is urging her friend that "it would be better for us not to talk about religion any more." She simply can't express what she thinks about the incarnation. She inclines now to the view that Christ is important as a "kingly example," but she is uncomfortably aware that that position is "shallow." All she can do is to quote Matthew Arnold, even though she has to admit that his poetry represents "the limit of sentimentality":

> Unaffrighted by the silence round them
> Undistracted by the sights they see
> These demand not that the things without them
> Yield them love, amusement sympathy.[5]

If one had to date this correspondence now by internal references to current public events, one would never imagine that it was written during the period of the great railroad strikes, the Molly Maguires, the rising industrial violence throughout the country. Insofar as religion remains the focus of these girls' relentless self-examination, one might as well be back in the early nineteenth century. The clue, however, to the later origin of these letters is the theological confusion

4. Ellen Starr to Jane Addams, Feb. 29, 1880, Addams MSS.
5. Jane Addams to Ellen Starr, May 15, 1880, Starr MSS.

of the correspondents, their utter inability to grasp points of Christian doctrine that earlier would have been taken for granted. The impulse to piety remains as strong as ever, but the effort to wed it to the speculative and analytical impulse founders on the rock of rationalism, which renders these young women incapable of intellectually accepting the central mysteries of the Christian faith.

What all this suggests—given the combination, in both women, but in Jane Addams especially, of a powerful moral sense and an equally strong taste for the kind of analysis formerly associated with theology—is that the social settlement, the ultimate solution to their difficulties, was for such people a secular outlet, among other things, for energies essentially religious. It is a commonplace to say that progressivism represented another outcropping of the old New England moralism.[6] Such observations are quite misleading, however, unless coupled with the observation that the old moralism now existed in a theological void. It was the waning of theology rather than the persistence of piety that created the cultural climate out of which the social settlement in particular and progressivism in general emerged. When Graham Taylor wrote in the manuscript of his autobiography that the settlement movement embodied the spirit of the Pilgrims, Jane Addams objected that "the settlement was rather a *revolt* against Puritan conceptions than a continuation of them—a substitute [sic] of 'works' for dogma."[7]

6. See, e.g., George E. Mowry: *The Era of Theodore Roosevelt* (New York: Harper & Brothers; 1958), p. 87 ("It seems likely that the intellectual and religious influence of New England was again dominating the land."); and Carl N. Degler: *Out of Our Past* (New York: Harper & Brothers; 1959), p. 370 ("In substance [progressivism] was the application of Christian morality . . . to the twentieth century.").

7. Jane Addams to Graham Taylor, Dec. 1, 1917, Graham Taylor MSS, Newberry Library. She added: "However that may be my Quaker reaction!"

Casting about for a calling, Jane Addams found herself faced with a choice between the kind of good works advocated by the seminary and a purely secular career—medicine, for example—divorced from any immediate and meaningful relation to piety. The alternatives proved equally untenable. But social work, as she came to conceive of it, ideally resolved the conflict; it combined good works with the analysis not only of the conditions underlying urban poverty but also of one's own relation to the poor. Those who see only the first side of the settlement movement miss the fact that for the people involved in it, it represented not only social service but sociology, the one as important as the other.

The case for combining the pursuit of knowledge with the immediate application of knowledge could be argued, of course, in secular terms. The work of John Dewey, which in so many ways ran parallel to Jane Addams's, was wholly secular in spirit. But the degree to which Jane Addams herself continued to conceive of the problem in religious terms makes itself evident throughout her writings. In an early essay, for instance, she summed up, in a revealing passage, her quarrel with the prevailing trend of higher education:

We recall that the first colleges of the Anglo-Saxon race were established to educate religious teachers. For a long time it was considered the mission of the educated to prepare the mass of the people for the life beyond the grave. Knowledge dealt largely in theology, but it was ultimately to be applied, and the test of the successful graduate, after all, was not his learning, but his power to save souls. As the college changed from teaching theology to teaching secular knowledge the test of its success should have shifted from the power to save men's souls to the power to adjust them in healthful relations to nature and their fellow men. But the college failed to do this, and made the test of its success the mere collecting and disseminating of knowledge, elevating the means into an end and falling in love with its own achievement.[8]

Universities, in other words, ought still to train ministers (not educated dilettantes), but ministers, now, of the *social* gospel.

This sort of complaint against education and against middle-class culture in general—their remoteness from "life"—became increasingly common around the turn of the century. It was the complaint that lay behind progressive education, of which Jane Addams was one of the pioneers. The religious roots of progressive doctrine help to account for its main weakness—an unawareness of the anti-intellectual implications implicit in defining education as a means of social control.[9] The proposition that education ought to be used, not for the "mere" dissemination of knowledge, but to "adjust" men "in healthful relations to nature and their fellow men" easily led to the conception of education as "life adjustment" which subsequently

8. "A Function of the Social Settlement," *Annals of the American Academy of Political and Social Science*, XIII (May, 1899), pp. 339–40. These themes—that knowledge must be applied to life, and that the proper application consists of using it as a means of "social control"—recur constantly in Jane Addams's writings on education. See the chapter "Socialized Education" in *Twenty Years at Hull-House*; the chapter "Education by the Current Event" in *The Second Twenty Years at Hull-House* (New York: Macmillan; 1930); *The Spirit of Youth and the City Streets* (New York: Macmillan; 1911), pp. 84ff., 109ff.; "A Toast to John Dewey," *Survey*, LXIII (Nov. 15, 1929), pp. 203–4; "Americanization," *Publications of the American Sociological Society*, XIV (1919), pp. 206–14; and "The Social Situation: Religious Education and Contemporary Social Conditions," *Religious Education*, VI (June, 1911), pp. 145ff. The last of these contains a characteristic passage: "[During the 1890's] the religious educator lost hundreds of young men and women who by training and temperament should have gone into the ministry or the missionary field, simply because his statements appeared to them as magnificent pieces of self-assertion totally unrelated to the world."

9. On this point see the chapter on John Dewey in Richard Hofstadter: *Anti-intellectualism in American Life* (New York: Alfred A. Knopf; 1963), pp. 359–90.

became so popular. Thus what began as a determination to make education serve the cause of social change ended in a concept of education deeply conservative—"education for citizenship."[1] Jane Addams and Dewey could later protest that the progressive educators had perverted their ideas by directing them toward conservative ends, but they had no philosophic grounds on which to resist the process they themselves had set in motion. They could only argue that "adjustment" ought to proceed along radical rather than conservative lines. But that was to introduce into discussions of education policy issues which did not belong there in the first place, issues which belonged rather to the sphere of political debate. By involving education with "social control," they themselves had made of the school a political battleground, and the fate of the school then became dependent on the resolution of the political conflict within the educational bureaucracy. When the battle went against the radicals, they had no recourse except to renew the battle—a battle, however, which very early became quite hopeless. Thus the religion that finally came to prevail throughout most of American public education—in accordance with the progressives' original insistence that teaching was still, in essence, preaching—was not the social gospel but the religion of the "American way of life."

In Jane Addams's case, the root of the difficulty lay in her misconception of what religious education had meant to begin with, in the days before education had become secularized—and this misconception, in turn, was a function of her ignorance of theology. Her conception of early religious education as "applied" knowledge, the success of which was to be measured in terms of the college graduates' "power to save souls," naïvely read back into an earlier period the jargon of her own. The early religious colleges had had a far greater respect for ab-

1. See below, pp. 155 ff.

stract knowledge than she realized. They had assumed, in keeping with the Protestant tradition, that knowledge was indispensable to a full understanding of the dark interior of the soul—without which religion itself became meaningless. That Jane Addams could imagine the religious college as a kind of technical school in soul-saving indicates in itself how far she had traveled from the intellectual world of early Protestantism.

[II]

Not Jane Addams's Protestant background itself, but the crisis that overtook Protestantism in her time, led her eventually to formulate an anti-traditional and even anti-intellectual position deeply critical of history and culture. The other social crisis that shaped her early life, the "domestic tragedy" of which she spoke so often, greatly reinforced her suspicions of history and culture, even as it led eventually, perhaps, to a partial relaxation of them.

From 1881 until 1888 Jane Addams underwent a prolonged nervous depression, from which she emerged with the decision to found a social settlement on Chicago's west side. A few weeks after her graduation from Rockford Seminary—she was now twenty-one—her father died, unexpectedly and prematurely. The impact of that event on his daughter was calamitous: as she had lived in "veneration" of him, to use her own word, and as her very reason for being since childhood had been to live up to his demanding standard of rectitude, his passing deprived her of the means by which to measure the success of her efforts. It deprived her of the incentive on which all this time she had been obliged, perhaps without realizing it, to rely. It was not surprising that the symptom of her breakdown was a paralysis of the will to act. Her sister Mary astutely identified the trouble: "You need not think," she urged, "that because he is gone, your incentive has perished. . . . He did not desire you to live for him but for the world, for humanity, for yourself & for Christ."[2]

Organized religion was no more help than before. By the summer of 1883 she was reduced to writing to Ellen Starr: "My experience of late has shown me the absolute necessity of the protection and dependence on Christ. . . . That the good men and books I used to depend upon will no longer answer."[3] Ellen herself in 1884 joined the Church of England. Her friend wrote wistfully: "You have found the Peace which passeth understanding . . . but I am afraid that I [am] almost as un-settled and perplexed as in the days when we were 'estimable young ladies.' "[4]

In 1885 she allowed herself to be baptized as a Presbyterian. The event did not represent a triumphal entry into the king-dom of God. It merely revealed the dimensions of her defeat: for the first time she had had to admit the need for support from without. "Many piteous failures" had undermined her "claims to self-dependence."[5]

In joining the Church she experienced no emotional con-version. Nor did her indulgent minister require her to sub-scribe to the finer points of Presbyterian dogma. Her baptism therefore settled nothing. A few months later she was writing

2. Mary Addams Linn to Jane Addams, Aug. 26 [?], 1881, Addams MSS.
3. Jane Addams to Ellen Starr, July 11, 1883, Starr MSS.
4. Jane Addams to Ellen Starr, June 22, 1884, Starr MSS. A small but revealing indication, by the way, of Jane Addams's progressive estrangement from middle-class culture is the increasing self-consciousness with which she used the phrase "young lady." Though here she already encloses it in quotation marks, it appears continually without them in her correspondence of this period. Years later she could still slip into the old usage, except that now she quickly apologized for unconsciously falling into this "false social distinction." It was, she once explained, "a remnant of former prejudice." (Jane Addams to Mary Rozet Smith, n.d., Addams MSS.)
5. *Twenty Years at Hull-House*, p. 78.

to Ellen Starr in the old vein: "I am always *blundering*, when I deal with religious nomenclature or sensations simply because my religious life has been so small. For many years it was my ambition to reach my father's moral requirements, & now when I am needing something more, I find myself approaching a crisis, & look rather wistfully to my friends for help."[6] But it was just this "something more" that neither church nor friends seemed able to provide.

Meanwhile she sank into a terrible lassitude, which deepened day by day. The deterioration of her health complicated her condition. Having set out in the fall of 1881, in spite of her father's death, to study medicine at the Woman's Medical College in Philadelphia, she soon developed a spinal condition brought on in part, probably, by the overwork with which she tried to drive out the thought of her deprivation. Although at its worst, therefore, her idleness was enforced by the breakdown of her health, she persisted in seeing it as only the symptom of a spiritual disease. "Failure through ill-health," she lectured herself, "is just as culpable and miserable as failure through any other cause. . . . I have been idle for two years just because I had not enough vitality to be anything else."[7]

In 1882 her stepbrother performed an operation on her spine. It was a success, but it left her, for reasons not altogether clear, unable to bear children. The significance of this latest disaster was not so much that it seemed, perhaps, to rule out marriage and to condemn her to celibacy, but that it raised the fact of her femininity as she had not had to face it before. Cut off now from a whole range of feminine experience, she must have begun to wonder whether she was not in danger of losing touch with her femininity altogether. A woman bent on a man's career, committed to her father's unyielding masculine

6. Jane Addams to Ellen Starr, Dec. 6, 1885, Starr MSS.
7. Jane Addams to Ellen Starr, June 8, 1884, Starr MSS.

example, she now ran the risk of finding herself altogether unsexed. To the invalid, turning over and over the meaning of her most recent misfortune, lying in bed with her books while the women around her busied themselves, in the immemorial tradition of women, with the details of her care, it must have seemed that she was in danger of losing contact with one whole side of her nature.[8] She began to compare the educated young women of her generation with their grandmothers and to wonder whether her contemporaries had not paid too great a price for their emancipation. She began to wonder whether they had not "taken their learning too quickly" and "departed too suddenly from the active, emotional life led by their grandmothers and great-grandmothers." Here lay another source of her argument with higher education. The education of young women "had developed too exclusively the power of acquiring knowledge and of merely receiving impressions." "Somewhere in the process of 'being educated' they had lost that simple and almost automatic response to the human appeal."[9] Thus her enforced idleness led Jane Addams to the discovery that troubled so many of her contemporaries: the "parasitism," as the feminists called it, of the educated woman of the middle class.

In July 1883, like so many "neurasthenic" girls of her class, Jane Addams set out for Europe with her mother, another

8. This fear persisted in later life, as is shown by a curious poem Jane Addams wrote to Mary Rozet Smith in 1895 after an attack of typhoid fever, a poem never finished and apparently never sent. In it she thanks her friend for delivering her from the loveless and unloving state into which she had fallen, she says, during the early Hull-House years. "I had forgotten Love,/ And only thought of Hull-House then." The poem continues: "That is the way with women folks/ When they attempt the things of men;/ They grow intense, and love the thing/ Which they so tenderly do rear,/ And think that nothing lies beyond/ Which claims from them a smile or tear." (James Weber Linn: *Jane Addams* [New York: Appleton-Century; 1935], pp. 79–80.)

9. *Twenty Years at Hull-House*, p. 71.

matron and her two nieces, and her college friend Sarah Anderson, in pursuit of health and culture.[1] The party stopped at Dublin, where she and Sarah "invested in some art books," proceeded to Edinburgh, an "enchanted city . . . filled with heroic associations," and then settled in London for six weeks —"more pleasing and interesting every day as one grows a little familiar with it"—before going on to the continent. Berlin she found "delightful." "The shops are much finer than any we saw in London, the streets are wide and clean, and the public buildings from the exterior at least are elaborate & splendid." Amsterdam, however, "was unclean & somewhat distressed [sic]." In Dresden she studied German and went assiduously to the opera. Passing on to Italy, she discovered that "the amount of history and wickedness that every spot holds is at times oppressive." "Everything," she wrote, "is in the great *Past*." In Venice she admired the lace; in Paris she bought fine dresses in which she and Sarah, "two country girls," could be comfortable only when they sat "perfectly quiet."[2]

Only once did she confess that her enjoyment of Europe was not "unalloyed." "Sometimes we get so tired of sight seeing that we wish as Sarah puts it 'Never to see another picture as long as I live,' but that is not very often."[3] Her autobiography, however, makes it clear that the trip was an

1. Henry James—"who I look at most of the time between courses at table"—was a fellow passenger. "He is very English in appearance, but not especially keen or intellectual." (Jane Addams to Alice Addams Haldeman, Aug. 27, 1883, in a collection of copies of letters from Jane Addams to her family written during the two European trips, now deposited in the University of Kansas Library; hereafter cited as Haldeman MSS.)

2. Jane Addams to Harry Haldeman, Dublin, Sept. 7, 1883; to Alice Haldeman, Sterling, Scotland, Sept. 30, 1883; to Alice, London, Oct. 23, 1883; to Alice, Berlin, Nov. 6, 1883; to Mary, Dresden, Dec. 6, 1883; to Alice, Dresden, Dec. 22, 1883; to Mary, Rome, March 31, 1884; to Alice, Venice, Feb. 20, 1884; to Alice, Paris, June 22, 1884. All in Haldeman MSS.

3. Jane Addams to Weber Addams, Rome, March 20, 1884, Haldeman MSS.

ordeal. Still completely conventional in her response to what she saw, she was enough at odds with convention to begin to reflect on the futility of the whole enterprise. Once again the sense of futility expressed itself in a contrast between generations. Speaking of the experience (as was so often her habit) obliquely, in generalized observations about young women of her class, she notes that in the course of the journey she met innumerable mothers and daughters, like herself, "who had crossed the seas in search of culture." What struck her again and again was the contrast between the mothers' spontaneous appreciation of the life about them and the daughters' distance from it. One found the mothers bargaining in the marketplace in their indifferent French or German; one found them visiting the kindergartens, "making real connection with the life about them." But the daughters were at ease only in the art gallery, the concert hall, the classroom. The odd part of it was that the mothers envied their daughters their cultural advantages. "If I had had your opportunities when I was young, my dear, I should have been a very happy girl." They never dreamed of the "sting" their words left. But the daughter knew only too well that she had no talent and would never fulfill the expectations of her friends. The daughter, in turn, envied her mother.

> The girl looked wistfully at her mother, but had not the courage to cry out what was in her heart; "I might believe I had unusual talent if I did not know what good music was; I might enjoy half an hour's practice a day if I were busy and happy the rest of the time. You do not know what life means when all the difficulties are removed! I am simply smothered and sickened with advantages. It is like eating a sweet dessert the first thing in the morning."[4]

4. *Twenty Years at Hull-House*, pp. 71-3.

It does not seem fanciful to suppose that Jane Addams referred to her own relations with her stepmother. Ann Haldeman, her father's second wife, was a woman of terrific energy and vitality—handsome, accomplished, gregarious. She rode horses, played the piano, and collected beautiful possessions. There was nothing in her of her husband's moral rigor, nothing of the stoic ideal that John Addams had passed along to his daughter. Her temperament was warm, sensuous, almost Latin in its passionate devotion to beauty and grace. "Wherever Ann went, beauty moved with her," one of her grandchildren later wrote. "I never saw her do anything more useful with her hands than adjust the objects in a room, care for her flowers and strum a guitar when she sang the ballads of Moore and Burns." At the same time she "loved to entertain and the circle of guests was widened. She drew her friends from people who, like herself, were interested in the arts and in literature." This same observer added that although Jane Addams soon adapted herself to "a control that was kind but positive," there was still "the clash of temperaments." Jane Addams, outwardly steady and reserved, "was never perfectly reconciled to the brilliant unevenness of Ann's nature."[5] Another woman, an old family friend who had visited the household in Cedarville not long after John Addams's death, wrote to Jane Addams afterward: "I remember how much more acceptable to you was the service of love from your eldest sister [Mary], than the word of authority from your step-mother. You doubtless in time, became more attached to the latter."[6]

It is not hard to imagine such a woman as Ann Haldeman Addams "making real connection" with the life around her,

5. Marcet Haldeman-Julius: "The Two Mothers of Jane Addams," Addams MSS.
6. Sarah C. T. Uhl to Jane Addams, Nov. 16, 1896, Addams MSS.

whether in America or in Europe. It is not hard to imagine her lecturing her stepdaughter on the girl's "advantages"—advantages she herself had bestowed. Nor is it hard, finally, to imagine her words, on innumerable occasions, "leaving a sting" of which she herself was quite unaware. She was not, one senses, deliberately harsh with her daughter. She simply had no way of understanding her.

Jane's urge to be useful must especially have baffled her. When the middle-class girl comes home from college, Jane Addams observed in a later essay, burning with the desire to serve humanity, "the family claim is strenuously asserted."[7] That this remark too was autobiographical—that is, that she arrived at her intuitions about middle-class family relations through pondering her relations with her own family—is indicated again by the facts of her early life. Ann Haldeman, as a matter of fact, asserted the family claim in an unmistakable form: she tried to arrange a match between Jane and her own son, George Haldeman, who had been Jane's playmate since childhood. Jane was devoted to George but equally determined not to marry him. At the same time she seemed powerless to prevent herself from being swept along in the current of her stepmother's plans.

Returning to the United States after two years abroad, Ann took her family to Baltimore, in furtherance of her desire to make Jane into a proper young lady; in furtherance also of her long-standing ambition, thwarted by John Addams, to get out of Cedarville.

7. "The Subjective Necessity for Social Settlements." This classic essay was first read as a paper at a conference of the Ethical Culture Society at Plymouth, Massachusetts, in 1892; then printed in a volume by Jane Addams and the other speakers, *Philanthropy and Social Progress* (New York: Thomas Y. Crowell; 1893), pp. 1–26; and finally reprinted as a chapter in *Twenty Years at Hull-House*, pp. 115–27. See also, for the same observation, "The College Woman and the Family Claim," *Commons*, III (Sept., 1898), pp. 3–7.

So to Baltimore they went, and "social" they became. Jane had brought back from Paris clothes, one "blue dress" in particular which seems to have particularly impressed her, and her mother launched her upon the gentle waves of Johns Hopkins University society. . . . She assisted her stepmother in giving parties, even card parties, having developed an acquaintance with whist; but on one occasion such a card-party produced a slight difficulty between them, Jane refusing to provide fresh cards for the company on the ground that "the old ones were clean enough."[8]

In Baltimore, Jane Addams later wrote, she "reached the nadir of my nervous depression and sense of maladjustment"; and the contemporary records bear her memory out.[9] "I am filled with shame," she wrote to Ellen Starr in 1886, "that with all my apparent leisure I do nothing at all. I have had the strangest experience since I have been in Baltimore, I have found my faculties, memory receptive faculties and all, perfectly inaccessible locked up away from me."[1] A few months later she wrote: "The nervous indications in this letter clearly show it should not have been written."[2] It was during this period, while on a visit to Cedarville, that she was baptized into the Presbyterian Church.

In December, 1887, she set out once again for Europe with Sarah Anderson.[3] At Munich they joined Ellen Starr, who was on her way to Italy to study paintings. Together, the three young women proceeded to Rome. There Jane's health broke down again. An attack of sciatica kept her in Rome for weeks,

8. Linn: *Jane Addams*, pp. 79–80.
9. *Twenty Years at Hull-House*, p. 77.
1. Jane Addams to Ellen Starr, Feb. 7, 1886, Starr MSS.
2. Jane Addams to Ellen Starr, July 17, 1886, Starr MSS.
3. The differences between this trip and the previous one made themselves felt at once. She was older, she traveled without her mother, and she had "lost that morbid thirst for information and doing that simply consumes American travelers and certainly did me the last time." (Jane Addams to Alice Haldeman, Florence, Jan. 26, 1888, Haldeman MSS.)

while her friends, at her insistence, continued their travels through southern Italy. She had had time, before her illness, to embark on a study of certain friezes in the catacombs; and now, attended by a trained nurse, she brooded over the conclusion suggested by her study: that "the early Christians, through a dozen devices of spring flowers, skipping lambs and a shepherd tenderly guiding the young, had indelibly written down that the Christian message is one of inexpressible joy." Twenty years later she could demand: "Who is responsible for forgetting this message?" Struggling in Rome with her flagging health, her mood, one imagines, was more tentative.[4]

Presently her doctors sent her to the Riviera, "to lead an invalid's life once more."[5] There Miss Anderson and Miss Starr rejoined her. Her health improved and they resumed their travels together. April found the party in Madrid; and it was at this point, according to Jane Addams's account, that the long-pent-up craving for action burst startlingly into life.

She had by this time begun to turn over in her mind the project which shortly was to put an end to her sufferings. She had begun to wonder, as she characteristically put it, whether it might not be a "good thing" to rent a house in the slums of some city, where educated and sheltered girls like herself would learn something of the life not taught in schools—where they would pursue a kind of postgraduate course in the con-

4. Her observations, moreover, were couched in the conventional style of the travel letter. "The early Christian symbols are so beautiful and attractive, as if they could scarcely find anything joyous and peaceful enough to express their eagerness for death and belief in immortality. . . . We went into the Church of St. Costanza near St. Agnes. It was built by Constantine & his daughter and the mosaics of the 4th cent. were almost as fine as those we saw at Ravenna," etc. (Jane Addams to Alice Haldeman, Rome, March 22, 1888, Haldeman MSS. The passage quoted in the text is from *The Spirit of Youth and the City Streets*, p. 10.)

5. *Twenty Years at Hull-House*, p. 84.

ditions under which the "other half" were forced to live.[6] The idea was as yet ill-formed. The visit to Toynbee Hall in London, which served to bring some of her thoughts into focus, came only after the decision to go ahead with the project had been made.[7] (It is a mistake, therefore, to treat the visit to Toynbee Hall, as some writers do, as providing the incentive for Hull-House.[8]) So far the project, insofar as it defined itself at all, defined itself not as a way of bridging the gap between the middle class and the poor but as a way of expressing her instinctual revulsion from the prospect of a lifetime of her stepmother's kind of culture—a lifetime of whist.

Even on the instinctual plane, the question was hardly settled in April, 1888, when Jane Addams and her friends arrived in Madrid. For all her growing revulsion against the

6. Ibid., p. 85. Just when the idea began to take shape she was not sure in retrospect. "It may have been even before I went to Europe for the second time."

7. The travel letters establish the chronology of both trips beyond any doubt. On the second trip her party, after touching at Southampton, went directly to the continent and visited England only on the way home; whereas on the first, they spent several weeks in England first.

8. Jane Addams's own sister Alice may have been the source of this particular legend. She gave to Carrie Chapman Catt (who visited Alice in Kansas in 1894) the following account of her sister's early years. "Jane Addams grew up in a most solicitous family. She had everything she wanted but was not well, and after a time, with so much attention, she began to think it was her due to be waited upon and petted. She became selfish and irritable, partly due to the pain she had to bear. Years passed, and the family got into the habit of thinking of her as having to be cared for and catered to, and then the family took her upon a trip to London, where she visited the settlement house there." (Minutes of a meeting of the Women's International League for Peace and Freedom, Sept. 6, 1935, in Lillian D. Wald MSS, New York Public Library.) There is not a scrap of contemporary evidence to bear out any part of this story. It sheds a great deal of light, however, on Jane Addams's relations with her family. It suggests that Ann Haldeman's untiring and unwelcome attentions to her stepdaughter's upbringing reflected in part her mistaken belief that Jane had to be "cared for and catered to."

life of cultivated ease, the aesthetic element in her make-up still exerted a powerful pull, still warred with the activist in her. And so she found herself an enthralled spectator at a bullfight. In the deep historic reverie which the excitement of the fight evoked, she was hardly aware of the waning of the afternoon. She lingered on; she saw bull after bull dispatched in "the most magnificent Spanish style," witnessed the slaughter of horses, heard the bloodthirsty yells of the crowd, smelled the blood of wounded animals and men. Hour after hour she sat transfixed.

> The sense that this was the last survival of all the glories of the amphitheater, the illusion that the riders on the caparisoned horses might have been knights of a tournament, or the matador a slightly armed gladiator facing his martyrdom, and all the rest of the obscure yet vivid associations of an historical survival, had carried me beyond the endurance of any of the rest of the party. I finally met them in the foyer, stern and pale with disapproval of my brutal endurance, and but partially recovered from the faintness and disgust which the spectacle itself had produced upon them. I had no defense to offer to their reproaches save that I had not thought much about the bloodshed; but in the evening the natural and inevitable reaction came, and in deep chagrin I felt myself tried and condemned, not only by this disgusting experience but by the entire moral situation which it revealed.

The experience, she says, opened her eyes to the truth about herself and her cherished project. It showed the project to be "a dreamer's scheme," a "mere paper reform" by which she had lulled her conscience into "going on indefinitely with study and travel." "It is easy," she concludes, "to become the dupe of a deferred purpose, of the promise the future can never keep, and I had fallen into the meanest type of self-deception in making myself believe that all this was in preparation for great things to come."

Thereupon she broke her long silence on the subject of

"the big house" and by doing so broke the deeper emotional silence which for nearly a decade had insulated her from the world about her. She broached the subject, not without misgivings—"in the fear of that disheartening experience which is so apt to afflict our most cherished plans when they are at last divulged, when we feel that there is nothing there to talk about"—to Ellen Starr. Ellen responded with enthusiasm; Jane Addams went to London to observe Toynbee Hall; and the next year they settled at Hull-House and opened its doors to their new neighbors.[9]

The bullfight was more than a reminder of her self-deception, her endlessly deferred plans and projects. It was the embodiment of the aesthetic principle toward which she was appalled to find herself so strongly drawn. Nothing could have made more clear to her what was wrong with a life devoted to beauty alone, the kind of life represented by her stepmother; for here was beauty intertwined with and depending upon the most outrageous cruelty—beauty bought with blood. And over the whole scene hung the sense of antiquity, the terrible weight

9. *Twenty Years at Hull-House*, pp. 85–7. There is an odd discrepancy between her autobiographical account of the bullfight and a contemporary letter describing it. In the letter she makes no mention of her friends' departure and of their disgust when she met them afterward in the foyer. On the contrary, the earlier account indicates that the entire party remained in the amphitheater until the fight was nearly over. "We were brutal enough to take a great interest in it." (Jane Addams to "Laura," Madrid, April 25, 1888, Haldeman MSS.) Why, in her autobiography, she took all the guilt upon herself and exonerated the others is not clear; but the discrepancy is by no means an isolated example. The autobiography almost invariably tends to read back more significance into earlier events than the contemporary records seem to warrant; more significance, at least, than she was aware of at the time. This fact alone is enough to refute those who insist that Jane Addams knew perfectly well from the outset what she was about, and that she merely followed an early inclination to good works to its logical conclusion. It suggests rather that the meaning of her early life became clear to her only after a period of intense self-examination, of which the bullfight itself was the beginning and the writing of her autobiography the culmination.

of the past; so that the total effect—the disclosure, for an American, of the full significance of the oldness of the Old World—must have been not unlike the effect Henry James attributes to Paris in *The Ambassadors*, when Strether comes for his last interview with Mme de Vionnet:

> The light in her beautiful, formal room was dim . . . ; the hot night had kept out lamps, but there was a pair of clusters of candles that glimmered over the chimney-piece like the tall tapers of an altar. The windows were all open, their redundant hangings swaying a little, and he heard once more, from the empty court, the small plash of the fountain. From beyond this, and as from a great distance—beyond the court, beyond the *corps de logis* forming the front—came, as if excited and exciting, the vague voice of Paris. Strether had all along been subject to sudden gusts of fancy in connection with such matters as these—odd starts of the historic sense, suppositions and divinations with no warrant but their intensity. Thus and so, on the eve of the great recorded dates, the days and nights of revolution, the sounds had come in, the omens, the beginnings broken out. They were the smell of revolution, the smell of the public temper—or perhaps simply the smell of blood.[1]

At such moments, writes F. W. Dupee in commenting on this scene from *The Ambassadors*, the American sees what America "in its idealism refuses to see: the amount of sheer sacrifice, the blood and tears, entailed in the perpetuation of any culture worth the name."[2] Such a revelation must have come with luminous clarity to Jane Addams in Madrid, only to be renounced the next moment in bitter revulsion and self-denunciation. It is this renunciation of culture, of the past, of history itself, so characteristically American, that precisely distinguishes Jane Addams from James, so alike in their receptivity to "odd starts of the historic sense," so far apart in the

1. Henry James: *The Ambassadors* (New York: Harper & Brothers; 1948), p. 396.
2. F. W. Dupee: *Henry James* (New York: Anchor Books; 1956), p. 215.

use to which they put those intuitions. It distinguishes the reformer from the traditionalist, and furnishes as precise a measure as one can find by which to judge their respective triumphs
and their respective failures.

In her mounting sense that the end-product of centuries
of sacrifice, this vaunted culture which she had come to Europe,
as a proper American young lady, to absorb, was not worth the
price, it might have crossed her mind (still filled with her study
of the catacombs, "hopelessly superficial" as that may have
been) that she stood in relation to the Europe of the nineteenth
century as the early Christians to the Roman Empire in decline.
Watching the bullfight, she thought of the matador as a "gladi-
ator facing his martyrdom"; and in the aftermath it is possible
that images of the decadence of Rome merged in her mind
with the growing sense of the decadence of her own time. In
any case she turned away from both in a spirit of early Christian renunciation. Henceforth not only the pursuit of beauty
for its own sake but all those intellectual pursuits which had
so long confused and misled her, those tangled theological
speculations which she could neither resolve nor put aside,
were to give way before her conviction that the only god she
could worship was a god of love—a god, that is, of doing rather
than of knowing. That was the lesson of the bullfight no less
than of the catacombs. In rediscovering the primitive church,
like so many reformers before her, she had discovered some
part of herself which, released, freed the rest. Her conversion
was complete.

[III]

When Jane Addams published her autobiography in 1910,
the world came into possession of at least a partial record of
her early struggles. But the world preferred to ignore its im-

port, even while professing to admire Miss Addams's candor. Her admirers fabricated instead their own version of her life, pious and sentimental, in which Jane Addams became a symbol of pure altruism, dedicated from earliest childhood to the service of suffering humanity. In the first pages of her auto-biography, Jane Addams recalled how she had gone with her father, when she was about seven, to the neighboring town of Freeport, after which she had conceived the fantasy that "when I grew up I should, of course, have a large house, but it would not be built among the other large houses, but right in the midst of horrid little houses like these." That was all she said about the incident; but her uncritical eulogists seized upon it to show that Jane Addams had never wavered from her youth-ful determination to help the poor. The "master-motive" of her life, wrote Graham Taylor, a friend and fellow settlement worker who ought to have known better, "began to possess her . . . from her sixth year."[3] Even Edmund Wilson made a pious bow toward the myth.[4] So did Robert Morss Lovett: "When a child of seven, she had had her first sight of 'the poverty which implies squalor.'"[5] As late as 1955 Violet Oakley wrote a "dramatic outline of the life of Jane Addams," in which she depicted Jane as a girl of seven discussing with her brother her plan to "have a lot of money saved up to build the Great Big House."[6]

All her subsequent uncertainty and confusion went by the board. When she went to Europe, "she was impatient with the art galleries in the capitals of Europe; her interest was in the

3. Graham Taylor: "Jane Addams's Twenty Years of Industrial Democracy," *Survey*, XXV (Dec. 3, 1910), p. 405.

4. Edmund Wilson: *American Earthquake* (New York: Doubleday; 1958), p. 449.

5. Robert Morss Lovett: "Jane Addams," *World Tomorrow*, VIII (Nov., 1925), p. 345.

6. Violet Oakley: *Cathedral of Compassion* (Philadelphia: limited edition; 1955), p. 12.

slums."[7] So wrote one admirer of the woman who described herself as feeling at home nowhere except in those art galleries, now so easily dismissed as irrelevant to her history. Another eulogist reduced even her revelation at the bullfight to a sentimental cliché: "Gradually a vision was taking shape in her mind. And this vision, strangely enough, became crystallized into a definite form while she was witnessing a bullfight at Madrid. The sight of the laughter and the brutal applause aroused within her a wave of resentment. She must do something to put an end to the cruelty of man."[8]

In time a reaction set in—part of a reassessment of American progressivism as a whole. Richard Hofstadter, writing from within the liberal tradition—a fact which most of his critics ignored—at the same time insisted that it was too simple to see reformers as disinterested champions of the downtrodden masses; at the very least, one had to ask what made the sons and daughters of the middle class so suddenly conscious of conditions they had previously ignored; for the conditions themselves were not new. Hofstadter accordingly suggested that middle-class intellectuals had themselves been cut off from the centers of power and authority in American society, and that their own loss of status and power in turn made them better able to understand the point of view of those who had never had power to lose. Of the ministry, for example, he wrote: "In the light of this situation, it may not be unfair to attribute the turning of the clergy toward reform and social criticism not solely to their disinterested perception of social problems and their earnest desire to improve the world, but also to the fact that as men who were in their own way suffering from the incidence of the status revolution they were able to understand

7. Robert M. Bartlett: *They Dared to Live* (New York: Association Press; 1938), p. 32.

8. Henry Thomas: *The Story of the United States: A Biographical History of America* (New York: Doubleday, Doran & Co.; 1938), p. 376.

and sympathize with the problems of other disinherited groups."[9]

But to inquire into the motives of the reformers seemed to a new generation of liberal or radical historians equivalent to dismissing the horrors against which they rose up in protest—in rightful protest, as it now seemed in the militant mood of the early sixties. By emphasizing the subjective sources of the reforming impulse, Hofstadter's critics complained, he had in effect set up an arbitrary norm or "consensus," and all deviations from it became irrational by definition; whereas in fact the evils against which Populists and progressives clamored were perfectly objective and real.[1] Thus the wheel came full circle: the reformers were rehabilitated and progressivism came to be seen once again (but without quite the sentimental extravagance of the earlier version) as a "response to industrialism."[2]

In an essay on Jane Addams written in 1961, Staughton Lynd commented on the tendency of revisionist writing, by calling into question the worthy motives of reformers such as Jane Addams, to explain the subject away. Boldly confronting the strongest piece of evidence in favor of a subjective interpretation of Jane Addams's career, her own "Subjective Necessity for Social Settlements," Lynd observed that "it is easy to see how such a frank confession of personal need to do good

9. Richard Hofstadter: *The Age of Reform* (New York: Alfred A. Knopf; 1955), pp. 151–2. For his own relation to the liberal tradition, see *The Age of Reform*, p. 12.

1. See Norman Pollack: "Hofstadter on Populism," *Journal of Southern History*, XXVI (Nov., 1960), pp. 478ff. For other attacks on what critics call the "consensus" theory, see John Higham: "The Cult of the American Consensus," *Commentary*, XXVII (Feb., 1959), pp. 93–100, and C. Vann Woodward: "The Populist Heritage and the Intellectual," *American Scholar*, XXIX (winter, 1959–60), pp. 55–72.

2. See Samuel P. Hays: *The Response to Industrialism* (Chicago: University of Chicago Press; 1957), and Norman Pollack: *The Populist Response to Industrial America* (Cambridge: Harvard University Press; 1962).

by a do-gooder provides an opening for those who have been questioning the validity of radical action by exploring its psychic origins." He went on to criticize Hofstadter for putting the essay, after praising it, into the context of the progressives' sense of guilt. The context seemed to Lynd to "erode the adjective." "Does [Hofstadter] mean to say that it was wrong or abnormal for a member of the urban middle class in 1900 (or for that matter, today) to feel guilt about living in comfort when millions of immigrant families battled tuberculosis and the sweat-shop in filthy and overcrowded tenements?"[3]

But the question is not whether it was wrong to pity the victims of industrialism or even to feel guilty about them; the question is whether that was what Jane Addams felt guilty about. She first saw industrial poverty in London in 1883, during her first trip to Europe. Many years later she evoked the scene unforgettably: "two huge masses of ill-clad people clamoring around two hucksters' carts," the final impression one "of myriads of hands, empty, pathetic, nerveless and work-worn, showing white in the uncertain light of the street, and clutching forward for food which was already unfit to eat."[4] At the time, however, the experience inspired no such outburst. In fact, her reactions hardly rose to the level of articulation. In all her dutiful letters home, there is only a single reference to the episode or to any like it, and that is of a curiously literary character, as if she could as yet confront such experiences only at second hand. "At one time," she wrote to her brother, "we found ourselves in a Dickens neighborhood. We took a look down into dingy old Grub St. It was simply an outside superficial survey of the misery & wretchedness, but it was enough to make one thoroughly sad & perplexed."[5]

3. Staughton Lynd: "Jane Addams and the Radical Impulse," *Commentary*, XXXII (July, 1961), p. 54.
4. *Twenty Years at Hull-House*, pp. 67–8.
5. Jane Addams to Weber Addams, Oct. 29, 1883, Haldeman MSS.

Jane Addams herself later commented on her tendency, at that time, to see life through literature. The tendency itself reminded her in turn of an essay of De Quincey in which the author, wishing to warn his coachman of a pair of lovers in the path of the coach, finds himself paralyzed by the effort to recall an appropriate passage from the *Iliad.* "It seemed to me too preposterous that in my first view of the horror of East London I should have recalled De Quincey's literary description of the literary suggestion which had once paralyzed him. In my disgust it all appeared a hateful, vicious circle which even the apostles of culture themselves admitted."[6]

There the matter rested for five years more. It can be argued that her feeling about the horrors she had seen was too deep to discuss with her family, and that her silence on the subject does not necessarily indicate an absence of concern. But she did not discuss her feelings even with Ellen Starr, with whom she showed no reluctance to discuss matters close to her heart; and it is hard to see, therefore, why she should have remained silent about this episode, if it troubled her so deeply.[7] What she did discuss, what she continued endlessly to discuss with her friend, was religion—that and her own uselessness. Later her sense of superfluity would acquire another dimension when she came to play it off against the wretchedness of her Hull-House "neighbors," whose grinding misery made a contrast to the leisure of her own kind.[8] But there was hardly a suggestion of such a point of view in anything she wrote during the

6. *Twenty Years at Hull-House,* pp. 70–1.

7. Miss Starr did not accompany her on the first trip. The correspondence continued throughout it.

8. And again she tended to project this way of thinking back into an earlier period. "For two years," she says, "in the midst of my distress over the poverty which, thus suddenly driven into my consciousness, had become to me the 'Weltschmerz,' there was mingled a sense of futility, of misdirected energy, the belief that the pursuit of cultivation would not in the end bring either solace or relief." (*Twenty Years at Hull-House,* p. 71.)

eighties. Her few surviving references to poverty have the conventional quality that characterized all her references to public questions in that period of her life. For example, she wrote to her brother after a visit to Pompeii that the ruins "showed the weak point of the old civilization every possible elegance & comfort for the few but nothing for the animals or the more wretched people." The very fact that she identified the condition with "the old civilization" shows how far she was from confronting the modern problem of industrial poverty. These reflections did not foreshadow Jane Addams's later critique of industrialism. They belonged rather to the line of thought that culminated in her reflections about the bullfight—European decadence, the cruelty that underlies high culture.[9]

As for politics, her reaction upon receiving news of Cleveland's election in 1884—"We still allow ourselves to hope [for the election of Blaine] until tomorrow morning"—shows that she accepted unthinkingly the genteel Republicanism of her family.[1] She herself later admitted her political innocence. Even as late as her second trip to England, "I did not, curiously enough, in any wise connect with what was called the labor movement, nor did I understand the efforts of the London trades-unionists, concerning whom I held the vaguest notions."[2]

What gleams out from her letters is her mounting frustration with the life her mother was trying to get her to lead. Her later essay, "The Subjective Necessity," recapitulates the experience in the form of a general analysis of the problem facing young girls of her class.

I have seen young girls suffer and grow sensibly lowered in vitality in the first years after they leave school. In our attempt then to give a girl pleasure and freedom from care we succeed,

9. Jane Addams to Weber Addams, Siena, May 19, 1884, Haldeman MSS.
1. Jane Addams to Alice Haldeman, Berlin, Nov. 5, 1884, Haldeman MSS.
2. *Twenty Years at Hull-House*, p. 81.

for the most part, in making her pitifully miserable. She finds "life" so different from what she expected it to be. She is besotted with innocent little ambitions, and does not understand this apparent waste of herself, this elaborate preparation, if no work is provided for her.

She burns with "the desire for action, the wish to right wrong and alleviate suffering," but society merely "smiles at it indulgently." But all the while the altruistic instinct in young girls is "persistently cultivated."

They are taught to be self-forgetting and self-sacrificing, to consider the good of the whole before the good of the ego. But when all this information and culture show results, when the daughter comes back from college and begins to recognize her social claim to the "submerged tenth," and to evince a disposition to fulfill it, the family claim is strenuously asserted; she is told that she is unjustified, ill-advised in her efforts.

Thwarted, "the girl loses something vital out of her life to which she is entitled." Her parents, meanwhile, are unaware of her unhappiness, "and we have all the elements of a tragedy."[3]

It was a cultural crisis, then—though a cultural crisis played out against the increasingly audible sounds of revolution, "the omens, the beginnings broken out"—that underlay Jane Addams's distress. At the end of the nineteenth century, middle-class parents found themselves unable any longer to explain to their children why their way of life was important or desirable. The children on their part found themselves equally unable to communicate a sense of why they could not pursue the goals their parents held up before them, unable to explain why they felt themselves "simply smothered and sickened with advantages."

Such an explanation of Jane Addams's early life, far from obscuring her later activities, makes it possible to understand

3. Ibid., pp. 118–20.

why the gap between the generations subsequently became one of the principal themes of her social writings. What she discovered at Hull-House was that the same thing was happening in immigrant families that she had already experienced in her own. The children of immigrants, driven by the timeless longing of youth for broader horizons, restlessly roamed the streets of the city, avidly drinking in the new culture about them. Their parents sought to keep them in the old ways. The children, maddened by everything in their parents that now seemed alien and queer, turned on them with loathing. Thus there came into being another domestic tragedy, no less poignant for Jane Addams than her own; and the breakdown of immigrant families upon contact with conditions in America came to seem to her, indeed, the measure of the immigrants' general degradation.

The conflict of first- and second-generation immigrants has now become a sociological commonplace, but Jane Addams was one of the first people to discover it and to subject it to analysis.[4] In view of her own struggles, one can understand why she was able to describe it with such sympathy and precision. In the end her sympathy not only with the rebellion of youth but with the plight of the parents, more pitiable still, enabled Jane Addams to see their conflicting points of view with equal clarity. Her growing admiration for the cultures of which the first-generation immigrants were the transmitters—a heritage their children proved so tragically unable to understand—even tended belatedly to reconcile her to the culture of her own class, tempering the despair that in other radicals led to forms of rebellion more destructive and ultimately nihilistic.

4. See especially *The Spirit of Youth and the City Streets.*

2 / Woman as Alien

[I]

RESTLESSNESS! RESTLESSNESS!" CRIED THE NOVELIST MARGARET Deland in 1910. Everywhere one found "a prevailing discontent among women," "a restlessness infinitely removed from the old content of a generation ago."[1] The figure of the "neurasthenic" woman haunted the period—"the woman of privilege, the woman of sane and sheltered life,"[2] whose possessions included everything except happiness. "One meets wives, young or mature, apparently happy, gay; suddenly they confide in you that they are bored to death. . . . Others . . . merely want a 'change.' If they live in California, they want to live in New York. . . . Many . . . fall into a state of depression, develop nerves, lose the taste of life."[3]

A literature of reproach and alarm sprang up around the discontented woman of leisure. For psychologists, called in when the symptoms defied medical explanation, she was an object of intense concern; indeed, so familiar were the symptoms of women—ennui, fatigue, inexplicable illnesses, fits of crying over the most trivial causes, "nerves," "melancholia"— that psychologists for a long time assumed that hysterical neuroses were purely feminine manifestations. Students of society found a portent of disaster in the "parasitism" of the educated woman of the leisure class—the "fine lady," as Olive

1. Margaret Deland: "The Change in the Feminine Ideal," *Atlantic*, CV (March, 1910), pp. 290–1.
2. Ibid., p. 290.
3. Gertrude Atherton: "The Woman in Love," *Harper's Bazar*, XLIV (May, 1910), p. 305.

Schreiner called her, "the effete wife, concubine or prostitute, clad in fine raiment, the work of others' fingers; fed on luxurious viands, the result of others' toil, waited on and tended by the labor of others."[4] To people already troubled by thoughts of overcivilization, the appearance of the female parasite seemed to herald an age of imperial decadence, a second Rome.

The fiction of the period abounds in speculation about the "emancipated" woman, whose newfound freedom seemed to be so much heavier a burden than her centuries of slavery. Robert Herrick, the most interesting of the so-called problem novelists around the turn of the century, saw in the restlessness of the modern woman the key to the social disorder about him: for it was the woman of fashion, he thought, freed by wealth and leisure to devote all her energies to competitive consumption, who drove her husband to sacrifice everything to the accumulation of wealth. Only by seeing economic competition as at bottom not economic at all, but social, could Herrick continue to deplore the "fierce competitive struggle" while at the same time celebrating the virtues of the old-fashioned entrepreneur. The entrepreneur might appear at first sight to have been himself implicated in the competitive struggle. But by distinguishing between the competition which centers on the production of goods and that which centers on consumption, and by investing the distinction with a moral value, Herrick avoided the utterly pessimistic conclusions to which his analysis so often seemed about to lead.[5]

4. Olive Schreiner: *Woman and Labor* (New York: Frederick A. Stokes; 1911), pp. 79–80.

5. Herrick was by no means the only novelist who wrote of the American woman in this light. The works of both Howells and James abound in matrons whose social ambitions and lust for power come to focus on the consumption of goods. Mrs. Westgate, in James's "An International Episode," is an example:

"An American woman who respects herself," said Mrs. Westgate, turning to Beaumont with her bright expository air, "must buy something every

"You drive him to the market-place," Herrick shouts at the despised "intellectual women" who were at once the objects of his censure and the most faithful readers of his fictions.[6] And in *Together*, his most ambitious production, he presented a whole gallery of restless, striving women, of the kind who leave destruction wherever their influence is felt: Bessie Falkner, whose social ambitions drive her husband first to bankruptcy and then to adultery; Connie Woodyard, the new intellectual whose first question is always, "What does it mean for *me*?"; Isabelle Lane, neurasthenic and effete, "too finely organized for the plain animal duties" of matrimony and motherhood, a victim, like the others, of the cult of "self-fulfillment."[7] Strangers to their husbands (as in the novels of William Dean Howells, the growing separation of the wife's and husband's spheres, she in the social whirl, he absorbed with business, is a persistent theme in Herrick's work), strangers to any conception of the traditional obligations of their sex, these women pass their lives in the pursuit of their own pleasure. They live in fear of pregnancy and have learned to prate of the family as an enslaving institution. The "atmosphere of the age" is epitomized for Herrick in Margaret Pole's adulterous affair with Rob Falkner—after which, however, he arranges her repentance and renunciation (not unlike similar renunciations in the novels of Henry James), an event which serves to throw into bolder contrast the unregeneracy of the others. Even in her moment of sin, Margaret distinguishes herself from the rest of Herrick's women by wishing nothing more than utterly to submit to her lover. She retains that intuitive sense of sexual differentiation the loss of which, in the others, is for Herrick

day of her life. If she cannot do it herself, she must send out some member of her family for the purpose." (Leon Edel, ed.: *The Complete Tales of Henry James* [London: Rupert Hart-Davis; 1962], Vol. IV, p. 275.)

6. Robert Herrick: *Together* (New York: Macmillan; 1908), p. 499.

7. Ibid., pp. 220, 155.

the most telling sign of their depravity. "You," she sighs to her lover, "are the Man!"[8]

Even *Together*, with its sustained and somewhat shrill indictment not only of feminism but of modernity itself, was too mild in its censure for some of Herrick's contemporaries. Indeed, many of them were shocked by it, attributing to Herrick the very opinions he sought to undermine. The tendency of his readers to mistake this profoundly conservative document for a manifesto of sexual freedom is an indication not so much of the ambiguity of the novel itself as of the confusion that had come to surround the whole question of the "emancipation" of women. It is an indication too of the depths of feeling, on either side of the question, which the question almost automatically evoked—beside which discussion of the other issues of the day, the trusts and the tariff and even prohibition, seemed amiable and innocuous. Howells, for instance, who had handled somewhat similar material in *The Rise of Silas Lapham* and had even taken up the question of divorce in *A Modern Instance*, was horrified by what he regarded as Herrick's sympathetic treatment of adultery. If Herrick was merely recording a phase of social history, Howells was willing to concede that he was within his "rights as an artist," but if he meant to portray adultery as "a thing to have done without shame or without sin," he opened himself to "the criticism deriving from such ethics as the world knows."[9]

Herrick was reduced to writing a long reassurance—in spite of his awareness that "an author's explanations are very doubtful things"—in which he set forth his intention as explicitly as he could. He was sorry that he had given rise to misunderstanding. "Certainly I never for one moment intended to hold a

8. Ibid., p. 390.

9. William Dean Howells to Robert Herrick, Feb. 16, 1909, Robert Herrick MSS, University of Chicago Library.

brief for free love, and there must be something wrong about
the book, about the conclusion, to lead people, you above all,
to think so." What he had meant to do was to present a series
of cases of "extreme individualism, which is the politely philosophical term we give to selfishness." The women in the book
were "all after the fulfillment of self—socially, sexually, and
economically"; and the failure of this "personal individualism"
to give happiness was the point of the novel. As for the admittedly "debatable" case of Margaret Pole and Falkner,
though written, Herrick conceded, with more sympathy than
the others, "it belongs, nevertheless, in the same category of
arrant individualism as the rest, only in this case there is presented flatly, and I believe honestly, the fact that for them this
fulfillment of self at the cost of moral love, was FOR THE TIME an
actual gain, a real enoblement [sic]." But Margaret after all
refuses to marry Falkner.

> Of course the commonplace thing for a woman like Margaret
> Pole to do would be to divorce and marry, a course that she has
> contempt for. The desire for her own life, her own greatest
> happiness led to her relation with Falkner, and it was only
> through this relation which aroused her whole being that she
> was enobled, or as a matter of fact did, come to the realization
> of the inadequacy of that solution.[1]

This explanation mollified Howells;[2] but Howells was only
one of many readers who misunderstood this curious book.
The British journalist W. T. Stead also objected to the affair
between Margaret and Falkner.[3] So did Neith Hapgood, not,
however, because she thought the passage immoral, but simply

1. Herrick to Howells, Feb. 17, 1909, William Dean Howells MSS, Houghton Library, Cambridge.
2. Howells to Herrick, Feb. 21, 1909, Herrick MSS.
3. W. T. Stead to Herrick, Oct. 6, 1908, Herrick MSS.

because "their ecstasy did not ring true." Like the others, however, she assumed that Herrick had intended "to realize the nobility of overstepping legal bounds."[4]

The most revealing of all these responses to the book came from a thirty-year-old woman in Washington, D.C., a stranger to Herrick, who not only admired the novel as "quite the greatest book . . . of the decade" but had tried to put its "theories" into practice—had "acted upon them as revelation."[5] On four legal-size, closely typewritten sheets Josephine Dixon poured out her autobiography—the unwritten autobiography of how many women of her time? She had married at eighteen a man thirty years older than herself, whom she idealized; a man, she thought, of poetic temperament and "almost ethereal" purity of mind. "From out of some source of those mistaken ideas with which girls are so liberally provided," she "conceived the idea that to him the sexual function was a more or less disagreeable necessity to be fulfilled as quietly and quickly and with as little emotion as the other physical necessities." Her husband became to her "a sort of priestly ideal" whom she "worshipped without understanding." By contrast, her own "*vivid* desires" and "*undefined* longing for an intense emotional gratification" made her ashamed. "Diabolical visitations," they rendered her "unworthy to be even in his presence." She was appalled to find herself strongly attracted to another man, "who aroused in me keen physical desire." "There was nothing more between us than the touch of hands but the consciousness of my passion and desire for him made me so degraded in the presence of the man to whom I was married that I was driven many times to the verge of suicide, and indeed made one ineffectual effort towards its accomplishment." The corrosive effect of this pas-

4. N[eith] H[apgood] to Herrick, Aug. 11, [1908], Herrick MSS.
5. Josephine Dixon to Herrick, n.d. [1908], Herrick MSS.

sion worked upon her for six years, "leading me to exaggerate as a solitary mind can, the virtues of my husband and my own private vicious unworthiness."

In the twelfth year of her marriage a chance event destroyed her illusions about her husband. A coachman in the service of the family was stricken with "a mysterious illness," which turned out to be a venereal disease. The other servants whispered about it, and the matter came to the attention of her husband. To Mrs. Dixon's consternation, he declared "that he could prescribe for the man better than the physician who was attending him." Then the whole story came out. Not only had he "suffered the same way," but he had lived with his previous wife, of whom Mrs. Dixon had known only that she was "coarse" and that she and her husband were eventually divorced, for more than a year without the sanction of matrimony. After she had run off with another man, he took up with "negresses, prostitutes, Paris women of the street and all the rest of the flotsam that I could not, would not, had never dared to think had touched him." These disclosures plunged Mrs. Dixon into "a bottomless sea" of "terror, horror, shock and hopelessness." She had once prided herself on her freedom from illusion. Now at the loss of the first illusion she "had gone insane."

At that point *Together* came into her hands.

If it were not true it would be unbelievable. Such a coincidence could not be used in fiction for its utter improbability. But it happened to be true. I read it as a drowning man catches at straws. I read that at thirty a woman is not done with life and romance and passion. It seemed to be an answer to me. . . . If one lost out in one venture in love there were other avenues open in which it might be found. What did I do? I did the obvious thing. I wrote to my straying man friend. He refused me on [my] terms but we met entirely by accident in another city and I gave myself to him, perhaps forced myself on him for I was

entirely mad. . . . I scarcely knew what I was doing but it is done.
I am back in my home. My husband comes and goes as placidly
as ever. . . . He knows nothing of my pitiful, shabby tragedy.
No one knows anything of it. The first word goes to you.

What Herrick made of all this is unfortunately not recorded. It is a remarkable letter. In fact, it reveals so many
pathological characteristics that one is tempted to treat its
writer as no more than the sum of her symptoms. With her
imagination, her intelligence, her "nerves," her false suicides,
Mrs. Dixon is a classic study in hysteria. Her sexual fears are
so strong that she discards her new lover after one night with
him—"My passion for him seems to have burned itself out in
the one sudden explosion"—and makes a confidant instead of
a distant author whom she has never seen: a symbol of wisdom
and sensitivity ("the only person likely to understand or comprehend") to take the place of the one she lost in her husband;
a love-object conveniently remote. But it is not the neurosis
which this letter betrays so much as it is the letter itself—the
fact of its having been written at all—that belongs to the study
of history. History is the record of consciousness; and it is
precisely Mrs. Dixon's self-consciousness about her symptoms
and the sophisticated relish with which she analyzes them (for
all her genuine suffering) that mark her letter as a distinctive
product of its period. Her narrative, moreover, is written in the
style of popular romance, the style of the ladies' magazines:
she "could not, would not, had never dared to think" that
Negresses and whores had touched her husband; the discovery
that they had threw her into "a bottomless sea" of suffering;
but when she read *Together* she realized that "at thirty a
woman is not done with life." It comes as no surprise to find
that Mrs. Dixon was herself an aspiring novelist. "I am trying
to write it out in book form," she confides at the end of her
letter.

All this suggests that the themes of feminine restlessness and of the unfulfilled craving for a larger life had already undergone a high degree of popularization. They had become sentimentalized; life began to pattern itself after romance. For the victims of this process, art ceased to serve any critical function and became instead a summons to "live." Thus Mrs. Dixon could see in Herrick's attack on the new woman—an attack, in effect, on herself—only another endorsement of her own fevered search for "life and romance and passion."

[II]

A further indication of the contemporary confusion surrounding the new woman is the fact that the opinions of antifeminists such as Herrick coincided in so many particulars with those of the feminists themselves. The feminists did not of course share the view that feminism embodied the "arrant individualism" of the times, but they were equally convinced that the fierce pursuit of self-fulfillment was the source of the social unrest deplored by feminists and anti-feminists alike. They were at one with Herrick in regarding the problem of the modern woman as essentially a labor problem; a problem, that is, created by the sudden superabundance of leisure, or as the feminists were fond of putting it, by woman's evolution from producer to consumer. In the latter role she was condemned, it seemed, to live on the labor of others. It was this condition that feminists like Olive Schreiner and Charlotte Perkins Gilman called "parasitism." As Olive Schreiner noted, the fact that feminism had "essentially taken its rise among women of the more cultured and wealthy classes"[6] seemed to

6. Schreiner: *Woman and Labor*, p. 124.

confirm this theory about its origins. Feminism apparently was a response—and an alternative—to the useless idleness which afflicted leisure-class women most immediately but which with the further advance of industrialism threatened to spread throughout modern society.

Rather than regarding this condition as originating in a moral flaw, the feminists reasoned that although it indisputably gave rise to uninhibited self-indulgence, its origins themselves were primarily economic. The family, they thought, once the most important unit of production, had gradually surrendered its functions to institutions outside the home—manufacturing to the factory, control over property to the state, the education of children to the public schools. This development, rather than the more obvious invasion of the home by labor-saving devices, was what the feminists had mainly in mind when they claimed that women's work had passed out of the home. The tasks formerly performed by the housewife and by the family in general were now performed elsewhere, and the function of the housewife in consequence was reduced to the passive role of consumption. The feminists did not regret the passing of the family; on the contrary, as staunch evolutionists, they regarded it as highly desirable, a necessary step in the "socialization" of mankind. They quarreled only with the refusal of their adversaries to see what these developments implied for the future role of women.

It was not only feminists who analyzed the problem this way. So common was the view that the family had lost its economic functions that by the turn of the century it was already a sociological truism.[7] Nor did it necessarily lead to

7. See, for example, William E. Carson: *The Marriage Revolt: A Study of Marriage and Divorce* (New York: Hearst's International Library Co.; 1915), pp. 21–2; Orison Swett Marden: *Woman and Home* (New York: Thomas Y. Crowell; 1915), pp. 23–31.

feminist conclusions. More often it led to conclusions midway between those of the feminists, who welcomed the demise of the patriarchal family but insisted that it dictated a larger role for women outside the home, and those of the anti-feminists, who held that women's claim to a larger role was itself the cause of the whole problem. More common than either of these arguments was the characteristically "progressive" contention that the emergence of woman as a consumer demanded above all that she learn to play her new role more effectively. Those who took this line did not urge her to adopt a new role altogether, to "follow her work out of the home," as the feminists put it. Rather, they wanted her to stay at home as before, but to learn to use her new "profession" as consumer as a strategic position through which to influence and finally control the national destiny. This argument was a somewhat more sophisticated version of the old cliché that women as wives and mothers ruled the world from behind the scenes. Now women were urged to see that the most humdrum details of marketing and household economics had repercussions felt in distant capitals of trade and commerce, repercussions which profoundly altered the course of public affairs.

It was this position—what one might call the pseudo-feminist position—that was expounded by the more advanced of the women's magazines and in particular by *Good Housekeeping* and *Harper's Bazar*. The former devoted itself to the premise that housekeeping ought to be seen as a science; it was an unofficial organ of the home-economics movement, which achieved its first successes around the turn of the century. *Harper's Bazar* was more genteel in tone, and concerned itself not only with household affairs but with fashions, "society," and the arts and letters. It addressed itself precisely to the woman of leisure and cultivation who was presumed to be the chief victim of technological unemployment. Politically

more adventurous than *Good Housekeeping* or the *Ladies'
Home Journal*, the latter of which, under the editorship of
Edward Bok, was strongly anti-feminist, the *Bazar* favored
woman suffrage and other progressive reforms. For Bok, on the
other hand, even the women's club movement represented a
threat to the family. "Twenty years ago," he wrote, "a change
in economic conditions, caused chiefly by the invention of
labor-saving devices, found thousands of women suddenly
thrown with leisure on their hands." But instead of using this
leisure to combat such evils as the laxity of the divorce laws
or the public drinking-cup, club women wasted their time on
activities that drew them still further away from the "great and
fundamental problems directly touching the marriage relation
and the home."[8]

Compared with *Ladies' Home Journal*, *Harper's Bazar*
was a model of enlightened progressivism. Nevertheless, it
rejected the feminist demand for the socialization of womanhood. To women in search of excitement, in search of careers,
the *Bazar* replied that the most ancient and honorable of professions was the home. A typical article, of the kind one can
find in any issue of the magazine for these years, deplores
"the spirit of unrest in the drawing-room" and enjoins on
women the higher fulfillment of "wifehood and motherhood."[9]

Home life in our busy day [the writer regretfully notes] . . . is
passing out of vogue. . . . Each [daughter] has her fad or mission,
keeping her for hours abroad, or else when in-doors bent over a
desk heaped with notes to answer, minutes to be made up, reports
to be prepared . . . papers to be written. . . . At breakfast she is too
absorbed in tearing open and digesting her correspondence to be
able to diffuse around her the aroma of gracious and sympathiz-

8. Edward Bok: "My Quarrel with Women's Clubs," *Ladies' Home
Journal*, XXVII (Jan., 1910), pp. 5–6.
9. Mrs. Burton Harrison: "Home Life as a Profession," *Harper's Bazar*,
XXXIII (May 19, 1900), pp. 148–50.

ing young womanhood which would help to arm the men of the family for their fight with circumstance downtown.

But at the same time—and this is what is so characteristic of the pseudo-feminist position—the writer makes it clear that she does not advocate a return to the family of former times. "Far be it from me to suggest a relapse to those dark ages of home life when a girl strummed on the piano or worked the cross-stitch tapestry what time she was not engaged in dressing or receiving 'beaux,' until she married and passed into a new arena." Not a "relapse" into culture and courtship, but modern motherhood, the ideal of "home life as a profession," ought henceforth to be the goal of women's efforts.

Full-blown feminists naturally had no patience with such counsel. To the home economists they replied that it was no use trying to make home industry a science. "It is just because it is home industry that all this trouble is necessary."[1] Home industry was inherently inefficient because it required the housewife, unspecialized and untrained, to perform a multitude of tasks each of which could better be performed by a specialist. It followed that homemade clothes were inferior to those made by a tailor, home cooking inferior to the products of the factory, home-baked bread inferior to the baker's. Bread, Mrs. Gilman noted, had "risen greatly in excellence as we make less and less at home."[2] In every sphere, progress came from without. If the home was safe, it owed its safety to the police; if it was clean, it had public sanitation to thank. And if such services as these were already "socialized," with obvious advantage to all, why not socialize the rest?—the education of children above all else. The kindergarten and the day nursery were encouraging signs. "There is no more brilliant hope on earth to-day than

1. Charlotte Perkins Gilman: *The Home: Its Work and Influence* (New York: McClure, Phillips & Co.; 1903), p. 93.
2. Ibid., p. 331.

this new thought about the child . . . the recognition of 'the child,' children as a class, children as citizens with rights to be guaranteed only by the state; instead of our previous attitude toward them of absolute personal ownership—the unchecked tyranny, or as unchecked indulgence, of the private home."[3]

If selfishness was the disease of modern society, in short, it was precisely because of the survival of the patriarchal family into an age in which it had no place. The family institutionalized selfishness; it gave sanction to every anti-social impulse. "Civilization and Christianity teach us to care for 'the child,' motherhood stops at 'my child.' "[4] Mrs. Gilman, who like so many radicals of the time tended to equate technological with cultural advancement, the division of labor with the progress of the spirit, analyzed the evolution of "love" as follows.

The primitive father, to feed the child, went forth himself and killed some rabbit—and the primitive mother cooked it: love, in grade A. The modern father, to feed his child, takes his thousandth part in some complex industry, and receives his thousand-fold share of the complex products of others' industry, and so provides for the child far more richly than could the savage: love, in grade Z.

But the modern mother, she complained, to feed her child still did nothing but cook for it. The modern mother "still loves in grade A, and the effect of that persistence of grade A is to retard the development of grade Z." "Mother-love," Mrs. Gilman concluded, "is the fountain of all our human affection, but mother-love, *as limited by the home*, does not have the range and efficacy proper to our time."[5]

What the feminists wanted to make clear was that not only women and the family, but society as a whole, would benefit

3. Ibid., p. 335. On the discovery of the child see below, chapter 3.
4. Ibid., p. 165.
5. Ibid., p. 167.

from the changes they proposed. Indeed, they managed at times to convince themselves that woman had as much to lose as to gain—looking at the matter in terms of her narrow and immediate self-interest—from her emancipation. She would be called on to make heavy sacrifices of leisure and comfort. It was "not for herself, not even for fellow women alone, but for the benefit of humanity at large, [that] she must seek to readjust herself to life"; and it was this fact, Olive Schreiner argued, that excused even the "passionate denunciations, not always wisely thought out," which some feminists leveled at the opposite sex.[6] It was woman's nature, after all, to work for others. Social consciousness was preeminently a feminine trait, and men acquired it, if they acquired it at all, through contact with women. The difference between men and women in this regard was inherent in the respective roles men and women, from time immemorial, had been required to perform. Women, as mothers, developed a sense of responsibility for others. Men, as providers, were necessarily dominated by the spirit of gain. As Rheta Childe Dorr put it: "Man, in the aggregate, thinks in terms of money profit and money loss, and try as he will, he cannot yet think in any other terms." But women had been trained for "constant service," and they were accustomed to look for "purely a spiritual reward."[7]

This line of argument was not without its difficulties. If it was domesticity that bred in women the social sense, would not women lose the social sense when they were no longer domestic? When exposed to the man's world, would they not take on what Mrs. Dorr called the "commercial habit of thought"? Answers to the question varied. Mrs. Dorr conceded that the danger existed and that in another age women might have

6. Schreiner: *Woman and Labor*, pp. 125–6.
7. Rheta Childe Dorr: *What Eight Million Women Want* (Boston: Small, Maynard & Co.; 1910), pp. 6, 11.

been contaminated by contact with the world of affairs. But it happened, she contended, that the new woman came into a world which was "already losing faith in the commercial ideal, and which is endeavoring to substitute in its place a social idea."[8] The time was singularly propitious, in other words, for woman's entry into the larger sphere of her responsibilities.

Others were not content to rest their case on the existing enlightenment of the age, perhaps because they could not concede that any age was enlightened which still discriminated against women. At the same time they insisted that women would not lose their womanly qualities by doing men's work. But that put them in the position of saying that woman's nature was unchanging and thus implied a rejection of the environmentalism to which feminists professed to be devoted. At this point, one begins to suspect that for many feminists the doctrine of evolution merely served to give scientific respectability to existing clichés about the nature of woman—her essential purity, her freedom from coarse or selfish motives, her "habit of service." A strict environmentalism would have forced them to reckon with the possibility that the nature of women, no less than that of men, might be changed, as Ellen Key observed, "by different vocations and surroundings." If women now believed they could achieve the "strength of men" without sacrificing something of the harmony of their lives, Ellen Key warned her more complacent colleagues, they believed "their sex capable of possibilities which thus far have been granted rarely and then only to the exceptional in both sexes."[9] But that was exactly what many American feminists did believe.

It is an added irony that the ideas about woman's nature

8. Ibid., pp. 12–13.
9. Ellen Key: *The Woman Movement* (New York: G. P. Putnam's Sons: 1912), p. 105.

to which some feminists still clung, in spite of their opposition
to the enslavement of woman in the home, were the very
clichés which had so long been used to keep her there. The
assumption that women were morally purer than men, better
capable of altruism and self-sacrifice, was the core of the myth
of domesticity against which the feminists were in revolt. Once
again, feminist and anti-feminist assumptions seemed curiously
to coincide.

According to Charlotte Perkins Gilman, civilization itself
was no more than that "common consciousness" which made
men something more than mere animals, and which it was
peculiarly the function of women to provide. In order for human beings to develop common consciousness, it was necessary
for them, in the beginning, to become aware of their mutual
need. The first step in this evolutionary process was the
mother's awareness of her child's need of her. The second step
was accomplished when the mother communicated her mother-
love, her sense of responsibility, to the father, making him a
partner in the work of bringing up the young. Woman domes-
ticated man, "to his immense improvement." "Man was made
part mother; and so both man and woman were enabled to
become human."[1]

These gains were accomplished, however, at the price of
woman's economic independence. When she took the man into
the family as provider, she ceased to provide for herself. She
sank into "a state of helpless slavery." She "was treated with
unspeakable injustice and cruelty."[2] Nor could she console
herself with the reflection that her sufferings, after all, were

1. Charlotte Perkins Stetson [Gilman]: *Women and Economics: A Study
of the Economic Relation between Men and Women as a Factor in Social
Evolution*, 3rd ed. (Boston: Small, Maynard & Co.; 1900), p. 128.

2. Ibid., p. 128.

necessary for the advancement of the race; for she did not, of course, know that. It remained for the science of evolution, applied to the study of society as well as to biology, to show that the whole process was "one of nature's calm, unsmiling miracles."[3]

But what had been necessary in the first stages of the evolution of humanity was now, at the beginning of the twentieth century, no longer necessary or desirable. The continued subordination of women worked nothing but evil. It had always worked evil, but formerly the evil was the price society had to pay for its advancement. That was no longer the case. A new stage had been reached in the evolution of consciousness. Thanks to the sacrifice of women, over the centuries, social consciousness in both sexes had now superseded sexual consciousness. Sex had served as the avenue by which man attained to the larger sense of his responsibilities not simply to his family but to all humanity. Now that the sense of community had at last been attained, sex was, so to speak, no longer necessary; and the old system of domestic relationships, whereby man went out to hunt and woman kept the home fires burning, had become an anachronism.

The period of women's economic dependence is drawing to a close, because its racial usefulness is wearing out. We have already reached a stage of human relation [sic] where we feel the strength of social duty pull against the sex-ties that have been for so long the only ties that we have recognized. The common consciousness of humanity, the sense of social need and social duty, is making itself felt in both men and women. The time has come when we are open to deeper and wider impulses than the sex-instinct; the social instincts are strong enough to come into full use at last.[4]

3. Ibid., p. 127.
4. Ibid., pp. 137–8.

The proof of this assertion was the simple fact of the existence of the "woman movement," that unprecedented upwelling of social consciousness. "Once it was of advantage to society that the sexuo-economic relation should be established. Now that it is no longer of advantage to society, the 'woman's movement' has set in."[5] Thus the very existence of a demand for change became for the feminists the proof of the validity of the demand.

[III]

As propaganda, all this was enormously effective. As an explanation of the sources of feminism, it left something to be desired. What neither the pleas of the feminists nor, for that matter, the despairing cries of their adversaries accounted for was the violence of the debate about the new woman. It was well to point out that the patriarchal family had lost its economic and social reasons for being, but that did not explain why women should have turned with such fury on an institution which according to their own reasoning was already defunct. One could argue, again, that women's eagerness to serve humanity excused their sweeping assault on the male sex, but that did not explain why the assault took place; it did not account for the enormous amount of sexual antipathy generated by the feminist movement. Nor did the evolutionist theories of Mrs. Gilman and Olive Schreiner throw any light on what in retrospect appears so marked a characteristic of American feminism, its preoccupation with the question of sexual identity. The whole "woman question," as it was debated in the United States, turned on the issue not simply of what roles women and men ought respectively to play, but of the respective

5. Ibid., p. 122.

nature of the sexes. What did it mean to be masculine or feminine? What did the adjectives signify? The intensity of the speculation about these questions discloses anxieties which lie much deeper than anything associated with the greater leisure of the modern woman or the flight of housework from the home. Those developments doubtless took place, but why they should have left such bitterness and passion behind them neither the feminists nor the sociologists and historians who adopted their theories about the family were able to explain.

Whatever one thinks of the justice of the feminists' cause, one has to admit that the envy of men was very pronounced in American feminism. Sometimes it amounted to outright antagonism. The feminists talked a great deal about the need for a freer and more spontaneous companionship between men and women, but in practice they often seemed to assume a state of perpetual war. Even when the envy of men did not reach the point of hostility—and it is possible to exaggerate the Lesbian and castrating aspects of the feminist revolt—the envy nevertheless remained. So did the unconcealed abhorrence of everything connected with the middle-class family and with middle-class life in general, an abhorrence of which the envy of men, in fact, was probably a single facet. Consider, for example, the autobiographical essays of Inez Haynes Gillmore, which she published under the deliberate and revealing title, "Confessions of an Alien."[6] In these memoirs one encounters at once the sense of superfluity that more than anything else identifies the feminist impulse. It was this "feeling of alienage," Mrs. Gillmore says, together with "a feeling of sex discontent" (i.e., envy of men), which pushed her into the "discoveries in regard to the life of woman" that made her a feminist.

6. *Harper's Bazar*, XLVI (April, 1912), pp. 170ff.; another installment appeared in the following issue. The editors published these articles with the explanation that the author's opinions "are not the opinions of the editors, nor are they in harmony with the editorial policy of the BAZAR."

For several years now I have felt myself alien to this world, and alien not because of race or color, but alien because of changing economic conditions. It seems to me that sociologically, so to speak, I hang in a void midway between two spheres—the man's sphere and the woman's sphere. A professional career . . . puts me beyond the reach of the average woman's duties and pleasures. The conventional limitations of the female lot put me beyond the reach of the average man's duties and pleasures.

But whereas her sense of alienation was "a comparatively recent growth," "that other feeling—sex discontent—has oppressed me all my life."

Not since I started to do my own thinking have I been in any doubt as to which sphere most attracted me. The duties and pleasures of the average woman bore and irritate. The duties and pleasures of the average man interest and allure. This seemed the most shameful of my discoveries. But I soon found that it was a feeling which I shared with the majority of my kind. I have never met a man who at any time wanted to be a woman. I have met very few women who have not at some time or other wanted to be men.

To uncover the reasons for her discontent, Mrs. Gillmore had to "go back to the very beginning" of her life. She grew up, a bookish and imaginative child, in genteel poverty, "poor enough to be dull, poor enough to be put to all the threadbare makeshifts of a faded gentility, but not poor enough to enjoy the hearty, vulgar social promiscuity of the frankly poverty-stricken." At first she attributed her unhappiness to her family's poverty. Then she discovered that poverty, "that strangling gray fog" bore harder on her than it bore on her brothers. "They were always escaping, not like me to an imaginative world, but to an actual, if invisible, world—that scarlet-and-gold country of the foot-loose male." She yearned for adventure, but "custom had decreed" that she could not go out in search of it; she must wait for adventure to come to her. Sometimes she was overwhelmed with a sense of the possibilities that lay before her, the sense that "almost anything can happen."

> But "almost anything" did not happen. . . . "Almost anything" can happen to men. . . . But to women adventure, excepting always what must be for most of them the only adventure—love and marriage—comes in the most casual way, comes, if at all, at such long intervals that it often finds them unready and afraid. Even the adventure of marriage is accidental. They cannot demand it of life.

At college she took courses in literature and philosophy and developed "an enormous curiosity about life." She and her friends argued and debated endlessly. But all the evidence on which they based their speculations came from books. "It never occurred to us that we were studying a second-hand world, that we were getting our life in translation, that we never really had a face-to-face encounter with it." Men, she thought—there was a men's college in the same town—didn't read as much and almost certainly didn't talk so well, but they *lived*.[7] "They were talking all the time to the man in the street, the cabman, the barber, the policeman. They were talking a great deal to the woman in industry, the shop-girl, the waitress, the stenographer." The world, she concluded, had "set up a double standard of experience—one for men, one for women."[8]

7. For the very similar comments of Randolph Bourne—but with the sexes exactly reversed—see below, p. 101.

8. There were a few experiences, she admitted, that were "essentially sexed," like fatherhood and motherhood. "But between those two classes there is a broad mass of experience essentially sexless, essentially human. My quarrel with life is that women are permitted to enjoy so few of the human experiences." Cf. Charlotte Perkins Gilman (*The Home*, p. 217): "It can never be too frequently insisted upon . . . that the whole area of human life is outside of, and irrelevant to, the distinctions of sex. Race characteristics belong in equal measure to either sex, and the misfortune of the house-bound woman is that she is denied time, place, and opportunity to develop those characteristics. She is feminine . . . but she is not human."

Eventually Mrs. Gillmore rebelled against her lot and determined to "play the man's game." She became a journalist and a writer. She went where she pleased and chose her own friends. Life favored her "above most women." "It has permitted me to do the man's work and it has paid me the man's pay." But she wondered whether she had not "paid high for my independence—in that feeling of alienage to which I have confessed." At the same time she continued to be tormented by the thought that after all, in spite of her exertions, she had not yet managed to confront experience for herself. "The fact that I've never seen life in the raw gives me an odd sense of bafflement. I am certain that . . . I shall at the end feel as much an amateur at life as I feel now."[9]

These "confessions" are not an isolated and solitary cry of despair. They were the common complaint of a certain kind of American woman in the period around the turn of the century—the middle-class woman of intellectual ambitions. Jane Addams, when she wrote of her own early sufferings, was describing the same experience exactly—the yearning for "adventure"; the sense of living at second hand and of "getting life in translation"; the fear of finding oneself "unready and afraid" in the face of experience. Few of the feminists of this period seem to have escaped the kind of nervous crisis described by Jane Addams—a period of utter aimlessness, in which all one's powers seemed to atrophy. Often the crisis was precipitated by marriage. Thus Charlotte Perkins Gilman, after tasting independence at twenty-one—a "tremendous surge of free energy"—stumbled into a disastrous marriage with Charles

9. See also Inez Haynes Gillmore: "The Life of an Average Woman," *Harper's Bazar*, XLVI (June, 1912), pp. 281ff.: "Woman is, after all, only a supernumerary in the great drama of the world. . . . The picture which, in imagination, I always draw of her is a slim, weak, pale, bowed, weary figure—weak, humorless, inarticulate, standing timidly on the threshold of life, peering through the open door, but not daring to enter."

Stetson, a painter, in spite of her premonition that she was entering "a future of failure and suffering."[1] Immediately she sank into an inexplicable illness. "A sort of gray fog drifted across my mind, a cloud that grew and darkened."[2] She bore a daughter, a "heavenly baby"; her husband was more attentive, more considerate than ever; but the gloom deepened day by day. "Here was a charming home; a loving and devoted husband; an exquisite baby, healthy, intelligent and good; a highly competent mother to run things; a wholly satisfactory servant —and I lay all day on the lounge and cried."[3] But when she went to California to visit friends, her spirits lifted at once. "From the moment the wheels began to turn, the train to move, I felt better."[4] She came home and within a month "was as low as before leaving."[5] One could not find a more conclusive application of the feminist contention that family life inhibited creative effort. Mrs. Gilman divorced her husband and went on to a brilliant career as writer and agitator.

Likewise Margaret Sanger, encouraged by the example of a revered father to develop her talents, embarked on a medical career, only to cut it off by an impulsive marriage to a young painter. Almost immediately she fell sick; in her case, with a real sickness, tuberculosis, from which she made a slow recovery. Thereafter she and her husband lived in Greenwich Village, cultivated the society of the artists and radicals whom they met at Mabel Dodge's salon, and to outward appearances led a busy life. Yet Mrs. Sanger was not happy, and as she grew older she realized that she had wasted too much of her life in "inactive, incoherent brooding." "I could not contain my

1. Charlotte Perkins Gilman: *The Living of Charlotte Perkins Gilman, An Autobiography* (New York: Appleton-Century; 1935), pp. 72, 84.

2. Ibid., p. 198.

3. Ibid., p. 89.

4. Ibid., p. 92.

5. Ibid., p. 95.

ideas, I wanted to get on with what I had to do in the world."[6]
Like Charlotte Gilman, she had to leave her husband in order
to do so.

[IV]

For women such as these, conscious of their intellectual
gifts but unable, it seemed, to make use of them within the
sphere of women's traditional duties, life, experience, "growth"
were always *out there*, they belonged to the great world beyond
the household and the family. But the sense of "alienage" was
by no means confined to women. When one sees the feminist
impulse as an aspect of a more general development—the revolt of intellectuals against the middle class—one begins to
understand the feminists' acute fear that life had passed them
by. For this conviction that life lay always outside the narrow
confines of one's own experience was common to all those, of
whatever sex, who felt themselves imprisoned in the stale room
of a borrowed culture.

The envy with which women looked on men had its
counterpart in the envy of intellectuals in general of what they
conceived to be the richer life of the proletariat (an envy which
in our own time has been transferred to Negroes).[7] Women
also, when they were not lost in wonder at the masculine world
of activity and adventure, often gave vent to this mingled fear
and envy of the working class. But when Inez Gillmore spoke
of "the hearty, vulgar social promiscuity" of the poor, to which
her own "faded gentility" made so poignant a contrast, she

6. Margaret Sanger: *An Autobiography* (New York: Norton; 1938), pp.
104–5.
7. See, e.g., Norman Mailer: *The White Negro* (San Francisco: City Lights
Books; n.d. [1957]). See below, pp. 344–5.

spoke not as a woman but as a middle-class intellectual gazing wistfully across the social chasm. She said no more than what every intellectual of the age must at one time or another have suspected, that his own class had somehow lost contact with life. To live fully, directly, spontaneously; to live to the outer limits of one's capacities; to immerse oneself in the stream of experience—all this was no longer something one took for granted as the essence of the human condition, but had become rather an objective to be strived after with all one's powers, an objective one was yet fated always to fall pitiably short of. It was precisely this mystical sense of the sanctity of experience, life, growth, and development that rendered the men and women of the period incapable of setting up an alternative to the cult of "self-fulfillment" the destructive possibilities of which they were so quick to discern. Charlotte Gilman could deplore the unbridled individualism which she saw as the curse of modern society and at the same time insist that personal "growth" was the law of life and the only goal worth pursuing.[8] And the "new religion" that Robert Herrick insisted was the alternative to the triumph of egotism turned out to be nothing more than the "religion of life"—a "faith in life apart from our own personal fate."[9]

The cultural and even the political history of the period, looked at in such a light, seems always to shine back some reflected facet of this religion of experience. One sees it in the vogue of literary naturalism; in muckraking journalism, with its celebration (under the guise of censure) of the teeming life of the cities; in the assumption, common to both, that "reality" was at once sordid and romantic, dirty and unspeakably exciting—whatever in short was the antithesis of genteel respectability. One sees it in the deep ambivalence with which men and

8. Zona Gale, foreword to Gilman: *Living*, p. xiii.
9. Herrick: *Together*, pp. 500–1.

women who called themselves progressives contemplated the doings of the "malefactors of great wealth"; their mingled fascination and horror, their outraged envy. Above all, one sees it in the discontent of intellectuals not only with the old conception of culture but with intellectual life itself; in their eagerness to escape from the isolation to which intellectuality seemed to condemn them; in the self-effacement and self-contempt which made them yearn to put their abilities at the service of the community. Nothing could have been more revealing than the pervasiveness of the ideal of "service" among the very people one might have expected to have been its most outspoken critics. Disinterested inquiry and speculation could no longer suffice. Intellectuals, like everybody else—even the poor, notwithstanding the full-blooded sensuality with which the intellectuals in their own minds endowed them—could find comfort and meaning, it appeared, only in large, encompassing movements of masses of people, of which they could imagine themselves a part.

But if all these things were true, why, it must be asked, did so many women ignore them? Why did they see only the "sexual question"? If, in fact, women shared with men of the same class this yearning for a larger life and for more direct encounters with experience, why did they not perceive the existence of this common ground? Why did they persist in attributing their sufferings not to class but to sex, not to their being middle-class intellectuals in rebellion against what had come to seem a sterile and meaningless existence, but to the simple fact of their being women? It is true, of course, that women such as Jane Addams saw the class issue as well as the sexual issue and in fact gave precedence to the first, but it is also true that the discussion of the new woman, considered as a whole, had a way always of coming back to the fact of "sex discontent," to the recital of women's age-old hardships and deprivations. Even Jane Addams could not altogether escape this resentment. Nor could she escape the suspicion that obsessed the feminist imagination: that in pursuing a masculine ideal she had betrayed her own femininity.

The resentment and the suspicion were inescapable because of the peculiar conditions of American life—or perhaps more accurately the peculiar conditions of life in English-speaking countries. In America the idea of culture was predominantly feminine to begin with. The care and preservation of culture had early been entrusted to women. Not only art but religion was considered to belong to woman's sphere, the more practical pursuits to man's, and in no other country in the world was the distinction between the two, in the popular mind, so uncompromisingly rigid. Women were the moral custodians of society. In a society that felt itself on the verge of chaos—a "frontier" in the broadest sense of the term—they came to represent cohesion, decency, and self-restraint; and the cult of the home, over which they presided, became the national religion. Under those circumstances the rebellion against culture necessarily became a rebellion also against the definition of woman's "place" with which the nineteenth-century concept of culture was so closely bound up.[1]

The association of moral and aesthetic refinement with femininity was more than an expression of the sentimental myth of woman's purity. It seems at one time to have served a more immediate and practical purpose. Artistic and intellectual accomplishments in a young woman, in the eighteenth and

1. On the feminization of American culture, see Denis Brogan: *The American Character* (New York: Alfred A. Knopf; 1944), part I, *passim*; Geoffrey Gorer: *The American People: A Study in National Character* (New York: W. W. Norton; 1948); Margaret Mead: *Male and Female: A Study of the Sexes in a Changing World* (New York: W. Morrow; 1949); Leslie A. Fiedler: *Love and Death in the American Novel* (New York: Criterion Press; 1960).

nineteenth centuries, were regarded as indispensable to her success in the marriage market, toward which from girlhood all her energies were supposed to be devoted. The feminists suspected, and with good reason, that not only the genteel ideal of culture but the whole system of genteel social intercourse had as its essential function the auctioning off of young girls to the most eligible bidders. When an eligible marriage was considered for one's daughters the *summum bonum* of existence, a vast body of convention grew up designed at once to facilitate and to regulate the frantic competitive quest for husbands which inevitably ensued. Fashion, "society," "culture" were all aspects of the same process. Their purpose, it seemed, was to cultivate a girl's attractions and then to provide a setting for their display. Even the business life of the middle class, if novelists like Robert Herrick were to be believed, came eventually to be pervaded by the social ambitions of American women; and the complaints one so often encounters around the turn of the century, that all life had been "womanized," would seem to reflect the degree to which social intercourse of every kind, at a certain level of society, had come to revolve inexorably around the demands of competitive matchmaking.

It is not surprising that images of slavery and prostitution figured so prominently in the rhetoric of feminism. The analogy between the condition of women and the condition of Negro slaves was always a favorite of feminists. It expressed the sense that women were legally the slaves of their husbands, but it may also have referred, more obliquely, to this sense of society as a kind of auction block, to which girls were bred (like Negro wenches) from birth. As for prostitution, the reference was perfectly obvious. When the feminists referred to the "parasitism" of the modern woman, they meant, among other things, that her only function in life was to be pleasing to men. Thus the difference between marriage and prostitution was hardly more than a legal nicety. There was "no sharp, clear, sudden-drawn line," Olive Schreiner maintained, between the "kept wife," living "by the exercise of her sex functions alone," and the prostitute.[2]

The practical effect of all this, for young girls of intellectual interests and serious disposition, was to make the society of their contemporaries almost intolerable. The lowest common denominator of the feminist revolt was simply a revulsion, formed early in life, against the sheer silliness of the life which a girl was expected to lead and which most girls apparently did lead. "My aim," said one feminist, "is . . . to make myself a true woman, one worthy of the name, and not to be one of the delicate little dolls or the silly fools who make up the bulk of American women, slaves to society and fashion."[3] One of Jane Addams's schoolgirl friends cried: "If anyone wishes to make himself particularly disagreeable to me just let him call me a *school girl*." Sentimental, "gushing, and *young*"; everlastingly "afflicted with the giggles"; having "nothing excepting the affairs of their neighbors to interest them"; lacking altogether the "faculty of reviewing what they read and enlarging upon it: digesting and discussing"—such were her companions. "How unhappy the quiet girl is deemed; she that can talk the most and gossip in an *easily hateful* [way] (do you understand?) is the popular girl."[4]

Another letter to Jane Addams, from a friend at a girls' seminary, captures at once the conditions against which the feminists rebelled and the difficulties inherent in the rebellion.

The girls here are afflicted with the same sentimental "spooning" malady, which, you say, infests Rockford. I heartily agree with

2. Schreiner: *Woman and Labor*, p. 104.

3. Caroline L. Hunt: *The Life of Ellen H. Richards, 1842–1911* (Boston: Whitcomb & Barrows; 1912), p. 57.

4. Vallie E. Beck to Jane Addams, Feb. 5, 1897, Addams MSS.

you, old fellow, that it is both disgusting & horrible, & demoralizing to us as women. . . . Indeed, the girls carried the thing so far
as to actually *flirt* with *one another*, in a way similar to the dif-
erent sexes. For a time there was quite an excitement over the
affair. Miss Bently brought it up in gen[eral] ex[ercises] in such
a sarcastic yet sad & reproving way, that we were all filled with
shame. I believe in kissing one's friends at the proper time, but as
to bestowing them—the kisses—promiscuously on one & all, the
sacredness of a kiss loses its charm. I believe that the true, deep
friendship & loves are those which make no obstreperous demon-
strations—as it were. Dear Pythias, I think that in you, I have
found my affinity & I picture to myself the delightful, quiet times
we might have "of an evening," reading aloud to each other, &
holding earnest conversations.[5]

It is touching and revealing that in their mutual revulsion
against the vanity and frivolity of their classmates—whose
casual flirtations among themselves, rehearsals for the more
important flirtations to come, were the logical end-product of
a system which elevated the drama of courtship to so central
a position—and in their pursuit of a life that would not be
"demoralizing to us as women," girls of more serious habits
should have found themselves addressing each other as "old
fellow," as "Damon" and "Pythias." It is an unimportant detail
in itself, this assumption of masculine pseudonyms; but it
symbolizes the feminist dilemma. The determination to be a
"true woman" forced one in effect to lead a man's life. That
was exactly the point made by the most uncomprehending
critics of the feminist movement. What was so maddening was
that there was finally no answer to this easiest of clichés. The
search for woman's nature led always in circles.

5. Unidentified correspondent to [Jane Addams], Dec. 5, 1877, Addams
MSS.

3 / Randolph Bourne and the Experimental Life

[I]

THE REBELLION AGAINST THE MIDDLE CLASS PRESENTS AN ever-changing face. From one point of view, it was a rebellion of women against the "family claim." From another point of view, it was a rebellion of intellectuals against middle-class culture. But it was also a revolt of youth, and as such it set a pattern which has been followed with variations only of detail by each subsequent generation of youthful rebels —the bohemians of the twenties, the radicals of the thirties and forties, the beatniks and hipsters of the fifties. The mass society, lacking the cohesive influences that make a society into a community, tends to break up into smaller communities, autonomous, self-contained, and having no viable connection with the whole. The existence of a "youth problem," a phenomenon mistakenly regarded as a problem of inadequate law enforcement or of a decline of public morality or of society's failure to provide adequate incentives for young people, in reality signifies the emergence of an autonomous youth-culture. Even "rebellion" no longer accurately describes the relation of young people— whether "delinquent" or merely "beat"—to American society, because their gestures of rebellion have long since lost their meaning and have become instead gestures of conformity to the culture of their contemporaries. With the decay of the older transmitters of cultural continuity—particularly the family and the school—the culture of their contemporaries claims young people almost from the instant of their exposure to influences outside the circle of their parents. They belong to it by default, for lack of alternatives.

The disaffection of the young is by no means a special case. On the contrary, it is only an instance—in many ways the most dramatic—of the condition of the mass man, who lives in societies within societies, cut off from the larger life around him and cut off also therefore from the cultural inheritance of the larger society—cut off from the past altogether, since the past derives its meaning from being shared and survives only to the degree to which the larger society remains intact. The culture of youth, the greatest attraction of which is precisely that it is wholly contemporary, is a particularly vivid example of the way in which the mass man is doomed (or privileged, depending on the point of view) to live out his life in the windowless room of the current event. Paul Goodman once chided the beat poets for cutting themselves off from the poetry of the past, to the impoverishment of their own work; as if it were an arbitrary act of willed defiance.[1] It would seem to be rather the necessary condition of all such rebellions. Pastlessness is their very essence.

It will be argued that the conflict of youth and age has a timeless quality and that it is a mistake to see it as a development of the twentieth century; for has not youth always believed in the existence of possibilities richer and fuller than the compromises, adjustments, and renunciations which its elders have held out as the best life can afford? It is in the nature of

1. Paul Goodman: *Growing Up Absurd* (New York: Random House; 1960), pp. 176–9. Goodman himself adds: "In a milieu of resignation, where the young men think of society as a closed room in which there are no values but the rejected rat race or what they can produce out of their own guts, it is extremely hard to aim at objective truth or world culture. One's own products are likely to be personal or parochial."

youth, then, to reaffirm the charm and beauty of existence, just as it is in the nature of age to insist on the virtues of moderation, restraint, and resignation. But it is apparent at once that this conflict, no matter how earnestly waged, never before led to the kind of generational segregation that has prevailed since the turn of the century. Before then, it worked itself out within the institutions of the larger culture, and the claims of class, religion, and family exercised a countervailing influence over the natural rebelliousness of the young, and in the end overrode it. It was only when those claims lost their force that youth became a class and a religion of its own.

Thereafter the attitudes of defiance very quickly tended to harden into a new orthodoxy. As early as the 1920's the pattern was set. Malcolm Cowley, who belonged to what one might call the second of the lost generations, the one coming to maturity at the end of the First World War, left a semi-autobiographical account of his youth—a somewhat patronizing account, written in the sober and responsible thirties—which shows the degree to which rebellion had already assumed a familiar shape. Even at seventeen, Cowley and his friends were self-consciously "disillusioned and weary."[2] Each of their successive enthusiasms quickly became passé; enthusiasm itself was passé; and having already lost sight of what it was they were rebelling against, having in fact no pressing need to rebel at all (since they were the children of indulgent parents), they found themselves reduced to going through the motions of what had become at once a ritual and a game, according to which one took whatever position was least expected and abandoned it as soon as others adopted it as their own. This exercise was what Cowley facetiously called the "theory of convolutions"; if you evinced a taste for Oscar Wilde because

2. Malcolm Cowley: *Exile's Return* (New York: Viking Press; 1961 [New York, 1934]), p. 18.

everybody else was still reading Tennyson, you were in the
first convolution, but if when your friends had taken up the
cult of decadence you went on to rediscover the animal vitality
of Kipling, you had advanced triumphantly to the second.[3]
However frivolous the amusement, and however frivolously
Cowley later chose to write about it, it was nevertheless a response to the inescapable question that had begun to confront
each successive generation of dissenters: when rebellion becomes orthodox, against what does one rebel?

The second generation of rebels began to envy the first, who
had originated what they themselves could only copy. His own
generation seemed to Cowley not only derivative in their rebellion but "spectatorial" in their relation to life in general.
His complaint was the familiar one: they had never experienced
reality for themselves, had never "lived." From the perspective
of the thirties, with its enthusiasm for public causes—which
was itself not necessarily a sign of maturity (as Cowley
thought), but in many cases no more than a further convolution of the cult of experience which had characterized the rebellion from the beginning—Cowley found it deeply mortifying
that in the First World War his contemporaries had been content to drive ambulances and write books about the futility of
war, while remaining indifferent "toward the cause for which
young Americans were risking their lives."[4] The older generation of rebels seemed to Cowley to have confronted life more
directly. The fact that many of them had in fact refused to
take part in the war at all did not diminish his sense that the
older generation had lived more fully than his own.

Under these circumstances, it is not surprising that the
heroes of the first generation—the prewar generation—achieved

3. Ibid., pp. 21-2.
4. Ibid., p. 43.

legendary status in their own lifetime. Their canonization would in any case have been inevitable, for every culture needs heroes, and even a culture of the contemporary tends to invent some sort of past for itself; but the rapidity with which the process went forward is another indication of the way in which rebellion had become an end in itself, fed only by the endlessly reiterated assertion of the need to rebel. It is an indication also of the remorseless publicity which is so distinctive an attribute of a contemporaneous culture. Federico Fellini's film *La Dolce Vita* (1961), which depicts another such culture—underscoring its pastlessness by setting the story amid the ruins and monuments of Rome—comments unforgettably on this point. The characters—film stars, "personalities," members of the "entertainment world"—are accompanied everywhere by reporters and photographers; the action unfolds in a blaze of flashbulbs and to the incessant accompaniment of loudspeakers, with the result that every event has the quality of being recorded the instant it transpires. The sense of time is thereby destroyed, and with it the meaning of action. It is as if action exists only to be recorded.[5]

Publicity is to a contemporaneous culture what the great public monuments and churches and buildings of state are to more traditional societies, an instrument of solidarity; but because publicity is only the generalized gossip of the in-group, the solidarity it creates is synthetic. Its myths are manufactured. It turns out products, in our own time an Ernest Hemingway, a James Dean, a Marilyn Monroe; and the legendary quality about these people attaches itself not to their memorable deeds

5. A confusion of races, nationalities, and tongues, the film captures not only the pastlessness but the placelessness of the "international set." Placelessness is an attribute also of the youth-culture, which now extends in one sweep from San Francisco to Moscow. Every capital in the Western world reverberates with the sounds of rock-and-roll.

but to their personal habits and idiosyncrasies, their liking to go barefoot or their fondness for cats or their love of motorcycles or their various phobias and neuroses. The whole process appeals not to the sense of history but to the voyeurism which is the strongest emotion, it seems, that the contemporaneous culture is able to evoke.

[II]

It was the fate of Randolph Bourne to become the first of the culture-heroes of the revolt of youth. His early death at the age of thirty-two made him eminently eligible for earthly immortality. The circumstances of his death, moreover, were picturesque; or so they appeared in the glow of retrospect. Although Bourne in fact died in the influenza epidemic of 1918, the belief gained ground that he had as good as starved to death because none of the magazines on which he depended for a living would print his pacifistic opinions. Thus Bourne became in the eyes of his admirers a persecuted martyr to the cause of nonconformity, driven to an untimely death because he refused to hew to the official line. Had he lived, it might have been more difficult to idealize him, for Bourne wielded a satiric pen which had always made him more enemies than friends. "I had a reputation for a sharp tongue long before I had a reputation for anything else."[6] His appearance likewise was elegant and distinguished only at a safe remove from the subject. His hunched back, ungainly hands, and too prominent brow, together with the long cape he sometimes wore, wrapped

6. Randolph Bourne to Carl Zigrosser, Sept. 18, 1911, Randolph Bourne MSS, Columbia University Library. All the letters to and from Bourne, cited hereafter, are to be found in this collection.

him in retrospective romance; Van Wyck Brooks spoke of "his vibrant eye, his quick bird-like steps."[7] But another friend, writing long after most people had forgotten that Randolph Bourne had ever lived—for the heroes of the youth-culture die twice untimely, constantly superseded by heroes more up-to-date—gave voice to what was a more common impression among those who had actually known Bourne. "There was no redeeming feature in his appearance," wrote Beulah Amidon, "—even his eyes had no magnetism, and his hands were clumsy and undistinguished."[8]

A legend in the twenties, Bourne was quickly forgotten in the thirties. These circumstances, together with the difficulty of classifying his interests—his works fall conveniently into neither literary criticism nor educational theory nor political commentary—probably explain why historians have paid so little attention to him. The only biography, by Louis Filler, deals almost exclusively with Bourne's political interests.[9] Meanwhile, Bourne's personal papers continue to gather dust in the Columbia University Library. Historians have occasionally examined them but have found it impossible to make much use of them, because most of them deal with intensely

7. Introduction to Randolph Bourne: *The History of a Literary Radical* (New York: B. W. Huebsch; 1920), p. xii.

8. Beulah Amidon to Alyse Gregory, Oct. 4, 1948, Bourne MSS.

9. Louis Filler: *Randolph Bourne* (Washington: American Council on Public Affairs; 1943). Two other short studies exist. Charles A. Madison: *Critics and Crusaders* (New York: Frederick Ungar; 1947) has a chapter on Bourne; so does Max Lerner: *Ideas for the Ice Age* (New York: Viking Press; 1941). Both these writers applaud Bourne's early pragmatism but deplore his opposition to the First World War. "With the Kaiser's military might let loose over Europe," says Madison (p. 440), ". . . he quixotically expounded a pacifistic anarchism." Lerner concludes (p. 141) that Bourne was valuable chiefly for his "affirmations." See also Lerner's introduction to Filler's *Bourne*, in which he criticizes Bourne for allowing himself "to be alienated from the main source of strength in American life, the people themselves" (p. vi).

private experiences. They seem to have nothing to do with "history" at all. It has apparently not occurred to anyone that that fact in itself might be of some importance.

Born in 1886, Randolph Bourne belonged to a generation which, as he put it, had "practically brought itself up."

School discipline, since the abolition of corporal punishment, has become almost nominal; church discipline practically nil; and even home discipline, although retaining the forms, is but an empty shell. The modern child from the age of ten is almost his own master. The helplessness of the modern parent face to face with these conditions is amusing. What generation but [our parents'] could have conceived of "mothers clubs" conducted by the public schools, in order to teach mothers how to bring up their children![1]

Bourne's own family, to judge from his account of them, provided a classic example of the helplessness of parents. His mother and father were overawed and intimidated by the brilliance of their son. His deformity, as so often happens in such cases, only provided them with a further reason for indulging his wishes in all things. It probably added also to their sense that their son was a stranger, a representative of some "rare and incomprehensible" species[2] who had unaccountably appeared, by a kind of parthenogenesis, in their midst. In any case, they left him to do "quite as I liked"[3]—for which he was both grateful and contemptuous. His mother was a well-meaning, addled woman, according to the account of her in Bourne's fragment of an autobiographical novel; and he found it easy to bend her to his will.[4] The father was weak, remote, and

1. Randolph S. Bourne: *Youth and Life* (Boston: Houghton Mifflin; 1913), p. 33.
2. Bourne to Alyse Gregory, May 20, 1914.
3. Ibid.
4. *History of a Literary Radical*, pp. 300-43, *passim*.

ineffectual, failing both as businessman and father. When Bourne was seventeen or eighteen, his father disappeared altogether, never to return.[5]

The family was ancient but shabby and narrow, not only economically but culturally. "The classics were stiffly enshrined behind glass doors that were very hard to open." Hawthorne, Irving, Thackeray, Tennyson, and Scott peered bleakly out, "but nobody ever discussed them or looked at them." *Outlook* and *Independent* were the intellectual nourishment of the household, and for Bourne and his sister the parents provided *St. Nicholas* and *Youth's Companion*, with the air of having conferred inestimable cultural advantages. In these circumstances, Bourne "gathered in" the New York *Tribune* "like intellectual manna."[6]

The family lived in the town of Bloomfield, New Jersey, under the reign of respectability. The village was twice invaded during Bourne's lifetime, first by industrial workers, who created the social split that he analyzed in an early article, "The Social Order in an American Town,"[7] and again by commuters from New York, who transformed it into a suburb. Bourne's Bloomfield, however, was the vanishing small town, the world of middle-class "Puritanism." The "annual contest with the saloon"—an issue that symbolized the conflict between workers and middle class—was the most exciting public event of the year, and a perfect example of "Puritanism" in action. The enthusiasm for moral causes, Bourne thought, argued "a relatively primitive state of civilization," when "philosophy" had made it clear that "the only valid solution of a problem is a scientific solution." It had never occurred to the ruling class of Bloom-

5. Filler: *Bourne*, p. 16.
6. Ibid., p. 12; *History of a Literary Radical*, p. 2.
7. *Atlantic*, CXI (Feb., 1913), pp. 227–36.

field that "the saloons might be regulated on some basis of a minimum demand."[8]

So wrote Bourne in 1913, at the height of his progressivism. It was the period of his life when he could still praise Walter Lippmann's *Drift and Mastery* as "a book one would have given one's soul to have written"—one which went to the heart of "the great problem" of the age, the problem, that is, of "what to do with your emancipation after you have got it."[9] Later the war would lead him to second thoughts about Lippmann's variety of progressivism and about "scientific solutions" in general. But nothing ever made him reconsider his opinion of the American small town. A trip to Europe in 1914 confirmed his worst impressions. After Germany, with its "charming villages" and "carefully laid-out towns," American town-life "seemed almost too grotesquely squalid and frowsy to be true;—the unkempt station surroundings and unhealthy factories and dingy workmen's houses."[1] Nor did he change his mind about Bloomfield and his family. On the contrary, the thought of them became more distasteful as he grew older. More and more he envied his friends, to one of whom he sent this despairing account of his family:

I have a home set in New Jersey in what used to be a country town, but is now surrounded by a thick blanket of cities. We have an old, dull and very uncomfortable house, and every summer I have spent there I have vowed would be the last. . . . I seem very queer out there and all my friends seem very queer. My family conveniently puts the corruption to the account of Europe. I am constantly confronted there by the immeasurable gulf between my outlook and theirs and I feel a constant criticism of my futile highbrowism and Godless pursuit of strange philosophers. My young sister is almost a passionate vulgarian, and takes with

8. Ibid., p. 235.
9. Bourne to Dorothy Teall, June 4, 1915.
1. Bourne to Carl Zigrosser, Nov. 3, 1913; to Alyse Gregory, Sept. 28, 1914.

really virtuous indignation my deviation from the norm of popular music, the movies, [R. M.] Chamber[s]'s novels, Billy Sunday, musical comedy, tennis, anti-suffragism, and the rest of the combination that makes up the healthy, hearty, happy young normal person of the well-brought up family of the day of the middle-middle class. I find her an index to current America, but we scarcely get along. I envy you your being so firmly and happily placed in a stimulating family, with backgrounds and connections and responsibilities and a place in things. My relatives are quite hopeless, and I feel at times like a homesick wanderer, not even knowing where my true home is.[2]

He could only conclude, in a more cheerful mood, that "this sacred institution of the family," with its "blind jealousy towards any assertion of individual ideals," was hardly worth the sacrifices it exacted. The only way to get along with it was to give up caring what one's relations thought—"to accept courageously the situation, act up to the affection I feel, and not torment myself into duties and attitudes which can never be mine."[3] But even this solution brought about at best only a modus vivendi. The "backgrounds and connections and responsibilities" which he envied in others were still missing in his own case, and nothing could ever quite make up for their absence.

[III]

Bourne escaped from Bloomfield, somewhat belatedly, by way of Columbia, Europe, and Greenwich Village. After a dreary period following his father's more dramatic escape, during which Bourne was obliged to work in a factory that produced paper rolls for player pianos, he won a scholarship to

2. Bourne to Elizabeth Shepley Sergeant, June 9, 1915.
3. Bourne to Alyse Gregory, May 20, 1914.

Columbia University. Entering at twenty-three, he cultivated literature, philosophy, and the art of personal friendship. A Gilder Travelling Fellowship following his graduation permitted him to spend several months abroad. He returned to America just after the outbreak of the war—of the approach of which his letters give no hint.[4] What impressed him about Europe and about Germany in particular was what had impressed Jane Addams and so many other American progressives: order, cleanliness, the scrupulous preservation of public places; all the visible symbols, in short, of the sense of community which was so completely lacking in the United States.[5] It almost made Bourne "want to renounce all ideals of individualistic freedom, if the German scheme will produce a civilization so superior."[6]

Europe quickened Bourne's political sympathies. A progressive, he became something of a socialist as well. After Europe, his writing acquired a certain sharpness and bite which it had lacked before; in his later work he was less the genteel

4. Except, perhaps, for his observation about England: "The whole country seems very old and weary, as if the demands of the twentieth century were proving entirely too much for its powers, and it was waiting half-cynically and apathetically for some great cataclysm." (Bourne to Carl Zigrosser, Nov. 3, 1913.) Afterwards Bourne wrote: "No one was more innocent than I of the impending horror." ("Impressions of Europe, 1913–14," in *History of a Literary Radical*, p. 231.)

5. Cf., for example, Richard T. Ely's account of his return from Germany in 1880: "I landed in New York on a hot and disagreeable midsummer day. As I walked through the streets of New York, my heart sank within me. The city was dirty and ill-kept, the pavements poor, and there were evidences of graft and incompetence on every hand. Is this my America? I asked myself. I thought of the clean, beautiful streets of Berlin and Liverpool, and the painful contrast made me want to take the next boat back to Europe." (Richard T. Ely: *Ground under Our Feet* [New York: Macmillan; 1938], p. 65. See also Frederic C. Howe: *Wisconsin: An Experiment in Democracy* [New York: Charles Scribner's Sons, 1912], which begins with a tribute to German civic-consciousness.)

6. Bourne to Alyse Gregory, Sept. 28, 1914.

essayist and more the critic of politics—and his critique, as time went on, became increasingly astringent and increasingly effective. Yet in the conventional sense Bourne had no politics at all. His politics remained largely an extrapolation from his own emancipation from the cultural stagnation of Bloomfield. Though he spoke glowingly of social and political advance, he conceived of it as a cultural progress. On the continent, he had noted, "life was enriched by a certain natural sensitiveness to art," the absence of which in England and America had a "brutalizing" effect. He advised a friend in New York, an architect, that if he could do anything "towards spreading that sensitiveness at home," he would have accomplished a work "as important as that of the best social reformer." "Until people begin to really *hate* ugliness and poverty and disease, instead of merely pitying the poor and the sick, we shall not have, I fear, any great social advance."[7]

Politics, in short, was important to Bourne as "a means to life."[8] Even his opposition to the war, on which his reputation as a public figure came to rest, was a politically negative act (however appropriate or correct) signifying his continuing preoccupation with the personal as opposed to the public. He opposed the war precisely because he saw that it represented a monstrous intrusion of the public on the private. It showed him the danger, if he had not known it before, of making politics a cult; and it was the reaction to this "cult of politics," he told Van Wyck Brooks, that had finally "driven so many of the younger generation back from the liberal camp." The war had "shown up what was really dearest to the liberal heart's desire. A change in institutions not as a means to life but as something pleasing in itself!" What the younger gen-

7. Bourne to Carl Zigrosser, Nov. 3, 1913.
8. Bourne to Van Wyck Brooks, March 27, 1918.

eration wanted, however, was "an idealism . . . which is more concerned with American civilization than with American politics."[9]

For these reasons the war could not engage Bourne's imagination—even after his whole career came to revolve around his relation to it—in the way it engaged the imagination of other progressives. He saw in it nothing but destruction, whereas they saw endless possibilities for the advancement of humanity—flowers growing from ashes.[1] Even Jane Addams, who also opposed the war, commended Bourne on his position. Even she, who certainly shared none of the illusions about the likelihood that the war might make the world safe for democracy, nevertheless had a certain stake in the war, for she thought she saw in it the beginnings of a new international cooperation. "A new internationalism was being established day by day," she wrote later; "the making of a more reasonable world order . . . was to some extent already under way, the war itself forming its matrix."[2] At the very least, she thought, the war would stimulate future agitation for peace. In the same letter in which she praised Bourne's attack on Dewey, she asked permission to make reprints of it on behalf of the Women's Peace Party.[3] Presumably he had no objection, but he would never have thought of such a thing himself. What mattered to him was the question the war raised about the relation of intellectuals to politics; he had no interest in organizing an opposition. As for Jane Addams's pacifism, he could hardly have cared anything about it, tainted, as it would have seemed to him, with sentimentality. He had long ago made up his mind about

9. Ibid.
1. For a discussion of the debate between Bourne and the war liberals, see below, pp. 205 ff.
2. Jane Addams: *Peace and Bread in Time of War* (New York: Macmillan; 1922), p. 84.
3. Jane Addams to Bourne, June 13, 1917.

Jane Addams, his contempt for her Christian idealism causing him to overlook their mutual interest in the revolt of youth and in questions of education. He saw her, as Beulah Amidon testifies, as a " 'Lady Bountiful,' condescending to her 'neighbors,' exploiting their old-world customs, crafts, music . . . a symbol of smugness and 'sweet charity.' "[4] Her support of his position, therefore, though it must have cheered him when supporters were so few, could hardly have commended her as an ally.

The only public issues that engaged Bourne's imagination for very long were questions, not of politics, but of culture: education, feminism, the rebellion of youth. These were the subjects of the three books he published during his lifetime, *Youth and Life* (1913), *The Gary Schools* (1916), and *Education and Living* (1917), and of many of his posthumous essays as well. But all his works came back in one way or another to the fact which from childhood had burned itself into Bourne's consciousness, the gap between the generations. His earliest collected essays—"Youth," "The Two Generations," "Virtues and the Seasons of Life"—stated the theme on which the rest of his work, even his political essays, was a set of variations. "The two generations misunderstand each other as they never did before." Youth felt itself "overpoweringly urged toward self-expression." Age, seeing in this impulse only an unbridled egotism, an irresponsible pursuit of pleasure, a want of "character," a softening of the moral fiber, sought to impose on youth its own stern conception of duty and self-control. The resulting conflict would end, Bourne thought, in the overthrow of the whole system of repression on which society until his own time had been based. It would end in the recognition that the vision of youth, after all, is always the "truest" and "justest."[5]

4. Beulah Amidon to Alyse Gregory, Oct. 4, 1948.
5. Bourne: *Youth and Life*, pp. 34, 3, 15.

These observations, drawn presumably from private rather than from public life, nevertheless had a way of slipping over into politics. *Youth and Life* was a political manifesto and a call to revolution. But in Bourne's politics, the source of injustice was seen not as the monopoly of the means of production or as the unequal access to privilege and power, but as the simple fact of age. The older generation ruled the world; "hence grievous friction, maladjustment, social war." More precisely:

> Youth rules the world, but only when it is no longer young. It is a tarnished, travestied youth that is in the saddle in the person of middle age. Old age lives in the delusion that it has improved and rationalized its youthful ideas by experience and stored-up wisdom, when all it has done is to damage them more or less— usually more. And the tragedy of life is that the world is run by these damaged ideals.[6]

Bourne was like other rebels before him in wishing to throw off the dead hand of the past; to that extent he belonged to a long line of radical thinkers. What was new in all this was his conceiving of the struggle quite literally as a struggle of youth against age, in spite of his awareness that youth is often more conservative than age itself. That only confirmed his opinion of the evil effects of the social domination of the middle-aged. If young people were conservative, when their natural tendency was to be radical, that was surely because they found the world in which they were expected to make their way "rather narrow and shallow."[7]

What was also new in Bourne's radicalism was the way in which the political problem, once it was formulated in this way, dictated nonpolitical solutions. To say that "friction, maladjustment, social war" had their origin in the ascend-

6. Ibid., p. 14.
7. Ibid., p. 4.

ancy of age over youth was to rule out politics altogether as a means of social advance. Specifically, it was to rule out the conventional radical solution of social revolution. Bourne could not urge the young to seize power as Marx had urged the proletariat to expropriate the expropriators. In the first place, a struggle for power was itself a form of "friction and social war." In the second place, Bourne saw clearly enough that revolutions are seldom led by men in their teens or even their twenties. Political power in most societies, traditional and radical alike, is a function of middle age. A revolution of youth is a contradiction in terms. But in the third place, it did not require a revolution, after all, to bring the young to power. The young would come to power as a matter of course, but in their middle age—there was the rub; and what would be the gain if by that time the rebels of today had become the reactionaries of tomorrow? The young must somehow discover how to take their youth with them into middle age.

> This is why it behooves youth to be not less radical, but even more radical, than it would naturally be. It must be not simply contemporaneous, but a generation ahead of the times, so that when it comes into control of the world, it will be precisely right and coincident with the conditions of the world as it finds them. If the youth of to-day could really achieve this miracle, they would have found the secret of "perpetual youth."[8]

Not Marx but the spirit of Ponce de León presided over Bourne's vision of the better world.

His statement of the problem took the problem out of politics and put it squarely into the realm of psychology. The key to politics was the process of aging. The root of social disorder was seen not as oppression but as repression: the destruction of freedom and spontaneity which was necessary to make children into adults. It was at this point that Bourne's analysis

8. Ibid., pp. 15–16.

coincided with John Dewey's, Jane Addams's, and the progressive educators' in general. It also ran parallel, for a while, to Sigmund Freud's, although how closely Bourne knew Freud's work, if he knew it at all at first hand, is not clear. The very fact that the point should be in doubt suggests what is indeed amply confirmed by other evidence, that the concept of the child as a different order of being from the adult—and in some respects a superior order of being—did not owe its existence to Freud. It was rather the general intellectual property of the age. It depended on one of those radical reversals of perspective in which the social literature of the period abounded. Instead of seeing the child as an undeveloped adult, one now saw the adult as an undeveloped child. In Freudian language, the child was "polymorphously perverse," accessible to a whole range of sexual experience which adults had learned to repress; by comparison, adults were emotionally impoverished. From a Deweyite perspective, the child, being physically dependent on others, was obliged to cultivate the gift of social intercourse, a gift which the adult in his overweening egotism thought he could do without. In Bourne's essays, the same idea appears in a form more lyrical still. The child sees things that must ever elude the adult. "The adventure of childhood is to get lost here in this every-day world of common sense which is so familiar to us. To become really as little children we should have to get lost again here." The "best substitute" adults can devise, Bourne adds, is "to keep exploring the new spiritual world in which we may find ourselves in youth and middle life, pushing out ever, as the child does, our fringe of mystery."[9] The notion that even so exalted an activity as the pursuit of knowledge is essentially a substitute for the lost joys of childhood—an echo of Freud's concept of sublimation—strikes the authentic note of the period. Previously

9. Ibid., p. 66.

it was childish pleasures that had been thought of as substitutes
—substitutes for the richer satisfactions that only maturity
could bring.

The nineteenth century, someone said, was the century of
the child. The coincidence, toward the end of the century, of
so many independent discoveries of the mystery and sanctity
of childhood leads one to think that childhood must have owed
its discovery not so much to a set of intellectual influences—
romanticism, naturalism—as to the social conditions of the
period; to some common experience through which an entire
generation had passed.[1] To look critically at the patriarchal
family was to see it, first and foremost, through the eyes of a
child. Psychoanalysis—which has been credited with opening
up the study of the child—appears to have acted more as con-
firmation than as revelation. It gave the weight of science to the
intuition which had already impressed itself on so many sons
and daughters of the middle class: that culture was founded
on repression.

But if psychoanalysis shared with American progressivism
this common ground, nothing could be more illuminating than
the way in which they diverged.[2] Freud was led by his evidence
to a stupefying irony: an ever-mounting burden of guilt was
the price men paid for civilization.[3] Freud was a European,
and such a conclusion was implicit, perhaps, in every detail of
the European scene. Jane Addams caught a glimpse of it in
Madrid. But the American, faced with Europe, found it easy
to repudiate its implications. Having no past, Americans could

1. On the "discovery of the child," see Richard Hofstadter: *Anti-intellectualism in American Life* (New York: Alfred A. Knopf; 1963), chapter 14.
2. On this subject see, in general, Henry F. May: *The End of American
Innocence* (New York: Alfred A. Knopf; 1959), pp. 232–6, and John C.
Burnham: "Psychoanalysis in American Civilization before 1918" (unpublished Ph.D. dissertation, Stanford, 1950).
3. Sigmund Freud: *Civilization and Its Discontents* (Garden City: Double
day & Company; n.d. [Joan Riviere, trans., London, 1930]).

look forward to an untroubled future. The American progressives drew back from the implications of psychoanalysis even as they embraced it. If culture and nature were in conflict, culture would have to go.

But in fact no such conflict was thought to exist. John Dewey's resolution of it was characteristic. In traditional societies, he explained—he was thinking of the primitive societies which anthropologists were just beginning to study—the young had to be brought up in the ways of their elders. These societies, being content merely to perpetuate themselves, were obliged to instill in new generations reverence for the customs and rituals of the old. Under such circumstances, socialization might indeed require repression; for "the natural or native impulses of the young do not agree with the life-customs of the group into which they are born." But in progressive societies the "life-customs" themselves are constantly changing. Progressive societies accordingly "endeavor to shape the experiences of the young so that instead of reproducing current habits, better habits shall be formed, and thus the future adult society be an improvement on their own."[4] If the better society of the future was defined as a "cooperative commonwealth" (as all of the new radicals, progressives, single-taxers, and socialists alike, defined it), and if it was true, moreover, that children were more adept in the art of cooperation than adults, then children themselves became the teachers in the school of social progress. Teachers became pupils. Far from repressing the natural impulses of the young, progressive societies—progressive schools in particular—tried to encourage their emulation by adults. "For certain moral and intellectual purposes," Dewey concluded, "adults must become as little children."[5]

4. John Dewey: *Democracy and Education* (New York: Macmillan; 1961 [New York, 1916]), pp. 47, 79.
5. Ibid., p. 42.

This discovery of Dewey's ran parallel to Jane Addams's discovery that it was the "neighbors" who educated the social worker by demonstrating socialized democracy in action, rather than the other way around; and the sentence in which Dewey summed up his philosophy of education reads almost exactly like a sentence of Randolph Bourne's—the one in which he spoke of adults becoming "as little children." Like Dewey and Jane Addams, Bourne thought that education could be used as an instrument of social reform. His quarrel with conventional modes of instruction (both at home and in the school) was that they produced reactionary conformists. Their typical victim, the "good" child—"the child, who at the age of five has a fairly complete knowledge of what God wants him and all around him to do and not to do"—grew up "into the conventional bigoted man."[6] Education under such conditions was nothing more than indoctrination. Real education would abandon "moral instruction," it would abandon the whole effort to make children into miniature adults, and it would accept instead the uniqueness of childhood as its first principle. It would admit to itself that children lived in "splendid isolation" in a world of their own, "hermetically sealed" off from adult interests and concerns.[7] Such at least was the condition of what Bourne called the "natural" as opposed to the "good" child. The good child alone was susceptible to the influence of adults. The natural child was "unconscious" of his elders. Educators would do better to leave such children alone. "The best thing they can do for [them] is to feed their curiosity, and provide them with all the materials that will stimulate their varied interests. They can then leave the 'influence' to take care of itself."[8] The object of education, in short, was to en-

6. Bourne: *Youth and Life*, pp. 60–1.
7. Ibid., pp. 67–8.
8. Ibid., p. 68

courage the child's urge toward self-expression. Self-expression, free and uninhibited, was the secret of youth, on which the progress of humanity, in Bourne's analysis, had come to depend.

[IV]

The new radicalism differed from the old in its interest in questions which lay outside the realm of conventional politics. It was no longer his political allegiance alone which distinguished the radical from the conservative. What characterized the person of advanced opinions in the first two decades of the twentieth century—and what by and large continues to characterize him at the present time—was his position with regard to such issues as childhood, education, and sex; sex above all. Politics by comparison was almost immaterial, if by politics one refers to the traditional business of government and statecraft: taxes, tariffs, treaties. But the new radicals had not so much abandoned politics as redefined it, bringing to political debate questions formerly reserved to art and letters. If politics is defined as the impulse to reform society, as the tendency to elevate ideas into programs, then it is clear that the political impulse was by no means dead. It survived even in such an apparent political skeptic as Randolph Bourne. Bourne thought he was repudiating politics, and he attacked other progressives as having subordinated everything else to political concerns; and yet his own conception of politics as a "means to life" represented an extension of the political into the most intimate areas of existence. To say that politics was of no use unless it could improve the very tone and quality of people's private lives was to argue in effect that every aspect of existence was ultimately a question for political decision.

The "sexual question," as it was called, was a case in point —and the fact that it presented itself to the new radicals as a "question" suggests what was happening. It was not enough for Bourne to appeal to the "new doctrines" in psychology as proof that "repression of unwelcome and shameful ideas and aspects of life causes all sorts of spiritual havoc." It was not enough that the new psychology showed the fallacy of equating sex with sin, by demonstrating—what was confirmed, Bourne thought, by his own experience—that the purest and most exalted thoughts could coexist with "erotic emotion and fantasy." If the erotic was in fact the source of "the sense of beauty," then Bourne could only conclude that "we need a lot more of it." So saying, he parted company with Freud. The student of psychology gave way to the psycho-sexual reformer, and the new psychology became the basis of a forward-looking program of sexual liberation. "If a man has a real sensitiveness to feminine charm," Bourne argued, "I don't see how he can physically bring himself to consort with dirty women. It is only because this Puritanical policy of repression brings everybody up to an idea of the complete divorce of the spiritual and the physical, to a concept of the 'nice' girl as all spiritual— as in the romantic novel—and of the prostitute as all physical, that the double life is possible."[9] The new psychology, in short, pointed the way toward the abolition of the double standard.

For some feminists the feminist movement was a crusade for women's "rights"; for Bourne it was part of a comprehensive assault on the cultural ascendancy of the *bourgeoisie*. On the continent he discovered that feminism was bound up with socialism, and the association, it seemed to him, was a natural one, as both movements represented a challenge to the middle-class way of life. "I wish it was that way in America," he wrote back, "and we didn't have progress blocked by the

9. Bourne to Henry [Elsasser], Oct. 10, 1913.

blind recalcitrancy of progressives and feminists of the Jane Addams type in the face of the socialist movement, which, international and proletarian as it is, is the only movement to make headway against a situation which is international, and from which the proletariat suffer most, and are therefore the most logical class to end it."[1] The socialist rhetoric, untypical of Bourne, does not quite ring true; if one considers his career as a whole, it is clear that what disturbed him on this occasion was not so much the sufferings of the proletariat as the unwillingness of American feminists to push their feminism to what seemed to him its logical conclusion. Nor did he really think that the condition against which feminism was a protest was international in scope. More often he spoke of it as something peculiar to the Anglo-Saxon environment. If the European had a stronger sense of beauty, he was also more sophisticated in his attitude toward women. In France, Bourne reported, he found "none of that patronizing, niggling tone" with which women were spoken of at home. Nor did European women feel called upon, as American women evidently did, to defend their husbands as "the kindest in the world." This last remark, thrown at him again and again in the debates about feminism he liked to "precipitate" among American women abroad, seemed to Bourne "an unconscious give away of that attitude of tolerant gallantry, which the American husband seems to[o] often to have towards his wife, as a pleasant child on whom it is a great pleasure to lavish the wealth which his 'brains and industry' have 'created.' "[2] Such observations seem to suggest that Bourne viewed the problem of women not as a problem of economic exploitation—his socialism notwithstanding—but as one of Anglo-Saxon culture, a problem of the

1. Bourne to Alyse Gregory, March 13, 1914.
2. Bourne to Alyse Gregory, April 10, 1914.

"values of Victorian England."[3] It was these values, Bourne decided after his visit to England made him "just about ready to renounce the whole of Anglo-Saxon civilization," that had to be overthrown if the world was "ever to have any freedom or any life or honesty or sensitiveness of soul." "Henceforth the Irish, the Welsh, the French for me," he exclaimed after his escape to the continent, "no Anglo-Saxons."[4]

Feminism, for Bourne, offered an alternative to "the old English way of looking at the world" in which he himself had been brought up and which he had "had such a struggle to get rid of."[5] It was a rejection not only of "Puritanism" but of the conventions of romantic love; for as Bourne discerned, prudery about sex and the glorification of women and court-ship were two sides of the same coin. Both built insurmountable walls between the sexes, which it was the purpose of feminism, he thought, to tear down. The feminists of his acquaintance seemed to Bourne to have put the relations between men and women on a new and freer basis. In the "Greenwich section" of New York he found "the most delightful group of young women" who constituted what he called "a real 'salon.'" Social workers and magazine writers, they were women of "decidedly emancipated and advanced" opinions.

They have an amazing combination of wisdom and youthfulness, of humor and ability, and innocence and self-reliance, which absolutely belies everything you will read in the story-books or any other description of womankind. They are of course all self-supporting and independent, and they enjoy the adventure of

3. Bourne to Alyse Gregory, Jan. 5, 1914.
4. Ibid.; Bourne to Carl Zigrosser, Dec. 13, 1913. "And my judgment," he added, "is all the more impartial because I was exceptionally well treated in England."
5. Bourne to Alyse Gregory, Jan. 5, 1914.

life; the full, reliant, audacious way in which they go about makes you wonder if the new woman isn't to be a very splendid sort of person. . . . They talk much about the "Human Sex," which they claim to have invented, and which is simply a generic name for those whose masculine brutalities and egotisms and feminine prettinesses and stupidities have been purged away so that there is left stuff for a genuine comradeship and healthy frank regard and understanding. . . . It is true that you shall not look for romantic passions in my salon, but I really believe that much of what we call romantic passion simply doesn't exist outside of the story book world; and this story book world is the worst sort of training for people growing up. . . . Not in the terms of romance and passion which poets have sung in, and the novelists have agonized and rhapsodized in for so long that we are incurably sick with it all, should these things be seen, but in terms of equality and cameraderie and frank hearty delight in personality and all the charm, physiological and spiritual, that goes with it. My salon says that their object is to restore "charm" to life, and that is one of the greatest revolutions that could be accomplished.

He concluded, as he so often did, on an autobiographical note. He himself, he said, had been brought up in a society "where everybody seemed to think it a duty to fall in love with each other and then desperately conceal it, or express it in a peculiarly hypocritical and insincere way." Under those conditions, the relations between men and women were based not on "whole-hearted comraderie [sic] and interest and attraction for each other's personality, which would grow and expand with friendship," but on "a crude instinct" overlaid with "a lot of conventions as to how it was 'proper' to behave, and what people would think of you."[6]

Such at least was Bourne's original estimate of the feminist movement. It was perhaps inherent in the nature of the conception that the feminists would disappoint him in the long

6. Bourne to Prudence Winterrowd, April 28, 1913.

run. What Bourne looked forward to was nothing less than a new era in sexual relations. To his dismay, he discovered that the girls who talked so convincingly about the "human sex" were not interested in the art of personal relations. They were more interested in asserting their right to enjoy the privileges formerly monopolized by men. The worst of it was that even the competitive impulse soon collapsed under the dull routine of the job. The career which was to open new avenues of experience became a daily grind, persisted in out of habit; the new woman began to acquire the soul of a clerk. One evening Bourne and his friends were turned out of a girl's apartment at ten o'clock, just when they were settling down to talk, because the girl had to be at work at nine the next day. This same girl, Bourne wrote bitterly, professed to be "not only anti-man but anti-woman too." The thing shook his "faith in womankind." He could "only ascribe it to some profound, incorrigible perversity of woman."[7]

By the end of Bourne's life, his disillusionment with feminism seems to have become complete. In a biting essay, "Karen," the new woman appears as a member not of a third sex but of a self-contained sorority; the desire for regard and understanding between the sexes has been swallowed up in a consuming resentment against men. "She felt the woes of women, and saw everywhere the devilish hand of the exploiting male." And even when his friend "Karen" had outgrown the more obvious forms of feminine hostility, even after she had ceased to agitate openly against the opposite sex and had taken up again the "tissue of personal relations," "all her friends," Bourne says, "seemed to be women. Her taste of battle had seemed to fortify and enlighten that ancient shrinking; her old annoyance that men should be abruptly different from what she would have them. She was intimate with feminists whose

7. Bourne to Alyse Gregory, Jan. 13, 1915.

feminism had done little more for their emotional life than to make them acutely conscious of the cloven hoof of the male."[8] Thus Bourne, more feminist than the feminists, came finally to the conclusion reached earlier by anti-feminists like Henry James.[9] The whole movement was founded, it seemed to him in his gloomier moments, on a deep-seated distrust of men. Far from clearing away the obstacles to a sexual *rapprochement*, it promised to bring hostility to the point of open warfare.

[V]

If Bourne was ultimately disappointed with feminism, he was disappointed also with most of his women friends. "I am so keen on girls' friendships," he once wrote;[1] yet they seldom lived up to his expectations. His correspondence with Prudence Winterrowd reveals the pattern of his enthusiasms. When she was twenty or twenty-one, she wrote from Shelbyville, Indiana, to praise an article of his in the *Atlantic*, and her letter led to a regular exchange. Bourne was at first delighted with his correspondent's intelligence and receptivity to his every suggestion. He showered her with names of books and authors—William James, H. G. Wells, Bergson, Maeterlinck; advised her to throw herself into suffragism; urged her to come to live in New York. He was particularly insistent on the last of these points. She had at all costs to get out of Indiana. He knew from experience "the bewildering, cramping effect of not hav-

8. Bourne: "Karen," in *History of a Literary Radical*, pp. 47–56.

9. See Henry James: *The Bostonians* (New York: Macmillan; 1886); William R. Taylor and Christopher Lasch: "Two 'Kindred Spirits': Sorority and Family in New England, 1839–1846," *New England Quarterly*, XXXVI (March, 1963), pp. 32–3.

1. Bourne to Prudence Winterrowd, March 2, 1912.

ing any one to talk to or understand."[2] But coming to the city was more than a matter of expanding one's horizons; it was a way of testing one's capacities, of transcending one's limitations. "It is worth a big fight to get finally standing on your own feet spiritually, with a feeling that you are a definite personality with something to say and something to do, and some kind of a career to follow. The feeling of being in control, more or less, of your own personality and career is the ideal to aim at, and until you are in that possession, you will hardly be effective."[3]

Miss Winterrowd came to New York—Bourne was then in Europe—but being quickly discouraged, returned to Indiana with the excuse that she could more easily pursue her studies there. Bourne warned her, in words reminiscent of Jane Addams's strictures on the "snare of preparation," that study was "only a substitute for work, a postponement . . . of the real duty of life." He too, he confessed, kept "postponing life," he too grappled with the constant temptation to lapse back into his limitations—limitations (though he did not reveal their exact nature to Miss Winterrowd) which in his own case, he intimated, were somehow more confining than most. But he nevertheless struggled against the temptation; and so must she, terrific as the struggle necessarily was for those cursed with an excess of sensitivity. "It's on the whole a very bad maladjusted world for people without an abounding vitality and self-reliance, and the only thing for such people to do is to acquire painfully and slowly that vitality and reliance."[4]

His protégée, however, refused to venture forth again from her provincial seclusion. The correspondence lagged. Bourne was content that it should, for as he wrote impatiently to a

2. Bourne to Prudence Winterrowd, Jan. 16, 1913.
3. Bourne to Prudence Winterrowd, Nov. 3, 1913.
4. Ibid.

friend, "her incapacity in following the very obvious leads which would have proved her sincerity and determination, began to weary me a little; though Heaven knows," he added with his usual self-reproach, "my own career has been nothing else but a demonstration of the same incapacity." Miss Winterrowd, however, had disappointed him in other ways as well. She transgressed the boundaries of a proper reserve; she called him "Randolph."[5] He himself, in point of fact, was the first offender, having written to "Dear Miss Prudence" as early as April 28, 1913, but her indiscretion brought him at once to a realization of the dangers of carrying the correspondence any further.

The whole thing [he decided] was an interesting and unconventional adventure tinged with certain dangers of thin ice, I must admit, on account of the difference in sex, which were all the more thin because I, as the ostensible hero, not being seen, could, I suppose, be pictured in any sort of personal colors desired. . . . I'm afraid I am very hard-hearted, but when these correspondences begun on a highly intellectual plane of apparent understanding of my ideas and a very pleasing radiant sympathy with them, suddenly take a swoop to the personal, it makes me very uncomfortable, and I see the dangers which sensible prudent people feel when they refuse to begin such a correspondence, or rather continue it at all. But my zest for the experimental life— a life lived in conflict with my natural constitutional timidity —makes me unable to resist interesting episodes of all kinds, correspondences with unknown women among them.

It would have pleased him immensely to have converted Miss Winterrowd from "Ingersollism" to socialism and pragmatism. "But she must not call me Randolph before she is fully converted."[6]

"A charming girl," Bourne once wrote, with "a mind of

5. Bourne to Arthur MacMahon, Oct. 23, 1913.
6. Bourne to Arthur MacMahon, Oct. 23, 1913; ellipses in original.

the same texture as yours," was "a heaven-sent companion, and the blessedest gift of the gods."[7] But how rare such creatures proved to be! "What is this feminine intuition, that breaks down so lamentably at such a crisis?" he complained when Miss Winterrowd assumed the familiar tone. "She should have known better."[8] His own standards of delicacy and mutual self-awareness appeared to be beyond the reach of most of his friends. At the same time he knew that his demands on them put them off—but knowing it did not make him able to modify the demands. He wavered between disappointment and panic, now turning his irony on those who fell short of his standards, now pleading with them not to desert him, not to treat him, as he once exclaimed, "like a precarious incident."[9] "He was in a constant turmoil of emotional upheavals and frustration," said Beulah Amidon thirty years later, "—devotion, disillusionment, anger, misunderstanding, anxiety." It was "tragic," she thought —since he gave his best efforts to friendship rather than to art—"that he was so much more successful in his thinking and writing than in his human relationships."[1]

It can be argued of course that all these disappointments and frustrations were the inevitable result of Bourne's deformity, which made him need other people more than they needed him;[2] and that they tell us nothing, therefore, about the society in which Bourne lived. But it was not so much the deformity itself as the conviction that it was a moral duty to resist it by plunging into the stream of experience—an attitude toward life Bourne shared with so many other radicals of his time—

7. Bourne to Prudence Winterrowd, March 2, 1913.
8. Bourne to Arthur MacMahon, Oct. 23, 1913.
9. Bourne to Alyse Gregory, n.d.
1. Beulah Amidon to Alyse Gregory, Oct. 4, 1948.
2. "I must confess, I find myself hopelessly dependent on my friends and my environment. My friends have come to mean more to me than almost anything else in the world." (*Youth and Life*, pp. 363-4.)

that explained the turbulence of his friendships. He himself provided the link between biography and history when he explained, in the case of his risky association with Miss Winterrowd, that it was his "zest for the experimental life" which drove him into such associations in the first place, when his "natural constitutional timidity" would have dictated a life of retirement and solitude. He raised his own misfortune to the level of an ethical issue. In his "philosophy of handicap," the adventurous life became a struggle against one's limitations; and in this broader view, the exact nature of the limitations came to seem at last almost immaterial. What was important was to resist the impulse to acquiesce. "Of course we are all Hamlets," he once wrote to a friend; "only you and I"—in contrast to a mutual friend, the latest in a long series, whose retreat into marriage they both deplored—"you and I have the firm conviction that some day our will will begin to operate freely and creatively, when we . . . get a certain poise and surety." The friend in question, on the other hand, seemed "to lack that ideal, to have no real point of view, and his drifting is not so much that of the learner and experimenter, as yours and mine is, as that of the aesthete who has already begun to feel pleasure in his own decadence. Our decadence is hateful to us; we struggle against it, and in so doing live to a far greater intensity than does the one who sits down and contemplates it."[3]

Bourne came to see—forced himself to see, against what must have been an almost overwhelming urge to give himself up to self-pity—that his condition was not unique. It was the "tragedy," after all, "of all the ill-favored and unattractive to a greater or less degree."[4] More broadly still, it was the tragedy of sensibility. "We are all Hamlets." And indeed the sense of being cut off from "life," the sense of being in some way

3. Bourne to Carl Zigrosser, Nov. 16, 1913.
4. "A Philosophy of Handicap," *Youth and Life*, p. 345.

disabled and deformed, weighed heavily upon a whole generation of American intellectuals. As intellectuals they envied the working class. As women they envied men. But so did men envy women, and for the same thing, their easier access to experience. In the life of a woman like Alyse Gregory, Bourne saw exactly what Inez Haynes Gillmore saw in the lives of her brothers.[5] "You cannot think how I envy you," he told Miss Gregory, "with all your hustle and adventure of work, your crowds of interesting friends, and your ostensibly—though you do so often hint differently—so easy command of life. . . . It would be so glorious to be 'in' something, making something go, or at least connected up with something or somebody to whom you were important and even necessary."[6]

The fact that it was possible for men to envy in women the very things women envied in men makes it clear that the sense of "alienage" was a highly subjective state of mind, one which cannot be traced to any such simple source as the deprivations of American women or even to so real a disadvantage as a physical deformity. The pervasiveness among intellectuals of the fear that life had somehow passed them by suggests that the fear reflected the growing isolation of the intellectuals as a class from the main currents of American life. It was both cause and consequence of their rejection of their middle-class origins. Seeking experience, they rejected a culture which seemed to them increasingly artificial, increasingly cut off from life; yet, having broken away from the middle class, intellectuals often found themselves no nearer to "life" than before. The act of severing their connections with their own class did not thereby make them members of the working class. They hovered instead in a classless void. It is little wonder that personal relations became for such people a kind of religion.

5. See above, p. 59.
6. Bourne to Alyse Gregory, Dec. 1, 1914.

Friendship had to supply the richness of the larger social and public life which had disappeared for good.

A man like Randolph Bourne brought to the art of friendship all the energies which in another age he might have expended on art and politics. He brought his enormous powers of observation and analysis to bear on the smallest details and the subtlest nuances of personal intercourse.[7] Friendship, however, could not bear such a weight of intensity; hence Bourne's recurrent disappointments. The kind of friendship he sought, moreover, was peculiarly an attribute of youth. Perhaps it was merely an attribute, more narrowly still, of a college environment. His happiest years—like those of so many Americans—were the ones he spent at college, talking with his friends far into the night. Nothing was ever quite like that again.[8] And as he grew older, he saw with mounting anxiety that his friends were going their separate ways, some absorbed in their careers, others in marriage; one by one they passed out of "that free, inexhaustible, spendthrift atmosphere that we used to know." One who had no work "except what he will initiate laboriously himself" and for whom marriage remained as always an im-

7. See, for instance, his description of an outing with Beulah Amidon: "The day was so much more glorious than I dared to expect. You could hardly feel all the innumerable little touches by which B. soothed and delighted my soul. There were those moments under the tree—Do you remember how she laughed when I threw acorns at her? How she hugged the brown ground? There were unpropitious moments in that unlucky corner where we halted and saw the lovers, but things flowed again when we started to walk, and even the nightmare of the trolley ride could not dissipate the high mood of the afternoon. And then the after-dinner discussion! . . . And how she dramatized her whole generation, and how hotly distressed she was as she gazed into her future, so passionate and yet so intellectual! Ah, a great mood, and a great day." (Bourne to Dorothy Teall, April 29, 1915.)

8. After his ejection from the apartment of the working girl mentioned above, he remembered how he and his friends "used to lie about the Columbia campus till two or three." (Bourne to Alyse Gregory, Jan. 13, 1915.)

possibility found himself "slowly beached high and dry"; "and how does one fortify one's self, do you think, against such a doom of isolation?"

At twenty-eight Bourne asked himself: "Is this what the world becomes? Am I really growing old?"[9] Age has always been more feared than welcomed; its comforts in the nature of things are compensatory. But under the peculiar conditions of modern culture it falls like a blight on the very prime of youth.

9. Bourne to Alyse Gregory, Dec. 1, 1914.

4 / Mabel Dodge Luhan:

Sex as Politics

[I]

MABEL DODGE LUHAN—born MABEL GANSON IN 1879—was the daughter of a rich banker in Buffalo, New York. She was educated in boarding schools; St. Margaret's in Buffalo, Miss Graham's School in New York, Chevy Chase School in Maryland. A summer in France with her mother completed her education. In 1900 she married Karl Evans, son of a prominent Buffalo family like her own. She bore him a son, but the marriage, she said later, was as loveless as that of her own parents, between whom she could remember only a single show of affection. ("He bent over her, with no more ease than he would have shown had he been trying to pluck berries with his lips from some thorny bush. He approached her gingerly. She gave him a brusque push backward as his mouth drew near her cold cheek. 'Oh, get out!' she said, and the kiss slid off and dissolved in the darkness."[1]) This first marriage ended abruptly when Evans was killed in a hunting accident in 1902. The widow suffered a nervous breakdown and was sent off to Europe—as standard a cure for neurasthenic young matrons as it was an education for girls. On the boat she met Edwin Dodge, a Boston architect of independent means, and in 1903 they were married and established residence in a villa near Florence. Mabel Dodge lived there until 1912,

1. Mabel Dodge Luhan: *Background* (New York: Harcourt, Brace; 1933), p 25.

when she returned to the United States and established her well-known *salon* at 23 Fifth Avenue. Estranged from her husband, she plunged into a highly publicized affair with John Reed, twice accompanying him to Europe. From the second of these trips she came home alone, to begin an affair with the painter and sculptor Maurice Sterne, whom she married, once more with a notable lack of enthusiasm, in 1916. They lived for a time on a farm near Croton, New York. In 1917 they went to Taos, New Mexico, already something of an art colony, so that Sterne could sculpt the Indians. There Mrs. Sterne fell in love with Antonio Luhan, a Pueblo Indian; bought a ranch outside Taos; and dismissing Sterne, began a new life in the desert. In 1923 she and Luhan were married. Thereafter she devoted herself to philanthropic efforts on behalf of the Indians, to collecting writers and artists (of whom the most renowned was D. H. Lawrence), and to writing her enormous autobiography, the published portions of which alone run to five volumes. She died in 1962.

Mrs. Luhan's autobiography consists of four volumes collectively entitled *Intimate Memories—Background* (1933), *European Experiences* (1935), *Movers and Shakers* (1936), and *Edge of Taos Desert* (1937)—together with a memoir of Lawrence, *Lorenzo in Taos* (1932), which is also autobiographical. (The last of these was published first, but written after the first two volumes of *Intimate Memories*, and a portion of the third, had already been completed.) In addition, Mrs. Luhan published two other books during her lifetime, neither of them of more than passing interest: *Winter in Taos* (1935) and *Taos and Its Artists* (1947). The bulk of her works, however, remain unpublished. Five other books were designated as part of *Intimate Memories* but withheld from publication, presumably on the ground that they might offend living people (although the same objection could have been raised against the published

volumes). These were "Green Horses," a 314-page continuation
of the account of her life in Buffalo; "Una and Robin" (1933),
a study of Robinson Jeffers and his wife; "Notes upon Awareness" (1938), "a consecutive summation of the attempts of one
manic-depressive character to discover how to free herself of
her disability & vacillation, & the various 'Methods' she encountered on her way thro' the Jungle of Life!"; "The Statue
of Liberty. An Old-Fashioned Story of Taboos" (1947); and
"The Doomed: A Tragic Legend of Hearsay and Observation"
(1953). Besides these, Mrs. Luhan also left a number of other
volumes described as having a "distinctly autobiographical
character": "Family Affairs, a Recapitulation" (1933); "Doctors" (1954), subtitled "Fifty Years of Experience"; "Mexico
in 1930"; "On Human Relations, A Personal Interpretation"
(1938); and two novels. All these works, together with her
correspondence after 1914 (the correspondence before 1914 was
accidentally burned), were deposited by Mrs. Luhan in the
Yale University Library, but her son, John Evans, has forbidden
anyone to look at the unpublished memoirs until the year 2000.[2]

2. Donald Gallup: "The Mabel Dodge Luhan Papers," *Yale University
Library Gazette*, XXXVII (Jan., 1963), pp. 97–105. For biographical details,
aside from the memoirs themselves, see Edward Nehls: *D. H. Lawrence: A
Composite Biography* (Madison: University of Wisconsin Press; 1958), Vol.
II, pp. 483–4. Mrs. Luhan has been written about only in passing, although
Emily Hahn has now undertaken a full-length biography. For brief references
see, e.g., Albert Parry: *Garrets and Pretenders* (New York: Covici-Friede;
1933), p. 273; Henry F. May: *The End of American Innocence* (New York:
Alfred A. Knopf; 1959), pp. 311–12; and the fictional portraits of Mrs. Luhan
in Carl Van Vechten's *Peter Whiffle* (New York: Alfred A. Knopf; 1922),
pp. 121ff., in which she appears as "Edith Dale"; and in Witter Bynner's
Cake (New York: Alfred A. Knopf; 1926), where she figures, more distantly,
as "the Lady." (D. H. Lawrence to Witter Bynner, April 13, 1928, in Harry
T. Moore, ed.: *The Collected Letters of D. H. Lawrence* [London: Heinemann; 1962], Vol. II, p. 1054.) See, finally, Gertrude Stein's *Autobiography
of Alice B. Toklas* (Carl Van Vechten, ed.: *Selected Writings of Gertrude
Stein* [New York: Random House; 1946], pp. 107ff.: "She was a stoutish
woman with a very sturdy fringe of heavy hair over her forehead, heavy
long lashes and very pretty eyes and a very old fashioned coquetry.").

Except for her vast memoir, an extraordinary effort of introspection, the life of Mable Dodge Luhan was that of another
rich and restless woman, a footnote in the cultural history of
Bohemia. It is as such that one occasionally hears of her; for
her autobiography is nowadays very seldom read. One comes
across references to her *salon*, where Bill Haywood and Emma
Goldman once held forth—"the only successful salon I have
ever seen in America," in the opinion of Lincoln Steffens.[3] One
reads that she had something to do with backing the Armory
Show of modern art; or again, that she helped to organize the
Paterson strike pageant staged in Madison Square Garden, in
which the workers themselves acted out the story of the strike.
For the rest, Mrs. Luhan hovers on the fringes of the Lawrence
legend, a marginal figure in literary as in social history. Her
memoirs created a small stir when they appeared in the thirties,
but except for the Greenwich Village volume, *Movers and
Shakers*, they have long since fallen into oblivion. Even at the
time, they seemed as dated as Mah-Jongg, relics of a period
which the depression had made ancient history. At a time when
political involvement was the fashion among intellectuals, Mrs.
Luhan's painstaking investigations of the intricacies of personal
intercourse could hardly have commanded a following. The
confessional had gone out of vogue; and even when it reap-
peared in the forties, in the form of "confessions" by ex-Communists, Mrs. Luhan by her continuing indifference to the great
issues of the day forfeited her chance for a reputation. She had
no sins to confess except those which were bound up with a
devotion to the private life as frivolous, it seemed now, as it was
impossibly selfish.

Yet those who read Mrs. Luhan's autobiography with care
are more likely to be struck by the familiarity of its theme and

3. Lincoln Steffens: *Autobiography* (New York: Harcourt, Brace; 1931),
Vol. II, p. 655.

tone than by the remoteness of the setting in which the story sometimes unfolds. One does not need to travel very far in the contemporary world—no farther, certainly, than the nearest academic community—to encounter the same intense involvement in group personal relations that was characteristic of Mrs. Luhan and her friends forty-five years ago; the same need jointly and publicly to analyze them in all their details; the same absence of compelling interests outside the circle of friendship which might relieve the pressure under which it is forced to operate. Literary fashions change; but if the intensely analyzed emotional life, of which Mrs. Luhan's autobiography provides such a classic record, was a passing literary fancy, it also represents a tendency inherent in modern life.[4] It is a result of the withering away of the larger social context of existence, which causes people in their loneliness to seek an intimacy even in casual friendships which hitherto was expected only of a few special relationships, if indeed it was expected at all.

The very idea of intimacy as a mutual baring of souls, a mutual examination of the psyche, seems to be an invention of the last two hundred years. When the community disappeared,

4. Changes in literary fashion probably signify nothing more than the temporary exhaustion of certain themes in the liberal weeklies and literary reviews. But even if in this case they signified a genuine disillusionment with the enthusiasm for intense personal intercourse which was so popular, among the avant-garde, in the first three decades of this century, it would have been very difficult for the generations which had outlived this enthusiasm to communicate their disillusionment to younger generations. Political history offers an analogous example of this phenomenon. It is a curious fact, as Theodore Draper has noted in his study of American Communism, that each new generation of radical intellectuals has had to undergo the same cycle of infatuation and disillusionment with the Soviet Union as the last; each generation seems equally unable to profit from previous experience. (Theodore Draper: *The Roots of American Communism* [New York: Viking Press; 1957], p. 130.) What is true of the Communist enthusiasm is true also of the passion for intricate and endlessly analyzed three- and four-way friendships. Both illustrate the lack of continuity between generations which, as I have argued in the previous chapter, seems to be a tendency intrinsic to postindustrial society.

intimacy not only displaced sociability as the ideal mode of human intercourse, it tended even to displace sexuality itself, notwithstanding the enormous apparent increase of interest in sex. The modern world in its ignorance of the past believed that it had discovered sex, had rescued it from the grip of "Puritanism"; but what had really happened was that sex for the first time had come to be seen as an avenue of communication rather than simply as a means of mutual pleasure. By insisting that sex was in fact the highest form of love, the highest form of human discourse, the modern prophets of sex did not so much undermine the prudery against which they appeared to be in rebellion (itself a comparatively recent development) as invert it. In effect, they took the position that sex, far from being "dirty," was more "spiritual" than the spirit itself, having its ultimate sanction in the communion of souls which sex alone, it was now thought, could provide.

[II]

When the community was a reality, most of life's events derived their meaning at least partly from that fact. As long as government remained essentially a local matter, the community represented the collective authority of the leading families, and the continuity between public and private life was therefore almost perfect. Birth, courtship, marriage, and death were public as well as private events, matters of general concern which could not be left to the discretion of the individuals most immediately involved. Marriage in particular, the union not merely of individuals but of families, involved questions of property and power in which the whole community had an immediate stake. In a sense, the private life did not exist at all. The concept of self-fulfillment as the aim of existence could not flourish, if it could exist at all, in a setting in which so much emphasis was placed upon the duties and responsibilities of life, so little upon its opportunities for new forms of experience. What one owed to others was always so much more apparent than what one owed to oneself. All the details of personal intercourse, moreover, were circumscribed by elaborate forms and conventions, as if to emphasize their quasi-public character; and under those conditions there was little opportunity for the naked embrace of the spirit which the modern world has since learned to understand as the essence of love and friendship, the essence of life itself. Communication even between lovers took the form of a stylized dialogue in which both participants remained acutely conscious of all that their respective roles, as defined by tradition, demanded of them. All this set limits to experience, but it also gave it a charm and beauty, a serenity and dignity, which it afterwards largely lost. Life was both enriched and impoverished by the waning of the conventions of communal existence.

By the end of the nineteenth century the close-knit communities which had once been the characteristic form of society throughout the Western world, eroded by a long process of national centralization, had disappeared, except in backwaters isolated from the mainstream of modern life. The most immediate evidence of what was happening was the dissolution of the old-style family, which had once served as the link between the individual and the community, the personal and the public modes of being. To some people this development came as a disaster; to others it symbolized better than anything else the release from outworn conventions which it seemed the special destiny of modern civilization to realize. The debate over the family, turning on the question of the rights of women and children, was waged with an intensity which suggests the importance of the changes that were taking place; but it missed what was perhaps the central point, that the dissolution of the family mirrored the dissolution of the community as a whole. The two institutions were intertwined. If the community was a collective family, the family was also a miniature state, the father a king, lord of all he surveyed. His authority over his wife and children was almost absolute in theory, however beneficently it was exercised. But it depended on his wider authority outside the family. The father was not only head of his household but the visible embodiment of the larger life beyond it. The whole community stood imposingly behind his authority at home. Not the winning of women's rights or the more permissive attitude toward children, but the disappearance of the community, destroyed that authority. When government was centralized and politics became national in scope, as they had to be to cope with the energies let loose by industrialism, and when public life became faceless and anonymous and society an amorphous democratic mass, the old system of paternalism (in the home and out of it) collapsed, even when its semblance survived intact. The patriarch, though he might still preside in splendor at the head of his board, had come to resemble an emissary from a government which had been silently overthrown. The mere theoretical recognition of his authority by his family could not alter the fact that the government which was the source of all his ambassadorial powers had ceased to exist.

The decline of patriarchal authority and the havoc it left behind make themselves immediately felt in Mabel Dodge Luhan's account of her early life, an account by turns nostalgic and harsh. "I like my Buffalo as I knew it," she announced at the outset, only to add in the same sentence that she had come to understand the adults who surrounded her as a child and to admire the gallantry and courage with which they endured "the terrible emptiness of their lives."[5] Her own life was empty too, insofar as the absence of familial authority left an emptiness at its center. Like Randolph Bourne, Mabel Ganson practically brought herself up. She might have been orphaned at birth, for all the demands her parents made upon her obedience or for that matter upon her affection. A stranger alike to love and authority, she knew only her father's sporadic gusts of impotent rage; and when this unfortunate man sought belatedly to arrest the anarchy in his own household, his wife undercut him with her silent contempt. Doubtless it was from her mother, in the first instance, that Mabel Ganson imbibed the scorn of men which was so often to assert itself in her later life. When her father flew into one of his jealous rages and "stamped and shouted and called her names," her mother hid "her cold, merciless, expressionless contempt behind her book or newspaper." The girl "tried to imitate her look." The father "would shout and fling his arms about and his face would seem to break up into fragments from the running passion in him," but her mother refused even to acknowledge his presence. "And when he could shout no more he would stamp out of the room and mount the stairs and presently we would hear his door slam far away in the house. Sometimes, then, she would raise her eyes from the pretense of reading and, not moving her head, she would glance at me sideways and drawing down the corners of her mouth, she would grimace a little message of very thin reassurance to me."[6]

Mabel Luhan's was the generation of which Walter Lippmann wrote: "We inherit freedom, and have to use it. The sanctity of property, the patriarchal family, hereditary caste,

5. *Background*, dedication, n.p.
6. Ibid., pp. 25–6.

the dogma of sin, obedience to authority,—the rock of ages, in brief, has been blasted for us. Those who are young to-day are born into a world in which the foundations of the older order survive only as habits or by default."[7] Beyond the chaos in the Ganson family, beyond the erosion of parental authority, one also senses the erosion of society itself. The Gansons belonged prominently to Buffalo "society," but society in the larger sense never seems to have entered their lives. Certainly it is completely missing from their daughter's autobiography. She never refers to a public event of any kind, never refers to her father's role in the world, gives only the barest hint of his occupation. Nor does her mother seem to have had any existence, in the girl's imagination, beyond the walls of the family mansion. Mabel suspected that her mother had "beaux"; but that was all.[8] She could imagine for her mother no connection with a world outside the family except one which was by definition clandestine and illicit—secret meetings with faceless men in unknown hotels. And even that, as she later realized, was perhaps no more than a fantasy of her own. "Was she a deep and secret woman . . . or did I invent all that about her?"[9]

The houses of the rich had become fortresses against intrusion. Even the architecture of the period reflected the tendency of each family to withdraw into a world of its own making. To the outsider these edifices presented a massive wall of impenetrable stone, into which doors and windows were deeply set, mere slits, like those of the medieval castles to which the buildings of Richardson and his imitators obscurely alluded. The effect of the heavy doors and ponderous draperies was not

7. Walter Lippmann: *Drift and Mastery* (Englewood Cliffs, N. J.: Prentice-Hall; 1961 [New York, 1914], p. 16). Cf. Randolph Bourne, above, p. 76.

8. *Background*, p. 25.

9. Ibid., p. 65.

only to shut out intruders but to stifle the human sounds within. A pervasive silence descended. Life came to be lived behind locked doors. In her mother's bureau, concealed in a handkerchief case, Mabel Ganson found a copy of Boccaccio.[1]

In such a setting the tenderer human emotions, muffled and stifled, thwarted and denied, could struggle to light only in shy and timorous gestures, taking on twisted and hardly recognizable forms. An aunt of a family down the street had a secret, like Mrs. Ganson. One evening when the other adults were away, she put on men's clothes, which she had hidden away in her room. She "wooed" Mabel and her friends with "an air of magical attractiveness." She danced with them, pressing them "to her hard shirt front." "She danced with us each in turn, and soon we were pushing each other aside to get into her arms again. She wrinkled her nose at us and laughed a kind of wild laugh and lighted cigarettes one from the other."[2]

Only twenty years, a single generation, separated Jane Addams from Mabel Dodge, but the disintegration of family life seemed already to have entered a new phase. Life in respectable families no longer seemed merely boring and pointless; it gave off now an atmosphere of actual decay. Or was it only that Mabel Ganson was a little obsessed with secrets? But if she was, that was significant in itself; it was the state of mind that middle-class family life now seemed all too often to induce. Whether her perceptions of that life were accurate or distorted, it is enough that they were of the darkest sort, intimations of a vast moral wreckage; and that they led very early to a longing to escape more urgent by far, more exaggerated, and at the same time more ambiguous and inconclusive in its expression, than anything Jane Addams seems to have felt. The very air in her family's house seemed to the girl unbearably oppressive

1. Ibid.
2. Ibid., p. 184.

and overripe. Even in the dead of winter, Mrs. Luhan says, she used to sleep with her head under a wide-open window.[3]

Very early, Mabel Ganson seems to have come to the conclusion that the world into which she was born was hopelessly corrupt, destined to imminent extinction. Yet it was not until forty years later that she announced her break with it, and even then the break was far from complete. The very depth of her loathing for middle-class life seemed ever more fully to implicate her in it. Long after she had undertaken her symbolic withdrawal to New Mexico, all the conflicts of her early life still remained unresolved. Jane Addams's more modest rebellion was much more decisive in its outcome than Mabel Luhan's melodramatic one. In Jane Addams's case, rebellion led at last to something like contentment; in Mrs. Luhan's it turned in upon itself, renewing old dissatisfactions. And although Mrs. Luhan's narrative of her struggle purported, like Jane Addams's, to be a record of the successful resolution of an emotional crisis, it was in actuality a prolonged cry of despair.

The crises themselves took outwardly similar forms. From the time of her first marriage, Mrs. Luhan displayed the now familiar symptoms of neurasthenia. Bored, weary, endlessly ill, she felt her life to be devoid of purpose. Lacking Jane Addams's Protestant conscience, she took a certain pleasure in her own misery. Perhaps the uninhibited self-indulgence of the one, the unremitting self-reproach of the other, was the great difference between them. Mabel Luhan liked to surround herself with sympathizing men: doctors, psychoanalysts, authors, anybody to whom she could recite her misfortunes. In Florence, she says, she grew to enjoy complaining to her doctor as she sat in her "shaded bedroom, away from the unbecoming light from the window." "But if I woke with early morning tears,

3. Ibid., pp. 233-4.

and felt too sad to get up and bathe and dress in one of my pretty peignoirs, then, when he came and the butler announced him, I would send down word I was not well enough to see him that morning, for I felt I could only receive him when I was looking my best."[4] For such women, confessors who should be at the same time objects of casual flirtation had become an abiding need.

Like Jane Addams, Mabel Luhan decided that her unhappiness was a function of the habit of living at second hand. Both women, moreover, saw the habit as the peculiar curse of their class, the curse of an excessive refinement and cultivation of the intellect at the expense of the emotions. Mrs. Luhan was appalled to find that the habit continued even after she moved to Taos. One day she came upon a garden in the desert.

> "Shakespearean," I thought, and then quickly dismissed the analogy. Was one to be forever reminded of something else and never to experience anything in itself at first-hand? My mind seemed to me a waste-basket of the world, full of scraps that I wanted to throw away and couldn't. I longed for an immersion in some strong solution that would wipe out forever the world I had known so I could savor, as though it were all there was to savor, this life of natural beauty and clarity that had never been strained into Art or Literature.[5]

The thought reminds one of Jane Addams's disgust when she discovered that even her own uselessness presented itself in the borrowed imagery of De Quincey. There is a further resemblance: in both cases, the realization that books and learning stood in the way of experience coincided with a mounting sense that excessive intellection cut one off also from the springs of femininity. Thus Jane Addams envied the

4. *European Experiences* (New York: Harcourt, Brace; 1935), p. 87.
5. *Edge of Taos Desert* (New York: Harcourt, Brace; 1937), pp. 301-2.

"active, emotional life" of her grandmothers. Mrs. Luhan
characteristically saw the matter in the context of a sexual
competition: if domination was masculine and submission
feminine, then her relations with men revealed an alarming
sexual inadequacy, since she seemed always to end by playing
the stronger part. The association of overcivilization with a
betrayal of woman's nature expressed itself in her conversion
to the simpler way of life of the Indians—an event analogous
to the revelation that came to Jane Addams at the bullfight in
Madrid. Her decision to turn her back on civilization coincided
with the discovery of a man to whom she thought she could
unequivocally submit. But the violence with which she expressed her resolution was all her own; there is no parallel to it
in anything Jane Addams ever wrote. When she came to
realize, she says, that she belonged to Antonio Luhan, that she
was "his" and could never dispute his decisions or seek to
impose her will against his, she began to wish to

> leave the world I had been so false in, where I had always been
> trying to play a part and always feeling unrelated, a world that
> was on a decline so rapid one could see people one knew drop-
> ping to pieces day by day, a dying world with no one appearing
> who would save it, a decadent unhappy world, where the bright,
> hot, rainbow flashes of corruption were the only light high spots.
> Oh, I thought, to leave it, to leave it all, the whole world of it
> and not to be alone. To be with someone real at last, alive at last,
> unendingly true and untarnished.[6]

Not only the intensity of her desire "to leave it all" but the
scope of her indictment of civilization distinguished Mabel
Luhan from Jane Addams and other radicals, for whereas
they tended to define the culture against which they were in
rebellion as the culture of a particular class or nationality (the

6. Ibid., pp. 221–2.

"Anglo-Saxon"), she brought the whole of the white race within the sweep of her rhetorical condemnation. Perhaps because she had not merely visited the continent but had lived there for a period of years, she could not share Randolph Bourne's belief that "Puritanism" was a peculiarly Anglo-American phenomenon. Nor did she look to the working class to find the spontaneity missing in the life of the middle class. She turned instead to the Indians, whom she proceeded to romanticize, however, exactly as other intellectuals romanticized Europeans, proletarians, and children.

There is one final difference between Mrs. Luhan and most of the other cultural radicals of her time. Like Jane Addams, like Bourne, like John Dewey, Mrs. Luhan upheld "experience" against intellection. But she defined experience much more narrowly than they did. Whereas they referred to any direct perception of life, any perception that was not filtered through the perceptions of others, she tended to restrict the concept of experience to the purely biological. All thought was treacherous in her view; the senses alone could be trusted to speak the truth. She insisted, moreover, on the primacy not of the senses in general but of the particular sensations associated with sexual excitement. Mrs. Luhan may be regarded as a pioneer in the cult of the orgasm, which has since not only captivated so many other intellectuals but permeated the entire culture. Her conversion in the desert presented itself as an upwelling of triumphant heterosexuality. Until her submission to Tony Luhan, she had known only a single "satisfactory sexual experience," as a more erudite generation would have put it. In Buffalo her first husband had rudely and abruptly taken her on the floor of the hall of her parents' house. Since that "first surprising involuntary orgasm," she maintained, "actually nothing real had happened" to her until she came

to Taos. But now "I was by grace born in that flash as I should
have been years, years ago; inducted into the new world."[7]

[III]

"It is indeed the happy woman who has no history, for by
happy we mean the loving and beloved, and by history we
designate all those relatable occurrences on earth caused by the
human energies seeking other outlets than the biological one.
. . . That I have so many pages to write signifies, solely, that
I was unlucky in love. Most of the pages are about what I
did instead."[8] Thus Mabel Dodge Luhan summed up the story
of her life: a sad story with a happy ending, her spiritual
regeneration "on the edge of Taos desert." Having found a
biological "outlet" for her energies, she had no further history
to record.

Unfortunately for the plausibility of this interpretation of
her life, Mrs. Luhan had already produced what was in effect
another volume of memoirs, in the disguise of an essay on
D. H. Lawrence, which gave a quite different version of her
life in Taos. Although it appeared before any of the volumes
of her *Intimate Memories, Lorenzo in Taos* dealt with events
more recent than any covered in that work. It showed how
little was changed by Mrs. Luhan's renunciation of the white
race and her marriage to an Indian. In fact, it showed that the
writing of the *Intimate Memories*, the ostensible record of her
triumph, was itself an act of desperation, undertaken as a kind
of therapy during a depression which appears to have been at
least as severe as anything she had experienced before. It may

7. *Edge of Taos Desert*, pp. 216, 219.
8. *Movers and Shakers* (New York: Harcourt, Brace; 1936), p. 263.

be that the therapy was so effective that it produced an un-precedented state of contentment which Mrs. Luhan, when she came to the last volume, then projected back to the beginning of her life in Taos. However that may be, the earlier account flatly contradicts the later, and since the former consists largely of contemporary letters, whereas the second is purely retrospec-tive, there is no question as to which is the more dependable of the two.

By the fall of 1924, seven years after her arrival in Taos and a year after her fourth marriage, Mrs. Luhan had reached a crisis in her affairs, one of those onsets of boredom, frustration, and melancholy which recurred at regular intervals throughout her life. In 1922 she had lured D. H. Lawrence and his wife to Taos. Lawrence had misgivings about coming, but "I willed him to come. Before I went to sleep at night, I drew myself all in to the core of my being where there is a live, plangent force lying passive—waiting for direction. . . . 'Come, Lawrence! Come to Taos!' became, in me, Lawrence in Taos. This is not prayer," Mrs. Luhan added, "but command. Only those who have exercised it know its danger."[9]

At first, Lawrence was captivated by Mrs. Luhan in spite of himself. He suggested that they collaborate on a novel based on her life. He drafted the first chapter of the book, but the project soon collapsed in a series of quarrels. The friendship itself collapsed. In October 1924 Lawrence went to Mexico, and although he returned to the United States for a few months in 1925, Mrs. Luhan had no further contact with him.[1] On

9. *Lorenzo in Taos* (New York: Alfred A. Knopf; 1932), p. 35.
1. "He, up on the ranch [Kiowa Ranch, seventeen miles from Taos, which Mrs. Luhan had given to Frieda Lawrence], avoided me, and I avoided him. . . . I never communicated with him until I completed the first volume of the *Intimate Memories* and wrote him that I wanted to send it to him in Europe, where he went the following autumn [September, 1925] and from where he never returned to America." (*Lorenzo in Taos*, p. 281.)

top of Lawrence's departure, she found herself at an impasse with her new husband. She now had to admit that their "different cultures" had "taken different directions." "There is practically nothing for us unavoidably to *do* together," she wrote to Lawrence. "For he likes Mexican dances and I don't. He likes the simple movements of life, like the plaza life, and I don't. And there is little we can talk about of *current* life. About general essentials and the eternities we are in agreement and can speak together about them. If we sit in a room, it is in silence."[2] Her boredom, as always, tended to immobilize her. The smallest decisions became "a kind of agony." She felt herself sinking under a "terrible inertia." From this familiar "gummed-up" state there were only two forms of release that she had been able to discover, falling in love and writing. "If one can do some writing for someone, then after it the world appears mild, sober, lovely, or interesting." She began to play with the notion of writing an autobiography. This thought, it is interesting to note, was bound up with her decision to return to psychoanalysis. She had been analyzed in New York some time before, first by Smith Ely Jeliffe and then by A. A. Brill, and she now decided to lease Finney Farm, where she had lived with her third husband, and to return to the care of Dr. Brill. After these arrangements had been completed, she wrote to Lawrence:

Now both you and Brill feel *I* have to do all the work this winter. With guidance I have to *do* the thing, whatever it is.
Can you tell me *what* this thing literally is? Finding myself? I believe I've been a kind of werewolfess.[3]

2. MDL to Lawrence, n.d. [Sept. 28(?), 1924], *Lorenzo in Taos*, pp. 276-7. In *Edge of Taos Desert* (p. 243), Mrs. Luhan glossed over these difficulties and noted only: "We didn't talk much. We never have talked much. But we were glad to be together."
3. MDL to Lawrence [Sept. 28, 1924], *Lorenzo in Taos*, pp. 275-6.

Lawrence had urged her to "try, above all things, to be still and to contain yourself."[4]

> *What kind* of control and discipline did you mean? *Would writing do* as a cure and a help? Shall I try to start a life-history or something? Save this letter if you think it would help Brill. It's so hard for me to formulate things, maybe it would aid him.[5]

Lawrence with characteristic bluntness told her that she hadn't enough "restraint" for creative writing but that she could "make a document." "If you want to write your apologia pro vita sua, do it as honestly as you can—and if it's got the right thing in it, I can help you with it once it's done."[6] Thus encouraged, Mrs. Luhan set to work and completed the first volume within a year—"a real effort," she thought, "*to see Mabel*."[7] Within another year she finished the second volume and sent it to Lawrence, as she had sent the first, for his opinion.

He was impressed with it in spite of himself. At the same time he found the manuscript "frightfully depressing"—"the most heart-destroying revelation of the American life-process that ever has or ever will be produced." Not art—"because art always gilds the pill, and this is hemlock in a cup"—it was nevertheless, he thought, "the most serious 'confession' that ever came out of America." It seemed to him "so horribly near the truth" that it made him "sick in my solar plexus, like death

4. Lawrence to MDL, n.d. [Sept. 19, 1924], *Lorenzo in Taos*, p. 274. Some of Lawrence's letters to Mrs. Luhan have been printed in Harry T. Moore's *Collected Letters of D. H. Lawrence*, but since Mrs. Luhan locked up the originals in a safe, Moore had to reprint them from *Lorenzo in Taos*. I therefore cite the latter source. In cases where the dates of Lawrence's letters are in doubt, however, I have followed Professor Moore's suggestions, wherever he offers them.
5. MDL to Lawrence [Sept. 28, 1924], *Lorenzo in Taos*, p. 276.
6. Lawrence to MDL, n.d. [*c*. Oct. 15, 1924], *Lorenzo in Taos*, p. 279.
7. MDL to Lawrence, April 3, 1926, *Lorenzo in Taos*, p. 294.

itself." "My dear Mabel, I do think it was pretty hard lines on all of you, to start with. Life gave America gold and a ghoulish destiny. Heaven help us all!"[8]

Notwithstanding her insistence (an afterthought, it would seem) that her childhood was "all right" and that she "would not have had it different," Mrs. Luhan knew that she had written a depressing book.[9] "It is indeed the happy woman who has no history." But it was not depressing for the reason she herself supposed—because it recorded the sublimation of biological energies into other channels. Mrs. Luhan's garbled interpretations of Freud and Jung, with which she unfortunately burdened so much of her narrative, were of little interest. What mattered, what rescued *Intimate Memories* from banality and at the same time accounted for the depressing quality of the work, was the "long, long indictment of our civilisation," as Lawrence noted; that, and what he called the "strange focussing of female power, upon object after object, in the process of decreation: or uncreation: as a sort of revenge," he speculated, "for the compulsion of birth and procreation."[1] This last theme, the theme of sexual rivalry and hostility, was the real subject of the work, the subject of practically everything Mrs. Luhan wrote, as it was the favorite subject of Lawrence himself. The difference between them was that Lawrence ruthlessly dragged what he knew about the battle of the sexes to consciousness and managed, moreover, to write about himself with a rare honesty; Mrs. Luhan, on the other hand, allowed most of her understanding of sexual conflict to remain only half articulated, buried under layers of ideology. Her chief fault as a writer was perhaps not so much artistic,

8. Lawrence to MDL, April 12, 1926, *Lorenzo in Taos*, p. 296.
9. *Background*, dedication.
1. Lawrence to MDL, Sept. 23, 1926, *Lorenzo in Taos*, pp. 309–10.

as Lawrence first suspected, as intellectual: a fatal susceptibility to intellectual quackery in all its forms. She was forever hitting upon some new nostrum that was to cure all her emotional complaints. First it was Freud, then Jung, then Dr. Gurdjieff's institute at Fontainebleau in France.[2] Her letters to Lawrence, filled with intricate diagrams of psychic principles and with talk of introverts and extroverts, made him despair of her. She reveled in the paraphernalia of pseudo-science, and her efforts to understand herself inevitably collapsed under this ponderous freight. Only when the descriptive writer triumphed over the ideologue did understanding struggle to the surface, too often to be crushed again under the weight of her latest intellectual enthusiasm.

The record of her unhappiness remains, however, and when one strips it of the dubious interpretations she herself inflicted on it, its outlines emerge with a good deal of clarity. Her Lesbianism is a case in point. Mrs. Luhan tends to treat it for the most part as a clinical detail, the consequence of an early breast-fixation. There is a whole section in *Background* on "The Breast," in which bosom after bosom is recalled in graphic detail: "round they were and with a deep cleft between them"; "white [and] flowery . . . with their pointed nipples leaning towards me"; "large, ballooning, billowing . . . , firm and resilient and with a stout, springing nipple."[3] What is important, however, is not that Mabel Ganson as a child was fascinated by breasts or that she later had a number of passing schoolgirl affairs, but that as she grew older her homosexual

2. This place, as she imagined it, had a certain uncanny resemblance to Dr. Renault's "life laboratory," in which Robert Herrick had Margaret Pole discover the secret of pure altruism—a place where the object of therapy was "to clean out their minds as well as their bodies, get rid so far as we can of the muddy deposits" left by a corrupt civilization; "give 'em a sort of spiritual purge," in the words of Dr. Renault. (Robert Herrick: *Together* [New York: Macmillan; 1908], p. 456.)

3. *Background*, pp. 208–9, 30–1.

tendencies revealed themselves more and more as an aspect of the will to power which pervaded all her sexual relations with women and men alike.

Consider her friendship with Violet Shillito, with its dreary sequel—the climactic episode of *Background*, and the central event, perhaps, of the entire autobiography. The friendship itself is described with tenderness; Lawrence found it almost "the only . . . touch of real love" in the book; but even that, he added, was "deathly."[4] Violet, the daughter of American parents living permanently in France, was the sister of Mary Shillito, a classmate of Mabel's at Miss Graham's School in New York. Her accomplishments, as Mary recited them, were legendary. She had taught herself Italian in order to read Dante, Greek in order to read Plato. Later she studied higher mathematics at the Sorbonne; "for the beauty," she explained.[5] Mary made a kind of cult of her absent sister, into which she inducted Mabel, a cult at the center of which was a shared passion for what Mary and Violet called "*la grande vie intérieure.*" Mary persuaded her new friend to make the pilgrimage to Paris. For Mabel and her mother it was a pilgrimage also, such as so many American girls and their mothers had undertaken before, to the temple of culture and tradition; and the daughter's reaction to Europe differed very little from that of innumerable other Americans who went abroad around the turn of the century. She came away with a sense that the old civilization had played itself out.

Violet herself was an intimation of the death of a way of life. Prematurely wise, she was to die prematurely shortly thereafter, hard on the Gansons' departure. High-strung, aristocratic, she lived in an atmosphere of overripe romanticism. She seemed to her friend "weary"; she suggested "civilization com-

4. Lawrence to MDL, May 21, 1926, *Lorenzo in Taos*, p. 303.
5. *Background*, p. 246.

ing to pieces." She had an intuition that Götterdämmerung lay close at hand; she spoke of the "debacle" ahead, "of everything going under."[6] She played Chopin and Beethoven while her sister wept. But it was Wagner to whom they were all three most perfectly attuned—Wagner, who "voiced for the white race its desire for annihilation."[7] At Bayreuth they strolled hand in hand about the grounds. In the Shillitos' country house Mabel turned to Violet in the night, and "there arose all about us, it seemed, a high, sweet singing." "*Je ne savais pas que je sois sensuelle*," Violet said, "*mais il paraît que je le suis.*" "*Et pourquoi pas?*" asked her friend, "for it seemed to me if that was what was meant by *sensualité* it was exquisite and commendable and should be cultivated." But Violet seemed more than ever weary and resigned. "That sweet, rueful, loving smile was on her face now all the time we were together, and it was called there by that glad life of our blood, which for want of a better term I must call music—but that she had named to me by the term *sensualité*."[8]

The Gansons went home to America, Mabel to the Chevy Chase School, her debut in Buffalo ("I was never so bored in my life"), her marriage to Karl Evans, his early death.[9] When she returned to Europe, Violet was dead and she herself was engaged to Edwin Dodge. Mary Shillito now lived with a girl named Marcelle, who had been devoted to Violet, "a girl with a strong, independent character, the kind of character that a man is supposed to have."[1] Both of them disapproved of Mabel's impending marriage; there were quarrels; Mabel went off to Florence with Dodge. By the time she next visited Mary, her own emotional life had settled into the pattern it con-

6. Ibid., p. 249.
7. Ibid., p. 269.
8. Ibid., pp. 264-6.
9. Ibid., p. 289.
1. *European Experiences*, p. 62.

tinued thereafter to follow. Finding Mary jealous and spiteful and the atmosphere in the château oppressive, she "began," she says, "to try to throw a little net around Marcelle." She succeeded without difficulty in "lighting a little fire in her," and "night after night Marcelle gave herself up to the luxury of streaming love that passed out of her across to me." Mary reacted with "rabbity alarm." One night she burst in on the pair; a terrible scene ensued; Mabel took Marcelle away to Aix-les-Bains for three days. Then she went back to her husband in Italy. "I missed Marcelle . . . I hated to grow cold again."[2]

Thus *la grande vie intérieure* played itself out in a sordid little struggle for power. "I began to try to throw a little net around Marcelle." One begins to understand why Mrs. Luhan's lovers are so often described as victims. Twice she uses a striking image in this connection, writing of a girl at the Chevy Chase School that she "lay in her bed like a sacrifice, straight and relaxed," and of Violet that "she lay beside me, a long, stiff effigy in the white light from the moon shining on the wall."[3]

It was in her relations with men that Mrs. Luhan, as she herself was at least intermittently aware, most fully gave play to her impulse to dominate. It was not, she explained, that she wished to dominate her men; it was only that she had never met a man to whom she could submit. "The fact is, like most real women, all my life I had needed and longed for the strong man who would take the responsibility for me and my decisions. I wanted to lie back and float on the dominating decisive current of an all-knowing, all-understanding man. I had never known any such man."[4] But why did sex present

2. Ibid., pp. 220–4.
3. *Background*, pp. 277, 263.
4. *Movers and Shakers*, p. 310.

itself in the first place as a struggle, a question of resistance or submission?

It was not simply that she had somehow never known "any such man." In her more candid moments Mrs. Luhan acknowledged a conflict within herself.

> Something in us wants men to be strong, mature, and superior to us so that we may admire them, thus consoled in a measure for our enslavement to them. . . . But something else in us wants them to be inferior, and less powerful than ourselves, so that obtaining the ascendancy over them we may gain possession, not only of them, but of our own souls, once more.[5]

Mrs. Luhan treated her husbands and lovers like possessions of the same order as the beautiful objects with which she filled her houses. She collected people and arranged them like flowers. Her New York *salon* was only one of many; wherever she went, she loved to combine people in startling new juxtapositions. Sometimes she staged a little tableau in which she herself played a part. In Florence she loved to torment her husband by engaging in harmless flirtations, just as she tormented Mary Shillito by "lighting a little fire" in Marcelle. Her pleasure lay in Edwin Dodge's having to be present at the scene of her conquests; the conquests themselves were nothing more than the amusement of a moment. When she tired of Dodge, she tired of the game as well. In Taos the pattern repeated itself. Lawrence was convinced that she had "*caused* [Luhan] to take a violent prejudice against" him. Not content with playing off Lawrence against Luhan, Mabel meanwhile sent her son around the neighborhood with the report that "my mother is tired of those Lawrences who sponge on her."[6]

5. Ibid., p. 228.
6. Frieda Lawrence: *"Not I, But the Wind . . ."* (New York: Viking Press; 1934), p. 136; Lawrence to MDL [Sept. 19, 1924], *Lorenzo in Taos,* p. 273; see also Lawrence to MDL, Oct. 17, 1923, *Lorenzo in Taos,* p. 118.

All the time she was pushing people here and there, she longed only to "lie back and float" on the current of dominating masculinity; so that her triumphs of manipulation brought her in the long run little satisfaction. She wanted her life to be "very comfortable and orderly"; she longed for "intimate, domestic pleasures."[7] With John Reed, the only one of her lovers whom she did not eventually marry, she tried particularly hard to adopt the role of the submissive wife and helpmeet. But it was impossible to submit to Reed because Reed himself was in so many ways a child. At the same time his masculine independence, which should have pleased her if she was "tired of trying to be emancipated," irritated her beyond measure.[8] When she went to Chicago to see him off to Mexico, where his articles on the revolution were to win him a reputation as a war correspondent, she was disappointed "that he looked merely rather glad instead of overjoyed." "The man in him was already on the job," she observed bitterly. "The woman's place was in the home."[9] And when she went with him to Europe in 1914, she found that Reed's real mistress was the war. "Panting with pleasurable activity, his eyes shining . . . he rushed with his friends into the affair of the war." Eventually Reed ran off with another woman. She herself lapsed back into invalidism. "I stayed in bed a good deal of the time. Lifeless."[1]

Maurice Sterne, her next acquisition, was more pliable than Reed, but his very pliability made him contemptible. When she met Sterne, he was a painter. She insisted he ought to be a sculptor instead. He obligingly turned to sculpture, changing his career to suit her. She pretended "a kind of deference" to

7. *Movers and Shakers*, p. 308.
8. Ibid.
9. Ibid., p. 247.
1. Ibid., p. 295. See also Granville Hicks: *John Reed: The Making of a Revolutionary* (New York: Macmillan; 1937), p. 163.

him. "For as long as I lived with him I had to try and look up to him, but it was an effort that constantly failed."[2]

Perhaps, after all, she had been "unlucky in men"; "or perhaps something in me had engaged me only with those men with whom I could successfully contend." But with Tony Luhan, she insisted, it was different. "From the first I never disputed his decisions."[3] So Mrs. Luhan claimed in her memoirs. She forgot all those occasions, which she herself had recorded in *Lorenzo in Taos*, when she successfully pitted her will against his. Luhan, for instance, at first disapproved of inviting Lawrence to Taos. "His instinct somewhat opposed it. . . . But I overruled it, and he gave way."[4] He also objected to taking Lawrence to an Apache festival, "but I made him!" "I am always *making* him do things," she added.[5] So much for her "submission" to Luhan.

Nor did she submit to the Indian way of life, though she was always talking about it. Having loudly renounced the "sick old world of art and artists,"[6] she still filled her life, as Lawrence reported, with "suppers and motor drives and people dropping in."[7] She loved "to play the patroness," he complained; and her relation to the Indians was that of the great lady to her wards.[8] In fact, it was exactly the relation Randolph Bourne mistakenly imagined Jane Addams had to the immigrants—a patronizing "appreciation" of their curious old folkways. As Lawrence quickly discovered, she "hates the white world and loves the Indian out of hate."[9] That is, she loved

2. *Edge of Taos Desert*, pp. 228–9.
3. Ibid., p. 227.
4. *Lorenzo in Taos*, p. 35.
5. Ibid., p. 47.
6. Ibid., p. 52.
7. Lawrence to Catherine Carswell, Dec. 17, 1922, in Moore: *Collected Letters of D. H. Lawrence*, Vol. II, p. 732.
8. Lawrence to his mother-in-law, Dec. 5, 1922, in Moore: op. cit., p. 730.
9. Ibid.

whatever was exotic and picturesque in Indian life, whatever was not white. The glory of the Indians, she once announced in public, was that they did not want progress; they did not want "a dismal accretion of cars, stoves, sinks, *et al.*"; "the blood of their fore-runners is still stronger in them than new needs for THINGS." She herself at that time had just moved into a new house, as Harry T. Moore has noted, "with soundproof bedrooms, a magnificent kitchen, and several fine bathrooms." A young Indian, addressing her in a letter to the local paper, angrily proposed that they exchange places. "You can have all the horse and buggies you want and I'll have your nice new cars. You drink muddy water from the mountains and I and my wife and five children will drink nice clean water from your faucets." What she did not understand, he said, was that "we want to live like humans and not like animals."[1] For Mrs. Luhan, however, their living like animals was the very source of the Indians' charm. It meant (as she erroneously believed) that they had not yet learned to sublimate their biological energies. If sublimation was the root of evil, the Indians still lived in an innocent Eden. It is a pity the Indians did not know more about Freud and Jung (as interpreted by Mrs. Luhan). They would have taken comfort in knowing that their illiteracy and squalor were enviable cultural advantages.

[IV]

When D. H. Lawrence cried: "Back to your tents, O America!" Americans such as Walter Lippmann and Mabel Dodge took him literally. When Lawrence urged Americans to "take

1. Harry T. Moore: *The Intelligent Heart: The Story of D. H. Lawrence* (London: Heinemann; 1955), p. 302.

up life where the Red Indian, the Aztec, the Maya, the Incas, left it off," and "to listen to your own, don't listen to Europe," they assumed that he was glorifying the noble savage.[2] Lippmann felt called upon to instruct Lawrence in the elements of American history: America had no native culture, but was "a nation of emigrants who took possession of an almost empty land."[3] Anyone who had read Lawrence's *Studies in Classic American Literature* might have seen that he was pleading with American writers to cultivate their own literary traditions; but it was characteristic of American radicals that they could see Lawrence only as a reformer with a bold new program for the regeneration of Western man. They forgot that he was first and foremost a writer whose chief concern was the process whereby life is translated into literature. That process was precisely what did not interest American radicals; they would have dismissed Lawrence as a believer in the heresy of "art for art's sake," had they suspected that he cared about it. It was as a prophet armed with a new religion that he caught their imagination and as a prophet that they accepted or rejected him. Mrs. Luhan solemnly explained: "Lawrence had a belief . . . that it was his destiny to [destroy] the old modes, the evil, outworn ways of the world" and "that if he could overcome evil and destroy it, he would have fulfilled his destiny."[4] She simply could not get it into her head that Lawrence was mainly interested in writing books. She could see him only as a Faustian figure wrestling with "Satanic powers." As for his writings, she seemed to have enjoyed only

2. D. H. Lawrence: "America, Listen to Your Own," *New Republic*, XXV (Dec. 15, 1920), pp. 69-70.

3. Walter Lippmann: "The Crude Barbarian and the Noble Savage," *New Republic*, XXV (Dec. 15, 1920), p. 70.

4. *Lorenzo in Taos*, p. 133. Admittedly, Lawrence did a good deal to encourage this picture of himself as a new Messiah.

his travel books, if indeed she had even read the others.[5] She cared so little about art in general that when she was presented with the manuscript of *Sons and Lovers*, in payment for the ranch which she tried to give to Frieda Lawrence and which Lawrence refused to allow his wife to accept as a gift, she gave the manuscript to Dr. Brill, "for helping a friend of mine." She took pride in this gesture, which symbolized her liberation from the "world of art and artists." "I suppose [Brill] still has it," she airily remarked. "I never asked him."[6]

Since Lawrence's American friends believed him to be essentially a propagandist who wanted white men to live like Indians, these friends were secretly pleased to find that real Indians made him uncomfortable. This discovery made them feel superior to him; they themselves, they imagined, had such easy and natural contact with red men. Witter Bynner, one of the ornaments of the Taos literary colony, professed amusement at the spectacle of Lawrence "extolling the noble savage in print while he dreaded or disliked him in person."[7] Mabel Luhan was convinced that Lawrence felt inadequate in the presence of her husband. When she and Luhan met the Lawrences' train, the car broke down and Luhan got out to fix it. Frieda Lawrence urged her husband to help him, whereupon Lawrence confessed: "I am a failure. I am a failure as a man

5. It was after reading *Sea and Sardinia* that she invited him to Taos. That book convinced her that Lawrence was "the only one who can really *see* this Taos country and the Indians." But she was also convinced that "of course one didn't really get the man in his books." (*Lorenzo in Taos*, pp. 3–4.)

6. Ibid., p. 192. See also Frieda Lawrence to Witter Bynner, Oct. 16, 1951, in E. W. Tedlock, Jr., ed.: *Frieda Lawrence: The Memoirs and Correspondence* (New York: Alfred A. Knopf; 1964), pp. 334–5.

7. Witter Bynner, foreword to Nehls: *D. H. Lawrence: A Composite Biography*, Vol. II, p. x. In Bynner's *Journey with Genius* (New York: John Day; 1951), p. 7, he also speaks of Lawrence's infatuation with "his noble savage."

in the world of men."[8] If Mrs. Luhan's account is inherently improbable—for, as Professor Moore has pointed out, Lawrence hated machines and "thought that Indians who knew how to fix them were corrupt"[9]—it nevertheless reveals once again her obsession with masculinity, femininity, and sexual rivalry. From the beginning, her relations with the Lawrences assumed in her mind a complicated pattern of competition, Luhan pitted against Lawrence, herself against Frieda Lawrence, Lawrence and Frieda against each other, and above all Lawrence against herself: a four-way battle of wills.

Thus she was convinced that "there was never a moment of sympathy" between Lawrence and her husband after Luhan laughed at Lawrence's first attempts to ride a horse.[1] Lawrence assured her that he had "nothing against" Luhan, but that altered in no way Mrs. Luhan's habit of seeing all human relations as a form of politics.[2] Love, friendship, and sex all continued in her imagination to constitute a struggle for mastery; life itself was a struggle for mastery; and she was later convinced that Lawrence had died, in fact, not of tuberculosis (a consideration altogether beneath her notice), but "because he scorned to learn the mundane mastery that may insure a long, smooth life if the living impulse is emasculated and overcome." He "made a mess of living and of friendship and love . . . because he never learned to 'control' himself, but let life rule."[3] Lawrence in turn thought that Mrs. Luhan was unhappy precisely because she was so intent on willing her happiness. "You have striven so hard, and so long, to *compel* life. Can't

8. *Lorenzo in Taos*, p. 39.
9. Moore: *The Intelligent Heart*, p. 297.
1. *Lorenzo in Taos*, p. 76.
2. Lawrence to MDL [Sept. 19, 1924], in *Lorenzo in Taos*, p. 273.
3. Ibid., pp. 14–15.

you now slowly change, and let life slowly drift into you."[4] But he had already answered his own question. Within a few weeks of meeting Mabel Luhan, he had discovered her "terrible will-to-power."[5] She had a "passion," he said afterward, "for breaking other people's eggs and making a mess instead of an omelette, which is really dangerous. She seems to hate anybody to care for anybody—even for herself—and if anybody *does* care for anybody, she must upset it—even if she falls herself out of the apple-cart." "A woman," he decided, "*must* upset any apple-cart that's got two apples in it: just for the fun."[6]

No sooner had the Lawrences arrived in Taos than Mrs. Luhan capitalized on the existing tension between Lawrence and his wife in order to drive a rift between them. Frieda Lawrence had to admire the "terrific energy . . . resources and intelligence" with which Mrs. Luhan set about her task; but "why were you so bossy?" she wailed afterward.[7] The proposed novel which Lawrence and Mrs. Luhan were to write became the means of rescuing him from what Mrs. Luhan regarded as a disastrous marriage. Frieda resisted the novel from the first. "I did not want this. I had always regarded Lawrence's genius as given to me."[8] Terrible quarrels ensued—"the vileness of 1923," Lawrence referred to them subsequently.[9] Mrs. Luhan told Frieda that she was not "the right woman for Lawrence," and Frieda was "miserable thinking that Lawrence had given her the right to talk like this to me." Lawrence railed by turns

---

4. Lawrence to MDL, Oct. 17, 1923, in *Lorenzo in Taos*, p. 119.

5. Lawrence to his mother-in-law, Dec. 5, 1922, *Collected Letters*, Vol. II, p. 730.

6. Lawrence to Witter Bynner, April 13, 1928, *Collected Letters*, Vol. II, p. 1054.

7. Frieda Lawrence: *"Not I, But the Wind,"* p. 137; Frieda to MDL, April 28, 1930, in Tedlock: *Frieda Lawrence*, p. 238.

8. Frieda Lawrence: *"Not I, But the Wind,"* p. 136.

9. Lawrence to MDL, Jan. 9, 1924, *Lorenzo in Taos*, p. 135.

at Frieda and at Mrs. Luhan. Finally he and Frieda "left
Mabel's ambient" and moved to a neighboring ranch.[1] In the
spring they escaped to Mexico.

The struggle with Frieda, Mrs. Luhan discovered, "released
. . . all my desire for domination."[2] She strove not only to win
Lawrence away from his wife but "to seduce his spirit so that
I could make him carry out certain things." She wanted him
"to take *my* experience, *my* material, *my* Taos, and to formulate it all into a magnificent creation." Knowing that "the
strongest, surest way to the soul is through the flesh," she simu-
lated a physical passion for him. "I persuaded my flesh and
my nerves that I wanted him." It was really "his soul I needed
for my purpose, his soul, his will." But "the only way to obtain
the ascendancy over these essential tools was by way of the
blood."

That is one of the things we know, Jeffers [she wrote, addressing
herself to the poet to whom her narrative was dedicated]; realists
like you know it. The idealists, as they call themselves—masking
under a nice word their short-sightedness—they never know it.
Of course some people stop short of the gate of blood. They are
satisfied with that. But others, all those who get things done—
they go on from there.

I was always trying to get things done: I didn't often even
try to do anything myself. I seemed to want to use all my power
upon delegates to carry out the work. This way—perhaps a com-
pensation for that desolate and barren feeling of having nothing
to do!—I achieved a sense of fruitfulness and activity vicariously.[3]

Beside her own confessions, Lawrence's strictures on Mrs.
Luhan's "will-to-power" seem mild enough; yet she became
convinced that Lawrence wished to "destroy" her.[4] After the

1. Frieda Lawrence: "*Not I, But the Wind,*" p. 137.
2. *Lorenzo in Taos,* p. 66.
3. Ibid., pp. 69–70.
4. Ibid., p. 270.

Lawrences' return to New Mexico in the spring of 1924, matters
came rapidly to a head. One night in July the caldron of accumulated bitterness boiled over. The Lawrences had come
down to Taos from their ranch, accompanied by Dorothy
Brett, a viscount's daughter who had worshipfully followed
Lawrence to the New World. Mrs. Luhan had two other house
guests, Alice Sprague, a childhood friend from Buffalo, and
her own latest admirer and retainer, Clarence Thompson, a
young aesthete from New York whom she described as "extremely sophisticated and exquisite."[5] After supper Tony Luhan
drove off on some errand, and the rest of the party "strolled
over to the studio." Lawrence and Clarence disappeared for
half an hour and returned surprisingly, for Lawrence rarely
drank, with a bottle of moonshine whiskey. "As the unaccus-
tomed alcohol ran through our veins, we all drew together,
feeling more convivial than usual, more cosy and reassured."
Somebody put a record on the gramophone and Clarence and
Mrs. Luhan began to dance. Then Clarence danced with
Frieda, "in a dignified, dreamy way." Mrs. Luhan seized
Lawrence, who danced as seldom as he drank, and "led him
round and round in a one-step." But when they stopped for
more drinks, "there began to rise between us all that feeling
of division and comparison that is so odious." They danced
again. Between the two couples "a fiercer and more sinister
emotion had sprung up." Clarence and Frieda, dancing gracefully "in an evident trance of self-satisfaction," pretended not
to notice Lawrence and Mrs. Luhan, who flew about the room
"bumping into them as hard as we could at every round!"
Gathering speed and momentum, the couples collided ever
more violently. "Lorenzo kicked Frieda as often as he could."
Mrs. Luhan was in transports of delight. "That night, for

5. Ibid., p. 115. "The instant he saw me standing in the doorway," Mrs.
Luhan reported, "he fell in love with me, or at least he thought he did."

once, and for only that once, I was able to join to his all my physical energy, and my will, destructive or not, in a mutual effort against the outside world. This was no deep, invisible 'flow' of life between us, reinforcing each the other [such as Lawrence was always commending to her as the best form of friendship]. No, it was his use of my strength for a battering-ram."

At last they all stopped for breath. Frieda and Clarence slipped silently out into the night. "I couldn't believe my eyes. That was simply not done among us. I mean, no one ever went out of sight of all the others. What one did we all did. There were no tête-à-têtes, no dialogues, nothing that was not in plain sight of all the others." But Frieda and Clarence, innocent of the rules, were gone. Lawrence went to bed. Tony came home. Mrs. Luhan went to bed and lay awake wondering what had become of the lovers, as she now imagined them. Finally she went out to look for them. She had reached the courtyard when Tony appeared, shouting: "Come back here!" She felt herself, however, "compelled to go on." Tony jumped in his car and drove angrily away; he did not return until the next morning. Meanwhile Mrs. Luhan found Clarence preparing for bed. "What *have* you been doing, Clarence?" He had been talking to Frieda, he said. "Frieda has told me *the Truth!*" The truth was that Lawrence had vowed to "destroy" Mabel Luhan. Mrs. Luhan "was shaking all over—trembling with the shock and the strangeness. It sounded true. It *was* true."[6]

Next morning Clarence confronted Lawrence. "You devil! I *know* you now!" The Lawrences and Brett went back to their ranch, in all likelihood none too clear as to exactly what had happened. Such were the hazards of group life. Couple

6. Ibid., pp. 224–30.

pitted against couple, the party had become a tiny court of intrigue, but a court with no world beyond itself, an oasis of intrigue in the middle of an uninhabited desert.

That such a scene could have taken place was a measure of the social vacuum in which modern life had come to be lived. But the central element in the scene was quite possibly a complete fabrication of Mrs. Luhan's. According to Dorothy Brett, usually a more reliable observer of facts, it was *she* who danced with Lawrence, bumping into Clarence and his partner, and Clarence's partner was not Frieda but Mrs. Luhan herself. ("Wild, elfish humour seizes [Lawrence]: as we pass Mabel and Clarence, decorously dancing the American dance, we bump into them, [Lawrence] with a wicked laugh, until Clarence, furious, rushes out of the studio. Frieda follows him— and Mabel vanishes, too. Then suddenly [Lawrence] tire[s]."[7]) But it makes no difference. What matters is that Mrs. Luhan could have imagined the scene as she did, seeing herself as Lawrence's "battering-ram."

In the fall of that year, she and Lawrence went their separate ways, Lawrence to Mexico, Europe, and death, Mrs. Luhan to her analyst in New York. She set out determined to will her will into submission. But how tedious, after all, these analysts were! One had to deal with them like babies, holding their hands. "With these analysts one has to be so careful, one has to weigh everything lest one give them more than they can swallow and they turn and rend one for it! Unless one fits oneself into their systems and formulas so they can pigeon-hole one into a type or a case, they grow puzzled or angry or sad. . . . One has, then, to be continually assuaging them and measuring down to them out of sheer, kind-heartedness. When I

7. Dorothy Brett: *Lawrence and Brett* (London: Martin Secker; 1933), p. 105.

think of the time I have spent assuaging analysts at twenty dollars an hour!"[8]

Happily, Mrs. Luhan could afford the sport; and she could take added consolation, if she needed it, in knowing that in the forthcoming struggle with Dr. Brill the odds, as usual, were all on her own side.

8. *Lorenzo in Taos*, p. 64.

5 / Politics as Social Control

NOT OPPRESSION, BUT WEAKNESS, BREEDS REVOLUTION. WHEN the nominally constituted authorities, whether of the state or of the family, combine weakness in action with an autocratic and overbearing manner, when they pretend to an invincibility which their actual resources can no longer sustain, their overthrow is close at hand. Louis XVI and Nicholas II, those celebrated autocrats, fell from power not because they were cruel but because they were contemptible. They fell because in their weakness, faced on all sides with a passive refusal to comply with their commands, they had more and more to circumscribe their claims to absolute authority; until at last people perceived the truth, that the old regimes were incapable of carrying on even the ordinary business of government. At that moment the old regimes melted away.

As in the state, so in the family: the very decadence of the patriarchal tradition—the weakness of fathers, the noninterference of parents—gave rise in the children of the middle class to a powerful contempt and revulsion. The men and women born around 1880 referred again and again to their curious sense that they had practically brought themselves up. Yet these men and women, on whom the weight of familial authority rested so lightly, rejected this authority most savagely. Their very freedom seemed to foster the discovery that they had been subtly enslaved.

At the same time, though they talked of the tyranny of the family claim, the freedom which they had undeniably enjoyed made it impossible for them to conceive of enslavement in the uncomplicated categories of the old radicalism, the radicalism of Mill and Marx. Men, they knew, were everywhere in chains, but the chains had become invisible. How could the new radicals talk of oppression when they themselves had been so little oppressed? Instinctively, they knew themselves to be the victims not of restraints imposed from outside but of a mysterious inner paralysis. Tyranny came to mean to them not oppression but repression, and the battleground between freedom and authority shifted from society to the self. The concept of freedom similarly acquired a new dimension: it signified the escape of the soul from a prison of its own devising, the triumph, to put the matter crudely, of instinct over intellect. The new radicals did not need Freud to tell them that men were divided against themselves. The lesson was inherent in their own experience. In their terrific struggles to realize themselves, they had met with none but the most perfunctory resistance from without. Who had forbidden Jane Addams to pursue a man's career? Her stepmother may have opposed it, but her own father encouraged her at every point. It was precisely her sense of her opportunities that made her consciousness of failure so painful; she had no one to blame but herself. It was the same with the others: neither Randolph Bourne nor Mabel Luhan ever complained that arbitrary obstacles had been put in the way of his self-fulfillment. Bourne might have taken refuge in such a complaint, but he did not choose to do so; and in Mrs. Luhan's case the assertion would have been absurd.

All of them complained, nevertheless, of the tyranny of the family. But this tyranny had not manifested itself in the imposition of the parental will against the will of the children. What then did they mean by the tyranny of the family? Presumably they meant that the very atmosphere of middle-class family life had come to be inimical to creative effort of any kind. The family, it seemed, gave off some subtle poison; and children, imbibing it, lost their natural, primitive creativity. The very "advantages" that their parents lavished upon them led to an excessive cultivation and refinement in which all the spontaneity of childhood was finally extinguished. Even at its best, the family was still the transmitter of a sterile and decadent culture, still the agent of "civilization"; and the child in every man and woman intuitively recognized these things as his enemies. "I been there before," said Huck Finn as he turned his back on civilization and Aunt Polly and lit out for the Indian territory. *Huckleberry Finn*, published in 1884, was a sign of things to come: by all odds Mark Twain's finest book, it owed its extraordinary power and lyricism to the device by which Twain solved at last the problem that had dogged him so persistently, the problem of tone, the problem of point of view, the problem, as Dwight Macdonald has put it, of learning to speak with his own voice.[1] In *Tom Sawyer* (1876) Mark Twain, himself the captive of the genteel tradition which in the other novel he attacked, saw childhood through the eyes of the grown-up world, reducing rebellion to a series of comic pranks. In *Huckleberry Finn* he saw the adult world with the eyes of childhood. Only as a child, apparently, could Twain see through the self-deceptions of the Victorian age.

As a very different sort of writer once observed: "For certain moral and intellectual purposes adults must become as little children."[2]

The great discovery of the turn of the century was the existence of uncivilized man; the existence, that is, of a buried part of the psyche which had never accepted the restraints of

1. Dwight Macdonald: "Mark Twain: An Unsentimental Journey," *The New Yorker*, XXXVI (April 9, 1960), pp. 173-4.

2. John Dewey: *Democracy and Education* (New York: Macmillan; 1961), p. 42; see above, p. 88.

adulthood or consented to become a responsible member of society. Hence the sudden interest not only in childhood but in primitive peoples. Hence also psychoanalysis, the most striking but by no means the only expression of the new preoccupation with buried levels of being.

These ideas represented the common achievement of the age. They were neither European nor American but Western. Nor were they in themselves radical or reactionary. In themselves they transcended political debate. It fell to the new radicals in America to convert the discovery of the hidden recesses of the spirit into a program of social and political action. In Europe, on the other hand, the new ideas helped to bring about a revival of the sense of the tragedy of the human predicament. They appeared to furnish evidence of human limitations rather than the promise of unfulfilled possibilities. In America, however, the discovery of the inner man encouraged the growth of a social, cultural, and political radicalism which had as its object the recovery of primitive modes of being, the lost innocence of the race. The recovery of the secret self was seen not only as something desirable in itself but as a means of bringing about far-reaching social changes as well; for as people like Jane Addams and John Dewey believed, the inner self represented above all a fund of natural affection and sociability. Man was a social being before he had been taught to think only of himself. The drawing-out of spontaneous selfhood, especially in children, became the primary means, therefore, of socializing democracy; the primary means, as the new radicals put it, of achieving "social control."

The new radicals assumed that it was possible, as William James had said, to find a "moral equivalent of war"—a moral equivalent of evil of all kinds. This idea, like the concept of uncivilized man, had a certain affinity with an idea of Freud's, the idea of sublimation. (Walter Lippmann noted the connection; so, apparently, did Randolph Bourne, when he observed that "the best kind of a moral equivalent is a moral sublimation.") But in arguing that the theory of moral equivalents ought to serve as a "guide post to statesmanship," in Lippmann's words, the new radicals ignored the limitations of the process of sublimation as described by Freud. Quite "apart from the fact that many people possess the capacity for sublimation only in a slight degree," sublimation, according to Freud, "can never discharge more than a certain proportion of libido." "To those who are not artists the gratification that can be drawn from the springs of phantasy is very limited; their inexorable repressions prevent the enjoyment of all but the meagre daydreams which can become conscious." And even to "the few," he added, sublimation "does not secure complete protection against suffering; it gives no invulnerable armour against the arrows of fate, and it usually fails when a man's own body becomes a source of suffering to him." No such reservations appeared in the writings of the new radicals in America. Lippmann could appeal to Freud in the same paragraph in which he spoke of the Boy Scouts—an organization which, he thought, had made boys' gangs "valuable to civilization"—as "a really constructive reform."[3]

Radical in its initial impulse, in its heartfelt rejection of the genteel tradition, the new radicalism nevertheless led to an attack on social problems which in some of its implications was the reverse of radical. The new radicals could speak of the need to liberate the creative energies of mankind and in the same

3. See Walter Lippmann: *A Preface to Politics* (Ann Arbor: University of Michigan Press; 1962 [New York, 1914]), pp. 41–3; Randolph Bourne: "A Moral Equivalent for Universal Military Service," in Carl Resek, ed.: *War and the Intellectuals, Essays by Randolph Bourne* (New York: Harper and Row; 1964), p. 146; Sigmund Freud: *A General Introduction to Psychoanalysis* (New York: Washington Square Press; 1960 [Joan Riviere, trans., London, 1922]), pp. 355, 384; Freud: *Civilization and Its Discontents* (Garden City: Doubleday & Company; n.d. [Joan Riviere, trans., London, 1930]), p. 21.

breath talk of "adjusting" men, as Jane Addams wrote, "in healthful relations" to one another. The study of the inner man could degenerate into a technique of manipulating him in accordance with your own designs; it could degenerate indeed into a technique of totalitarian control. Totalitarianism was hardly the goal toward which American progressives were even unconsciously striving. But the manipulative note was rarely absent from their writings: the insistence that men could best be controlled and directed not by the old, crude method of force but by "education" in its broadest sense.

If the new radicalism was the product of a revolutionary social upheaval, the exhaustion of the cultural tradition of the middle class, it generated no revolutionary appeal to action. Its politics, at the same time that they reflected a profound dissatisfaction with older conventions of analysis and perception, ended in a design for "adjustment" which was almost as innocuous, in the challenge it posed to the political and social *status quo*, as the genteel and effete liberalism which the new radicalism displaced as the reigning creed of the educated classes. That was one reason, perhaps, why the new radicalism never reached much beyond those classes.[4] Another reason was that the experience which generated it was not felt throughout all levels of society or even throughout the middle class itself. The sense of grievance, of an intolerable waste of inner resources, afflicted chiefly the kind of people who in any age are likely to find themselves at odds with convention. At the end of the nineteenth century such people found themselves at odds not only with convention but, increasingly, with society itself. Their disgust was analogous in its fervor to the great

4. "American liberalism," an English writer notes, "is an academic creed which flourishes hardly anywhere outside the schools and universities." (George Lichtheim: "Introspectives," *New Statesman*, LXVII [Feb. 7, 1964], p. 214.)

waves of revolutionary enthusiasm which have convulsed the modern world, but it led to no new social and political synthesis. It produced a ferment of new ideas, but these ideas, most of them, were evidently destined to remain the exclusive possession of a small minority. They did not spread throughout the rest of society, as the ideas of the *philosophes*, for instance, seem to have pervaded the Western world at the end of the eighteenth century. Nor did they inspire in masses of men a new sense of solidarity, such as accompanies revolutionary movements. On the contrary, their effect was everywhere divisive. In the people as a whole—"the people," in whose interests the new radicals so often professed to speak—they aroused indifference at best and resentment at worst, not merely because they flew in the face of accepted orthodoxies but because they were irrelevant to the conditions under which most people continued to live. The revolt of the intellectuals had no echoes in the rest of society.

[II]

The originality of the new radicalism as a form of politics rested on a twofold discovery: the discovery of the dispossessed by men who themselves had never known poverty or prejudice, and the mutual self-discovery of the intellectuals. The combination of the two accounted for the intensity with which the intellectuals identified themselves with the outcasts of the social order: women, children, proletarians, Indians, and Jews. At the very moment when they became aware of the other half of humanity, they became aware of each other and came to see themselves as yet another class apart. In time, their very sense of kinship with one another made them all the more painfully conscious of their collective isolation from the rest of society.

Then the "submerged tenth" came to be seen not only as the visible representation of the unsublimated selfhood of mankind but, more immediately, as a potential political ally. The intellectuals came to court the dispossessed with an ardor doubly endowed.

At the first moment of their mutual self-discovery, however, exhilaration rather than anxiety was the dominant mood. What Edward T. Devine said of the social workers applied to the intellectuals as a whole: "the mutual discovery of one another's existence" constituted one of the "extraordinary developments of the opening decade of the twentieth century."[5] The discovery that others had fought the same fight against bourgeois surroundings, the discovery that one had after all taken part in a general awakening that one's own struggles were the struggles of sensitive people everywhere, endowed the moment with the sense of a thousand possibilities. It suggested hidden treasures of aspiration, yet unfathomed, lying beneath the surface of an outwardly contented and corrupt society. The awareness of their own emancipation made intellectuals see what might be accomplished by the liberation of the repressed energies of the social organism as a whole. "Individuals and groups who represent what might be called the underdog, when they are endowed with energy and life, exert pressures towards modification of our cast-iron habits and lay rich deposits of possible cultural enhancement, if we are able to take advantage of them."[6] The new radicals sought not only justice for the exploited but the enrichment of the cultural life of the whole nation. The terms in which the social workers spoke of their clients made it clear what they expected of them. "More and

5. Edward T. Devine: *The Spirit of Social Work* (New York: Charities Publication Committee; 1911), p. vi.

6. Hutchins Hapgood: *A Victorian in the Modern World* (New York: Harcourt, Brace; 1939), p. 567.

more," one of them wrote, "I feel how much we have to *learn* from these people whom too often we are expected to teach. They are braver, simpler, better than we are; more generous, more helpful—and it is because they are daily *doing* the things of which we are only thinking."[7]

Where expectations ran so high, disappointment was sure to follow. The new radicals found to their dismay that the poor clung obstinately to the saloon, the church, and the captains of the ward machine—symbols of their unenlightened state which the new radicals, for all their generous understanding of the problems of poverty, never managed to accept with equanimity. Perhaps the intellectuals retained more of their middle-class prejudices than they realized. Or perhaps they were in truth a little frightened by the poor, frightened of the violence of working-class life at the same time that they were charmed by its spontaneity. In any case, the new radicals proposed to extend to the working class the very "advantages" which they themselves professed to reject—as Jane Addams explained, in order "to bring them in contact with a better type of Americans."[8] And even when they had outgrown the shallow progressivism of the muckraking era, with its almost exclusive reliance on moral indignation as a means of reform, the new radicals continued with undiminished emphasis to deplore the bawdyhouse and the saloon, those ancient enemies of respectable society.

The career of Fremont Older, one of the most outspoken of the radical journalists of the period, shows how the broadest social sympathies often coexisted with a surprisingly conventional attitude toward "vice." Like so many of his contem-

7. Alice Lincoln to Jane Addams, June 29, 1902, Jane Addams MSS.
8. Jane Addams: *Twenty Years at Hull-House* (New York: Macmillan; 1910), pp. 231–2.

poraries, Older came to his radicalism only after a kind of conversion, a crisis of self-contempt. He began as a yellow journalist, and it was in search of good copy rather than good government that he launched an editorial assault, in his San Francisco *Bulletin*, against the Democratic machine led by Abraham Ruef. Ruef's henchman, Mayor Eugene E. Schmitz, had been elected in 1901 as the candidate of the workingmen of the city. In attacking Ruef, Older was aligning himself with the "best people" of San Francisco, the people who wanted to "clean up" politics by applying business methods to public administration. Older's methods were no more savory than his motives. Like other vice crusaders, he adhered to the custom of obtaining confessions by threats and bluffs coupled with promises of immunity.[9] In the *Bulletin* he published an intemperate attack on Golden M. Roy, one of Ruef's allies, in which he intimated—what was in fact not the case—that he had evidence that would send Roy to the penitentiary. He called in Roy and repeated his threat. Frightened, Roy agreed to tell everything he knew about Ruef, in return for which Older generously promised not to expose him.

It happened that Golden M. Roy was the proprietor of a skating rink, Dreamland. After his defection, the town supervisors in retaliation passed an ordinance prohibiting any girl under eighteen from visiting a skating rink without her mother. The ordinance threatened to undermine the economic foundations of Roy's enterprise. Roy now suggested to Older that he attempt to bribe the supervisors into killing the ordinance, so that Older and his fellow reformers might apprehend

9. Fremont Older: *My Own Story* (New York: Macmillan; 1926), pp. 96–7. According to Lincoln Steffens, the crusading attorney Joseph W. Folk used the same techniques in St. Louis. (Lincoln Steffens: *The Shame of the Cities* [New York: Hill and Wang, 1960], p. 28.)

the supervisors in the very act of being bribed. The sins of the Ruef machine were notoriously elusive; what the reformers needed was concrete evidence of corruption.

With great attention to detail, Older, Roy, and detective William J. Burns laid the trap, carefully rehearsing the scene in Roy's office at Dreamland. In his autobiography Older describes the preparations with relish. He and Burns hid in a little room off Roy's office, peering through peepholes they had bored in the door. Roy proceeded to enact the scene he intended to play with the supervisors. " 'Tom, I want that skating rink bill killed. I'm willing to pay $500 for it, and here's the money.' " The rehearsal, Older says, was "perfect." "It was beyond my imagination to conceive of anything like that being fulfilled." He said to Roy: " 'It's too much of a melodrama for me. I don't believe it's possible that anything like this will ever happen.' " The scene went off, however, exactly as it had been planned; and it was the evidence thereby obtained, along with other evidence obtained by similar methods, that eventually sent Ruef and Schmitz to the penitentiary—not before Older himself had been kidnapped by his enemies, spirited away to a mountain hideaway, and dramatically rescued.[1]

No sooner were Ruef and Schmitz convicted than Older suffered a curious change of heart. It occurred to him that Ruef and Schmitz had been made the scapegoats for the sins of society. He regretted his own part in their conviction. A few years later, in 1914, he delivered himself of a public "confession":

It never occurred to me in those days that these men were very much like all other men in our civilization. They were not especially evil men. They were just doing evil things. We made the mistake then in assuming that it was a moral question. It was

1. Older: *My Own Story*, pp. 99–101.

not. It was economic pressure—a desire for money to meet the one standard by which society measures success—which is possession and the private ownership of the valuable things of the earth.[2]

If not quite a socialist, Older had moved much nearer the socialist than the progressive view of capitalism. The shock of his self-disgust made him a radical, and his radicalism, moreover, reached even to international affairs—something very rare in the period of the First World War. When the United States entered the war, Older attacked the government for surrendering to what seemed to him a universal madness—an act that required considerably more daring than his exposure of the unpopular Ruef machine.

A fuller account of Older's conversion appears in a letter he wrote to Jane Addams in 1910 in praise of her book *Democracy and Social Ethics*; and this earlier account shows that although he now assigned deeper causes to it, Older was as disturbed as ever by the problem of vice. It was not until he read *Democracy and Social Ethics*, he said, that he understood what a mistake he had made "in condemning the masses of the people" for not living up to a higher moral standard. Jane Addams's "psychology of the minds of the poor" had been "by far the most helpful aid" he had ever known. "Formerly I sat in my office after an election where the poor had voted crooks into office, and raged at them. I did not understand them as you do, and as you have taught me to understand them." But even after he had abandoned progressivism, Older continued to give voice to the progressives' typical horror of drinking, dancing, and prostitution. The tenderloin continued at once to repel and to fascinate him.

Within the last week [he went on] the barons of our night life have commercialized the passions of the young men and young

2. Speech to the Council of Jewish Women, March, 1914, in *My Own Story*, pp. 171, 173-4.

women by throwing open all of the saloons to them, all of the cafés to them, and allowing them to dance and drink all night. After having worked them all day industrially, they have turned them over to the kings of the tenderloin to be exploited throughout the night. The saloons obtained this privilege upon a petition which was signed by a thousand merchants asking that dancing might be permitted in these resorts. The venders [sic] of jewelry, millinery, lingeries, etc. felt that by creating more prostitutes out of their neighbors' daughters they could gain more dollars for themselves. Our little group here is helpless to alter it. It is the result of a race gone money mad.[3]

In Older's case, the horror of vice cannot simply be attributed to the persistence of middle-class attitudes. Older was not a "puritan." In fact, like other radicals he was in full flight from Puritanism. He understood the futility of trying to legislate against immorality. His impatience with the kind of reformers who wanted to save mankind by a stricter enforcement of the blue laws resembled that of Randolph Bourne— whose social philosophy, in fact, was essentially the same as Older's. Both men, reformers who had transcended the limitations of reform, spoke for a kind of philosophical anarchism quite common among "progressives" of the time, an anarchism rooted in the moral relativism of Dewey and James. Brand Whitlock and Frederic C. Howe, the Ohio progressives, were others of this type. No "reformers" had less use for reform.[4]

If men like Older retained what seems to us a rather exaggerated horror of alcohol, prostitution, and the rest, it was

---

3. Older to Jane Addams, April 2, 1910, Jane Addams MSS.

4. See, e.g., Brand Whitlock: *Forty Years of It* (New York: D. Appleton; 1914), p. 239: "Your true reformer is not only without humor, without pity, without mercy, but he is without knowledge of life or of human nature, and without very much of any sort of sweetness and light. The more moral he is, the harder he is, and the more amazingly ready with cruel judgments; and he seldom smiles except with the unction that comes with the thought of his own moral superiority. He thinks there is an absolute good and an absolute bad, and hence absolutely good people and absolutely bad people."

because they sensed the rebelliousness and alienation these forms of vice were so often an expression of; and this knowledge made them uneasy. In the actions of juvenile delinquents in particular they recognized a contempt for middle-class culture much deeper than their own. The new radicals' attitude toward delinquency, their insistence that a policy of repression perpetuated the evils it was supposed to eliminate, represented a striking departure from the conventional attitude. Indeed, their sympathy for juvenile delinquents and for criminals of all classes made them almost as objectionable, in the eyes of respectable citizens, as the criminals themselves. What the new radicals did not allow themselves to see, however, was that their sympathy stopped short of a full endorsement of the "rebellion of youth," the nature of which they did so much to explain. Their own rebellion seemed to demand from them the decisive step not merely of understanding the revolt of youth but of upholding it as in some sense a valid response to the brutality and vulgarity of industrialism. Instead, they tried to "turn it into more productive channels," in the jargon of the day. Lincoln Steffens's account of Ben Lindsey, the humane and courageous judge of the juvenile court in Denver, catches at once the hardboiled realism of the new radicals, the badge of their own revolt, and the sentimentality which so often underlay it.

It will be noticed [Steffens wrote] that Lindsey made effective use in this case of the "gang" which the police and all prematurely old reformers seek only to "break up." The "kids' Jedge" never thought of breaking up such organizations. His sense is for essentials, instinctively, and there's nothing wrong about gangs as such. They are as natural as organizations of men. The only trouble with gangs is that they absorb all the loyalty of the members, turning them from and often against the home, the Law, and the State. But that happens in grown-ups' gangs, too. Railroad and other corporations are gangs which, in the interests of their "business," corrupt the State. Churches are "gangs" whose members submit to evils because, if they fought them, the church might be hurt. So with universities, and newspapers, and all kinds of business organizations. Tammany Hall is only a gang which, absorbing the loyalty of its members, turns it, for the good of the gang, against the welfare of the city. Judge Lindsey simply taught the members of his kid gang what many gangs of grown-ups have to learn, that they are citizens also, and he turned the loyalty of the Kid Citizens' League back to the city, using the honour of the gang as his lever.[5]

Steffens's reference to "prematurely old reformers" sought to show that his own sympathies were unequivocally on the side of youth; yet he upheld Judge Lindsey's attempt to use the gang as a "lever" by which to turn the loyalty of disaffected young people back to the very society in which, by his own account, corruption flourished so freely under the guise of respectability.

[III]

The same ambivalence appears in the work of Jane Addams. She wrote feelingly of "the spirit of youth," yet proposed to force it into socially acceptable channels. Having experienced in her own life the conflict of youth and age, and having seen the same conflict daily reenacted in the immigrant quarter, she could understand that it was not immorality but the romanticism and idealism of young people which made them impatient with the restrictions their elders imposed on them. She saw too that the outcry against juvenile delinquency, the shaking of heads, the resort to repression, were more than anything else manifestations of a profound indifference. "Society cares more for the products [young people] manufacture than for

5. Lincoln Steffens: *Upbuilders* (New York: Doubleday, Page; 1909), pp. 124–5.

their immemorial ability to reaffirm the charm of existence."
That explained why young people were permitted in such
numbers "to walk unattended upon city streets and to work
under alien roofs."[6]

These reflections might have led Jane Addams to attack the
indifference at the source to which she traced it—capitalism
itself, which values individuals only for their labor power.
Instead she came to a very different conclusion. If juvenile
delinquency sprang from "the quest for adventure," she reasoned, then the problem was to find substitutes for crime which
would satisfy the same yearning and make use of the same
energies. Jane Addams searched for these substitutes in the
same spirit in which her intellectual master, William James,
cast about for a moral equivalent of war. Her proposal to substitute "a more wholesome form of public recreation" for the
popular stage was characteristic. Shocked to find that the leading themes of the five-cent theater, according to an investigation
of 466 plays in Chicago, were marital infidelity and revenge,
she instituted a theater at Hull-House, where the children of
the neighborhood performed Shakespeare and Molière.[7] She

6. Jane Addams: *The Spirit of Youth and the City Streets* (New York:
Macmillan; 1911), p. 5.
7. *Ibid.*, pp. 84–92. A later generation of educators would discover that
even the classics were unsuitable for children. Shakespeare and Molière also
dealt with marital infidelity and revenge. The day was not far off when
even Beatrix Potter would have to be marketed in the United States in
expurgated editions. In a new version of Miss Potter's *Peter Rabbit*, "specially
edited" by Nova Nestrick ". . . to meet the reading needs of the young child,"
all reference to Peter's father's "accident" in Mr. McGregor's garden ("he
was put in a pie by Mrs. McGregor") has been dutifully deleted; and the
story ends, not with a dose of camomile tea, but with "Mother" Rabbit's
bland assurance: "Peter, you will feel better soon." "And he did!" the
editor adds. "And, horrors," notes a reviewer, "over his bed . . . is a framed
slogan, vintage 5-and-10-cent store, on which is printed: 'Good bunnies always
obey.'" (Mary Bingham: "Flopsy, Mopsy and Plain Boredom," *St. Louis
Post-Dispatch*, Nov. 16, 1961.)

hoped incidentally that the artistic impulse thus developed might eventually be brought to the service of industry so as to free it from "its mechanism and materialism." Better workers, better goods.[8] But the important thing was to "organize a child's activities with some reference to the life he will later lead." The trade schools at Hull-House therefore attempted to explain the relation of each particular stage in the manufacturing process to the finished product. Miss Addams argued that if a girl entering a sewing factory knew something about her material and the processes to which it was subjected, knew something also of the history of art and decoration, her daily life would be "lifted from drudgery to one of self-conscious activity."[9]

The trouble was that Jane Addams was asking, in effect, that young people be adjusted to a social order which by her own admission was cynically indifferent to their welfare. She confronted a moral problem with a manipulative solution. Having laid bare the brutalizing effects of industrial labor, having made clear that the demands of the factory and the sweatshop and of the whole economic system of which they were the tangible expression were incompatible with the demands of human dignity, she proceeded to look for ways of reconciling people to their work. Industrial society, according to Jane Addams, was a terrific engine of repression; yet her own efforts seemed often to have as their aim only to make its parts run more smoothly.

If Jane Addams's radical intuitions about modern society led both in theory and in practice to solutions far from radical, the same thing was true of the educational ideas of John Dewey, with which her own ideas had so much in common.

8. Jane Addams: *The Spirit of Youth*, pp. 127–9.
9. Ibid., pp. 109–10.

The settlement movement and the movement for progressive education ran parallel at every point. Originating in a criticism of middle-class culture, they attempted to institutionalize this criticism by incorporating into philanthropy and education the point of view of outsiders (immigrants in the one case, children in the other), only to end in a reaffirmation of the liberal values of wholesomeness and adjustment.

The two movements not only ran parallel, they influenced each other. Between Hull-House and Dewey's experimental school at the University of Chicago there was a constant exchange of ideas and personnel. One of the teachers in Dewey's school was a resident of Hull-House. Dewey himself delivered a series of lectures at Hull-House on social psychology. Like William James, who told Jane Addams after reading *The Spirit of Youth* that she did not so much seek reality as "inhabit" it, Dewey greatly admired his neighbor's uncanny instinct for social observation.[1] Her essay on the Pullman strike moved him to exclaim: "It is one of the greatest things I ever read both as to its form and its ethical philosophy."[2] Jane Addams reciprocated with many acknowledgments of Dewey's influence on her own thought. As early as 1899, she was citing Dewey and James in support of her contention that knowledge was useless unless it was related to action.[3] And she was quick to see the implications for social work of Dewey's ideas about the proper relation between the teacher and his pupils. "His insistence upon an atmosphere of freedom and confidence between the teacher and pupil, of a common interest in the life

1. See William James to Jane Addams, Dec. 13, 1909, Addams MSS.
2. Dewey to Jane Addams, Jan. 19, 1896, Addams MSS.
3. Jane Addams: "A Function of the Social Settlement," *Annals of the American Academy of Political and Social Science*, XIII (May, 1899), p. 35.

they led together, profoundly affected all similar relationships, certainly those between the social worker and his client."[4]

Dewey, it will be recalled, maintained that in "progressive" societies, where the "life-customs" of the group were constantly changing, children had as much to teach their teachers as they had to learn from them. It was his contention—arrived at, characteristically, by a process of deduction rather than by systematic observation—that children had a more highly developed talent for social life than adults. They had to have, he reasoned, because their physical weakness rendered them dependent on their ability to convey to others an understanding of their needs and wishes. He insisted that observation bore him out. It showed that "children are gifted with an equipment of the first order for social intercourse," which few adults retained.[5] It followed that in the ideal school the children would themselves be in some sense teachers. The ideal school would be child-centered and by the same token future-centered, aiming not to transmit a dead past but to encourage social progress and growth.

This conclusion followed, that is, once one made the important assumption that the purpose of education was the socialization of the individual, not only in the general sense of adapting him to the life customs of the group into which he was born but more specifically in the sense of eliminating the selfish ambitions that presumably generated social conflict. Dewey's educational reforms depended on the premise, stated quite explicitly, that education itself was to be considered a means of reforming society. "Men have long had some intimation of the extent to which education may be consciously used

4. Jane Addams: "A Toast to John Dewey," *Survey*, LXIII (Nov. 15, 1929), p. 203.

5. Dewey: *Democracy and Education*, p. 43.

to eliminate obvious social evils through starting the young on paths which shall not produce these ills, and some idea of the extent in which [sic] education may be made an instrument of realizing the better hopes of men. But we are doubtless far from realizing the potential efficacy of education as a constructive agency of improving society."[6]

The very act of defining the purpose of the school in these terms forced Dewey back into the conception of education he wished particularly to avoid, the idea of education as a form of indoctrination in the values of the grown-up world. It was out of a wish to avoid such a conception of education, and instead to make education "creative," that he proposed to put the child at the center of the school. The act of putting him there, however, encouraged Dewey to go on to formulate a theory of education in which education was seen as an agency of progressive social change. He advised educators "consciously" to use education "to eliminate obvious social evils." In doing so, he was in effect simply substituting one set of values for another, progressive values for conservative ones. The indoctrination remained. Worse, the social evils that were "obvious" to Dewey were not obvious to all of his followers. In the hands of educators of narrow social sympathies and thoroughly conventional opinions, progressive education could become an instrument not of reform but of conformity. Dewey's concept of eliminating social evils "through starting the young on paths which shall not produce these ills" came in practice to mean "training for citizenship"—precisely that early and ruthless inculcation of the norms of an older generation that Dewey had been so eager to eliminate from the public schools. By 1925 the dean of Teachers College could say in triumph: "Good citizenship as an aim in life is nothing new. . . . But

6. Ibid., p. 79.

good citizenship as a dominant aim of the American public school is something new. . . . For the first time in history, as I see it, a social democracy is attempting to shape the opinions and bias the judgment of oncoming generations."[7]

Dewey cannot be blamed for the perversion of his doctrines. It is curious, however, that although he repeatedly complained that his ideas were being distorted, the evident ease with which they were distorted did not cause him to reexamine the ideas themselves. He might at least have reflected on the possibility that they contained ambiguities which made them peculiarly susceptible to misinterpretation, if misinterpretation was in fact what was taking place.[8]

Part of the difficulty was that the repressive implications of progressive education, and of the new radicalism in general, were not immediately apparent. They became apparent only when the new ideas began to harden into an orthodoxy of their own, to be taken up by men who had not experienced the rebelliousness, the questioning of established truths, the impatience of convention that had initially given those ideas life; and by that time it was too late for men like Dewey to change their minds. At the dawn of the century, however, the prospects for the rational progress of society and for the liberation of the human spirit still appeared uncommonly bright. Not merely physical force but compulsion of any kind, whether imposed by man or by nature, seemed on the point of disappearing as a factor in human affairs. That was the lesson, it seemed, of science and experience alike. The new psychology, the child-study movement, the new education, the idea of scientific management, the philosophy of pragmatism, the science of

7. Quoted in Robert S. and Helen Merrell Lynd, *Middletown* (New York: Harvest Books; 1956), p. 197n.

8. On this question, see Hofstadter: *Anti-intellectualism in American Life* (New York: Alfred A. Knopf, 1963), pp. 361-2.

evolution, all confirmed the experience of a century of unimpeded material and social progress, that the turmoil and conflict which had so long troubled the course of history could at last be eliminated by means of a scientific system of control. The old techniques of social discipline, the old agencies of institutionalized violence, would soon be obsolete. The mark of progressive societies was precisely their ability to govern themselves without resort to force.

For the new radicals, conflict itself, rather than injustice or inequality, was the evil to be eradicated. Accordingly, they proposed to reform society not through the agencies of organized coercion, the courts of law and the power of the police, but by means of social engineering on the part of disinterested experts who could see the problem whole and who could see it essentially as a problem of resources—natural and human—the proper allocation and conservation of which were the work of enlightened administration. Exploitation presented itself as a matter not of injustice but of waste. It was a problem of management rather than of morals. In place of the older view that "misery is moral," the social worker Edward T. Devine wished to substitute the view that "it is economic; the result of maladjustment."[9] When he cast about for an image with which to capture the brutality of child labor, Devine could condemn it sufficiently only by comparing it to the exploitation of natural resources. "The exploitation of children resembles nothing so much as the indiscriminate destruction of young trees for pulp."[1]

Conservation, then, was the battle cry of the day. Walter Lippmann in his dispassionate way outlined what needed to be done.

9. Edward T. Devine: *Misery and Its Causes* (New York: Macmillan; 1912), p. 11.
1. Devine: *The Spirit of Social Work*, p. 20.

You have to make a survey of the natural resources of the country. On the basis of that survey you must draw up a national plan for their development. You must eliminate waste in mining, you must conserve the forests so that their fertility is not impaired, so that stream flow is regulated, and the waterpower of the country made available. You must bring to the farmer a knowledge of scientific agriculture, help him to organize cooperatively, use the taxing power to prevent land speculation and force land to the best use, coordinate markets, build up rural credits, and create in the country a life that shall really be interesting.

You had, in a word, literally "to *educate* the industrial situation, to draw out its promise, discipline and strengthen it."[2]

The idea that it was possible by means of proper planning to create "a life that shall really be interesting"—an idea so characteristic of the manipulative mind—points up once more the confusion between political and cultural issues that was the essence of the new radicalism. The new radicals proposed political solutions for cultural problems and cultural solutions for political problems. On the one hand, they proposed to improve the quality of American life by means of public administration. On the other hand, they proposed to attack such public problems as the conflict between capital and labor by eliminating the psychological sources of conflict, by "educating" capitalists and laborers to a more altruistic and social point of view—in other words, by improving the quality of men's private lives. Most of the new radicals would have preferred a secular to a religious formulation of the problem, but they would all have agreed with the substance of Washington Gladden's assertion that there could be "no adequate social reform save that which springs from a genuine revival of religion; only it must be a religion," Gladden added himself,

2. Lippmann: *Drift and Mastery* (Englewood Cliffs, N. J.: Prentice-Hall; 1961 [New York, 1914]), p. 98.

"which is less concerned about getting men to heaven than about fitting them for their proper work on the earth."[3]

The older methods of control appeared to the new radicals not only offensive in themselves, since they rested on external coercion of the crudest type, but inexcusably inefficient. It was the latter point which they were at particular pains to drive home. "We are likely to take the influence of superior force for control," John Dewey argued, "forgetting that while we may lead a horse to water we cannot make him drink; and that while we can shut a man up in a penitentiary we cannot make him penitent." You could not make him penitent, that is, by shutting him up in jail, but there remained the intriguing possibility that you could make him penitent by other means—make him, in the language of a later day, into a useful member of society. There remained the possibility that means could be found "of enlisting the person's own participating disposition in getting the result desired, and thereby of developing within him an intrinsic and persisting direction in the right way." That possibility was lost, however, "when we confuse a physical with an educative result."[4]

Stated in its simplest terms, what the social planners had found was that "if you wanted to get a firebrand out of the hand of a child," as Newton D. Baker explained, "the way to do it was neither to club the child nor to grab the firebrand, but to offer in exchange for it a stick of candy!" Reformers had discovered from experience that passing laws and getting policemen to enforce them solved nothing.

For a long time . . . we imagined that our salvation lay in the passage of laws. . . . And I can remember when I was mayor of [Cleveland], that every now and then some movement would get

3. Washington Gladden: *Social Salvation* (Boston: Houghton Mifflin; 1902), p. 30.
4. Dewey: *Democracy and Education*, pp. 26–7.

its start to have a curfew law passed in that city, to make everybody go to bed at a particular time. Some laws of that kind were passed, and some supreme courts held they were unconstitutional, and some held they were constitutional, but no court had any right to pass on the real fact involved, which was that they were ineffective.

What was effective was "to offer adequate opportunity for wholesome recreation and enjoyment." Social reformers had learned to use the techniques of progressive education: "the inculcation throughout the entire body of young people in the community of substantially the same form of social inducement which the American college, in modern times, has substituted for the earlier system of social restraints."[5]

At its worst, the idea that education was the answer to all social problems degenerated into the jargon of the efficiency experts. The studies of F. W. Taylor and others evoked widespread enthusiasm at this time. Norman Hapgood thought that they suggested "almost unlimited possibilities." Harrington Emerson, for instance, had shown in his book *Efficiency as a Basis for Operation and Wages* "that men, women and children starve," as Hapgood put it, "not because there is not abundance, and not because a few have appropriated the portion of many, but because there is a quite unnecessary waste."[6] According to Edwin L. Earp, Professor of Christian Sociology at Drew Theological Seminary and author of *The Social Engineer*, conflict in society was a matter of "consciousness," and the solution was, of course, "education." If men are taught to think of themselves as members of a class and to despise those below them, class conflict results. If they are taught to appre-

5. Newton D. Baker: "Invisible Armor," *Survey*, XXXIX (Nov. 17, 1917), pp. 159–60.
6. Norman Hapgood: *Industry and Progress* (New Haven: Yale University Press; 1911), p. 69. Emerson's book was published in 1909 (New York: The Engineering Magazine).

ciate the interdependence of classes, the result will be predictably different. "Tell the city boy how the farmer boy must go without many good things because the unscrupulous commission man cheated his father out of nearly all the profits of his season's toil in raising his crop for market; or tell the boy in the country how some poor man in the city was robbed of his property by some unscrupulous 'loan shark' when he was in need, because he was unable to push his case with any hope of success in the courts."[7] Earp's most characteristic advice concerned the labor problem. "How can the church help the labor movement?" he asked. And the answer was: by promoting the "*socialization* of workingmen." Provide for their recreation; bring beauty into their drab lives; help them "to develop personality and to broaden their social horizon." "Take the Church to the people."[8] In other words, make the working class middle-class in its outlook.

Earp's book reminds one of the ease with which the settlement movement, like the movement for progressive education, degenerated into a form of propaganda—in the case of the settlements, a form of missionizing. One social worker whom he quotes, Isabelle Horton of Chicago, addressed a conference of Methodist social workers as follows:

It is hard for one brought up under the droppings of the sanctuary, drawing in with every breath the influences of early religious training, to understand how far away from this world in which he lives are the multitudes that we speak of as the "unchurched masses"—how life becomes narrowed by long hours of heavy toil, how embittered by pinching want, how brutalized by intemperance, how chained by Old World superstitions and habits. The Christian worker who goes among them must have faith to do pioneer work and trust God for results that may be most apparent

7. Edwin L. Earp: *The Social Engineer* (New York: Eaton & Mains; 1911), p. 57.
8. Ibid., pp. 245–6, 252.

in the next generation. She . . . must root up weeds of false teaching, dig out rocks of ignorance and prejudice, break up the fallow ground, and be glad if it is given to her to drop a seed of divine truth here and there.[9]

The new industry of advertising, the unattractive, the downright sinister, aspects of which have now become so familiar, appeared to the social engineers of an earlier time as an exciting exercise in mass education. Even before the First World War showed that it was possible to mobilize public opinion in overwhelming support of predetermined policies—showed, in the words of that super-salesman, George Creel, "how we advertised America"—the more advanced planners had glimpsed the implications of advertising for the science of social control.[1] Ellen H. Richards, in her book *Euthenics: The Science of Controllable Environment*, argued that advertising could even take the place of religion as a stimulus to good behavior. Indeed some such substitute was urgently needed, for "in the confusion of ideas resulting from the rapid, almost cancerous growth of the modern community," people had lost their "power of visualizing their conception of right and wrong." It was its immediate appeal to the visual sense which had made "Puritanism" such a force. Heaven and Hell were tangible realities. Their disappearance deprived people of a "spur to good behavior." But the "psychology of influence" could discover other means of internalizing social restraints. "Perhaps the sword of Damocles must be visualized by such exhibits as the going out of an electric light every time a man dies, by the ghastly microbe in the moving picture, by the highly colored print or

9. Ibid., p. 254.
1. Creel's book *How We Advertised America* (New York: Harper & Bros.; 1920) deals with the activities of the Committee on Public Information during the First World War; it bears the subtitle, *The First Telling of the Amazing Story of the Committee on Public Information that Carried the Gospel of Americanism to Every Corner of the Globe.*

by a vivid reproduction of crowded quarters." Hitherto, reformers had unwisely left such methods to those who used
them to advertise "less worthy subjects." Men "skilled in promoting commercial interests" had learned "how to apply the
right stimulus at the right time in order to arouse the desired
interest." All the more reason for reformers to appropriate the
new techniques for their own purposes. The power of what
Edward A. Ross called "social suggestion" must no longer be
monopolized by those with only selfish ends to serve.[2]

[IV]

The new radicals were torn between their wish to liberate
the unused energies of the submerged portions of society and
their enthusiasm for social planning, which led in practice to
new and subtler forms of repression. The rage for planning
reflected the planners' confidence in themselves as a disinterested elite, unbound by the prejudices either of the middle
class or of the proletariat. It reflected also their abiding anxiety
lest the voice of reason be overwhelmed by the uproar of social
conflict. The fear of conflict was natural enough at a time of
mounting industrial violence; and it was by no means confined
to intellectuals. The middle class as a whole had for some time
instinctively preferred order to anarchy, regularity to uncertainty and risk; and in the long period between the Civil War
and the First World War the spokesmen of the middle class
had dwelled again and again on the advantages of social peace
and tranquillity. They advocated an end to reconstruction,
avoidance of war with Spain, avoidance of politics altogether.
"Too much politics, too little attention to business," said Presi-

2. Ellen Richards: *Euthenics* (Boston: Whitcomb & Barrows; 1910),
pp. 117–20.

dent Hayes, was the bane of the postwar South; he might have said, as far as the middle class was concerned, of the whole nation.[3]

But when their immediate interests were in question, the business classes had been ready enough to reply to violence with violence, indeed to instigate it. They were perfectly willing, if the need arose, to call out the federal troops to put down strikes and to recruit armies of Pinkerton detectives in the name of harmony and peace; and they were supported in these policies by respectable citizens everywhere. The middle class feared not violence so much as a threat to the *status quo*. The intellectuals, however, having no resources of their own to throw into the social struggle—no resources, as a class, except argument and exposition—had a class interest in nonviolence for its own sake. In a struggle of force against force the intellectuals, possessing neither property nor the force of numbers, had everything to lose. Hence their insistence that the way of progress was necessarily the way of peace. Their confidence that "education" could take the place of force was more than an expression of the prevailing faith in the scientific solution of social problems and in the applicability of the laws of biological evolution to the study of society; it was also, to borrow Jane Addams's phrase, a subjective necessity. Sometimes, indeed, it seemed only to rationalize a crude will to power on the part of the intellectuals themselves. Certainly their reiterated assertion that "government is a profession, not a business," as Richard T. Ely put it, carried with it the unmistakable implication that intellectuals, not businessmen, must govern. "*We must have a class of office-holders,*" said Ely, and he went on to urge the universities "to train experts for every branch of the public service."[4]

3. C. Vann Woodward: *Reunion and Reaction* (Boston: Little, Brown; 1951), p. 104.

4. Richard T. Ely: *The Coming City* (New York: Thomas Y. Crowell; 1902), pp. 39, 46, 55.

One of the clearest statements of the confidence of the new radicals in the manageability of society and in the ability of intellectuals to manage it was Edward A. Ross's widely read textbook, *Social Control*. Published in 1901, the book influenced a decade of speculation on the subject of scientific planning. It also inaugurated Ross's own brilliant career as a sociologist— a career which suggests how strong, in some intellectuals, was the drive to dominate, and how deep were the anxieties underlying it.

Ross suffered from quite immediate and specific anxieties as well as from the anxieties that seem to have become common to his class. As a student in Germany, he underwent a spiritual crisis which came to focus on the intellectual's familiar sense of being cut off from a real and vital contact with life; but his sense of superfluity, which afflicted so many others of his generation, was superimposed, it appears, on feelings of inferiority originating in earliest childhood. Orphaned at eight, Ross lived with a succession of aunts until he was taken in by a family of Iowa farmers—proper Presbyterians, "reserved, stiff, undemonstrative." His temperament as well as his birth made him an outsider in the household of "Squire" Beach, for he was a dreamy, bookish child. Not only that, he was undersized and weak. (As so often seems to happen in such cases, he grew eventually into a great, raw-boned giant, vain and self-assertive, delighting in his physical prowess.) The cruelest stroke of all was that although he in no sense belonged to his new family, he inherited their social status and was scorned by the townspeople as a rustic. "In those days," Ross explained in his autobiography, "town looked down on country much more than it does now," and the farmers' muddy clothes "gave the townspeople a means of identifying and sneering at the countryfolk—and they used it."

Ross was thus doubly an outsider; but the passage in which he recalls his early humiliation ends on a characteristically cheerful note, or rather, on a note of slightly forced cheerfulness. "It was a good thing for me that, during my more sensitive years, I was a member of an element that was *looked down on*; it saved me for life from the vice of snobbery."[5] Ross's autobiography, and indeed his entire life, reflected the unremitting effort to put the best face on things, to see in every handicap a hidden asset, and to fight off despair, that one encounters in so many other men of the period similarly burdened with handicaps real or imagined. Not puritanism, which historians have so often seen as an influence on American reform (but from which the new radicals at least were in full retreat), but these early struggles against uncongenial surroundings, would seem to explain why the literature of the liberation insisted again and again on the importance of discipline, mastery, and control, the control of the environment by means of the will. No words evoke more clearly the desperation which gave rise to the search for social control than the words with which the most enthusiastic exponent of that doctrine described how at length, summoning up a tremendous resource of will, he triumphed over the powers of darkness. "I renounced pessimism," says Ross, "not for being false, but for being unendurable."[6]

In Berlin, to which he made his way in 1888 after two years' teaching at a denominational college in Fort Dodge, Iowa, Ross exchanged Presbyterianism for philosophy. Like many other American students in Germany, he also lost faith in orthodox economics. It was evidently the collapse of his accepted ideas

5. Edward A. Ross: *Seventy Years of It: An Autobiography* (New York: D. Appleton-Century; 1936), pp. 7–10.
6. Ibid., p. 28.

about the world that brought on what he called his period of "storm and stress." Perhaps he was only lonely, a country boy in a strange city. What matters is that his loneliness associated itself in his mind with the philosopher's remoteness from humanity; so that in the end, for reasons that were highly personal, he came to the general conclusion that knowledge was worthless unless it was somehow related to "reality." In a letter written in 1889 (a year after Jane Addams's similar revelation), he announced his discovery that a person "who plants himself on the shore of some remote idea," in order to get a panoramic view of the world, "is sure to be overwhelmed by an awful feeling of loneliness." The view was grand but the chill "deadly." The philosopher, "dying of loneliness and purpose-lessness," envied "the heats of passion, intensity of desire, energy of will, warmth of love and fierceness of hate felt by those struggling and shouting amid the multitude."[7]

Having worked himself free of the "spell of philosophy," Ross went so far as to renounce thinking in general. Thinking was "an evil of a very positive kind and I banish it."

> The texture of a happy life [he wrote in another contemporary letter, reproduced in his autobiography] is woven of dreams, of instincts unrepressed, of passions yielded to, of abandonment for the moment, to whims, caprices, etc., of a vivid sense of freedom, of self-willed acts. Where reflection has no wiser course of action to suggest but can only disturb the joy and harmony of the moment, I repress it. This refusal to reflect makes possible the complete surrender to the object and the moment which makes possible the poet.

He had confidence now "only in that philosophy which begins by renouncing philosophy." What counted was not thought but feeling. "Love and hate," he wrote, "are the two finest things in life. Strong attractions and strong repulsions,

7. Ibid., p. 32.

strong loves and strong hates, great successes and great reverses enable one to say at the close, 'I have lived.' "[8]

Ross renounced philosophy not for poetry, as these letters might lead one to believe, or for the passionate love affair of which their exalted tone might suggest he was on the verge, but for science. Science alone enabled one to see things straight; and Ross had a horror of the "subjective and delusional."[9] (He traced it to early exposure to insanity. An uncle went mad; so did Squire Beach.) He also had an exaggerated fear of alcohol (which he traced to another childhood root); that is, of the process of "wilfully fogging the only lens through which we see the world."[1] For all the lyricism with which, in the moment of his release from philosophy, he celebrated the instinctual life, Ross, like others of his kind, searched above all for a means of control—control over self and over others. The catalogue of his happy life, the life of "instinct unrepressed," incongruously ended with "self-willed acts." Elsewhere, when he sought to sum up what he had achieved by throwing off the "needless inhibitions" of his boyhood, he measured the gain not in terms of spontaneous enjoyment of life but in terms of influence. "Since my early twenties," he wrote, "I have had a big advantage in influencing people owing to my complete release from early clamps."[2]

It was appropriate that Ross's masterpiece should have been a book about influence on a grand scale. If his autobiography recorded Ross's own rise to personal power, a triumph over early adversity, *Social Control* celebrated the impending rise to power of the intellectuals as a class. Ross based his prediction of the intellectuals' increasing influence on the complexity of modern society, which gave rise, he argued, to a demand for

8. Ibid., pp. 30, 32.
9. Ibid., p. 7.
1. Ibid., p. 2.
2. Ibid., p. 7.

specialized knowledge that was greater than the public schools could meet. The result would be to widen the gap between higher education and public education. "As the enlightenment of the public wanes relatively to the superior enlightenment of the learned castes and professions, the mandarinate will infallibly draw to itself a greater and greater share of social power."[3] As late as 1901, the term "intellectual" was still so unfamiliar that Ross had to coin a clumsy substitute; but the import of his analysis is perfectly clear. The future belonged to the manager, the technician, the bureaucrat, the expert.

As a tribute to the social planner, *Social Control* distinguishes itself from many other books in the same vein only by virtue of having been one of the first. What gives the book more than passing interest is the uneasiness that periodically breaks through the bright vision of a better world. Even Ross's enthusiasm for social reform could not quite suppress the book's sociological realism. Thus, although he agreed that great advances had been made in public education, Ross also foresaw the growth of an educational bureaucracy in the hands of which the new education would become a peculiarly insidious instrument of oppression. His observations on this danger, surely among the most prophetic in the vast literature on education which flooded the country in these years, need to be quoted in full.

A state educational machine with its semi-military organization of little children, its overriding of individual bent and preference, its appeals to head instead of heart, its rational morality, its colorless and jejune textbooks, its official cult of ethical and civic principles, its cold-blooded fostering of patriotism, is far from attractive. . . .

The coalescence of physical and spiritual forces in the modern state may well inspire certain misgivings. When we note the enormous resources and high centralization of a first-class educa-

3. Edward A. Ross: *Social Control: A Survey of the Foundations of Order* (New York: Macmillan; 1916 [New York, 1901]), p. 88

tional system; when we consider that it takes forcible possession of the child for half the time during its best years, and submits the little creature to a curriculum devised more and more with reference to its own aims and less and less with reference to the wishes of the parent; when we consider that the democratic control of this formidable engine affords no guarantee that it will not be used for empire over minds—we may well be apprehensive of future developments.[4]

The only consideration that made the thought of these things tolerable to Ross was that the alternative was a state church and church schools, as in the dynastic states of Europe; for some form of social discipline, Ross argued, was indispensable. In frankly acknowledging the coercive function of public education, even of progressive education, Ross distinguished himself from other educational reformers, who gave so little thought to the machinery that would be necessary to carry out their reforms. Ross saw the modern state as a menace (even as he conceded its necessity); but at the same time he believed that "other spiritual associations lying over against the state" would be able to "redress the balance" of power.[5] He had chiefly in mind, one imagines, the universities. Had he foreseen the degree to which even they would be drawn into the educational bureaucracy and into the network of the "national purpose," he might have been less sanguine.

Like other radicals of his time, Ross deplored the disorder of American society. Like Jane Addams, he pointed out that modern societies were organized economically but not socially, the social order, as he put it, having parted company with the sociable impulse.[6] Ross was practically alone, however, in calculating the costs of imposing order on such a system. He was alone in confronting the fact that what the reformers of his

4. Ibid., pp. 178–9.
5. Ibid.
6. Ibid., p. 19.

generation really proposed was not, as they thought, to create a new community, but to replace the old one, now hopelessly shattered, with an artificially devised system of controls and restraints. These controls, Ross believed, would keep order, but they would not restore the sense of community. Most of the reformers of the progressive period believed that the success of their program depended on the development of untapped social instincts in a people given over wholly to the bourgeois pursuit of self-interest. Ross maintained, on the contrary, that the effect of social control was precisely to render sociability unnecessary. He cast this observation in the form of a rather dogmatic evolutionary formula, but history, for once, seems to have borne out a Darwinian view of the social future:

> In the same way that the improvement of optical instruments checks the evolution of the eye and the improvement of tools checks the evolution of the hand, the improvement of instruments of control checks the evolution of the social instincts. The goal of social development is not, as some imagine, a Perfect Love, or a Perfect Conscience, but *better adaptation;* and the more this adaptation is artificial, the less need it be natural.[7]

Even this much an unwary reformer might have accepted. But what followed was a challenge to the social planners deeper perhaps than Ross himself was prepared to admit. He went on to raise the possibility that the planners might not only succeed but succeed beyond their expectations. When he reflected that "the art of domesticating human beings may succeed only too well," he contemplated the utopia of the near future with a sense of "mournfulness and even disgust." A grim spectacle raised itself before his eyes: "the great agencies of Law, Public Opinion, Education, Religion, and Literature speeded to their utmost to fit ignoble and paltry natures to bear the moral strains of our civilization, and perhaps by the very success of

7. Ibid., p. 437.

their work canceling the natural advantage of the noble over the base, and thereby slowing up the development of the most splendid qualities of human nature."[8]

Since he shared the racist assumptions so common to his time—another fruit of the Darwinian tree—Ross could take at least temporary refuge in the thought that the Aryan race, though it would have to be subjected to social control if society were to continue to function, would have to be controlled through appeals to its pride and its historical individualism. Thus the institutionalized propaganda of the modern state might keep alive the heroic qualities of the race. Time has dealt harshly with such hopes and has eroded their racist underpinnings; no student of society could today find comfort in such arguments. Ross's hopes have one by one been refuted; only his forebodings remain.

[V]

Thirteen years after Edward A. Ross published the first edition of *Social Control*, a general war broke out in Europe— the first in a hundred years. Two and a half years later, the United States herself entered the war, and the "educational" machinery of the modern state was set in motion to persuade Americans that the destruction of imperial Germany would make the world safe for democracy. The "spiritual associations lying over against the state," which Ross had hoped would prevent the "state educational machine" from tyrannizing over the minds of men, not only failed to resist the official war propaganda but often anticipated it, so that it became impossible to tell whether the government was teaching the people to hate or whether the people themselves were forcing the hand

8. Ibid.

of the government. Citizens' groups took it upon themselves to ferret out subversives and punish dissent. They descended on the public schools, tore up German books, abolished the German language. A lynching party in Montana murdered Frank Little, an official of the IWW.[9] In a suburb of Cincinnati, vigilantes seized Herbert S. Bigelow, a liberal whose support of the war his neighbors deemed not sufficiently ardent, threw him into an automobile, took him to a wood, stripped him, tied him to a tree, and flogged him until he was covered with blood, then left him to wander alone until he was finally rescued next morning.[1]

The universities—at such a time the last refuge, it might have seemed, of the critical spirit—proved to be as weak a line of defense as any other. It was not merely that university administrations yielded to outside pressure, as in the celebrated case of Professor Dana at Columbia, and dismissed unpopular teachers. The professors themselves, most of them, fell eagerly into step. Distinguished historians wrote tracts for George Creel's Committee on Public Information, proving that the Germans were Huns, inhuman beasts guilty of unspeakable atrocities. Two of the foremost scholars in the country, John Franklin Jameson and Samuel Harper, made a perfunctory examination of the notorious Sisson documents, which purported to show that the Germans had even sponsored the Russian revolution, and upheld their authenticity, although the documents were widely recognized as forgeries even at the time. Professor Harper privately believed that although the documents might be genuine, they did not sustain the inference drawn from them by Creel and Edgar Sisson, that the Bolshe-

9. H. C. Peterson and Gilbert C. Fite: *Opponents of War 1917-1918* (Madison: University of Wisconsin Press; 1957), pp. 56-8.

1. *Pearson's*, XXXVIII (Jan., 1918), p. 313; Walter Nelles to Beatrice F. R. Hale, Dec. 19, 1917, and Daniel Kiefer to Mary Ware Dennett, Jan. 5, 1918, American Civil Liberties Union MSS, Princeton University Library.

viks were German agents; for "there was clear evidence in [the] documents," he thought, ". . . that Lenin constantly had in mind the possibility of double-crossing the Germans." But he and Jameson were told by the administration "that such a statement would not help to promote that emotional upsurge necessary for the mobilization of all our resources to be thrown into the struggle." Accordingly, the historians refrained from commenting on the matter at all, thus encouraging the delusion, in the words of one journalist, "that Lenin et al. were a band of cheap adventurers who took the stand they did in order to earn German pay."[2]

Even passive acquiescence in the war spirit was not always enough to prove one's loyalty. Ross himself, returning from a trip to Russia in the winter of 1918, was accused of a want of aggressive patriotism. An outraged citizen who heard him speak on Russia objected to his address not because of what he said but because of what he failed to say. "There is a vast difference between a silence of non-disloyalty and the few spoken words of open and aggressive patriotism which one should like to hear on all occasions from professors of our State University." Ross hastened to apologize. Having been out of the country for eight months, he said, he was unaware of "the struggle between loyalists and others in some parts of this State." It had not occurred to him "that a vigorous statement" of his "entire sympathy" with the war effort would be "appropriate or helpful." But he would by all means take care in future addresses "to make my position clear on this point."[3]

2. Harper to Jerome Landfield, Nov. 15, 1918, Harper MSS, University of Chicago Library; Samuel N. Harper: *The Russia I Believe In* (Chicago: University of Chicago Press; 1945), pp. 111–12. See also the unpublished draft of Harper's autobiography, Harper MSS, in which he admitted that he and Jameson had contributed to the "war spirit." For the Harper-Jameson report, see the New York *Evening Post*, Nov. 11, 1918.

3. E. P. Sherry to Ross, Feb. 9, 1918, Ross to E. P. Sherry, Feb. 12, 1918, Edward A. Ross MSS, State Historical Society of Wisconsin.

By June, Ross was writing even in private: "I am delighted to find on what a high plane the war is pitched in this country and I am heartily with the administration in its policies. I accept entirely the view that the Potsdam gang actually contemplated the conquest of the world."[4]

Thus Ross, who had discerned in the idea of social control almost unlimited possibilities for establishing an "empire over minds," fell victim to the very process against which he had once so persuasively warned.

4. Ross to Frank C. Goudy, June 26, 1918, Edward A. Ross MSS.

6 / The New Republic
and the War:
"An Unanalyzable Feeling"

[I]

AT FIRST THE WAR IN EUROPE SEEMED AT ONE STROKE TO refute all the assumptions on which the social planners had built their elaborate design for orderly progress. Its unexpected scope, its unprecedented devastation, the rapidity with which it resolved itself into a deadlock which it seemed madness to pursue but to the terrible logic of which all the parties to the struggle seemed as in a nightmare bound— these things appeared to put an end, once and for all, to the hope that human societies could order their own advance. Where now was the evidence of man's abiding reasonableness, his strong but undeveloped social instincts?

Walter Lippmann, the year before, had written of "mastery" as the alternative to "drift." He "was beginning to shake me," a friend reflected in the fall of 1914, "in my very firm belief in *original sin*—this war has restored it triumphantly." "Bad education" was not the source of social conflict. "It's not education, it's the thing that can never be educated—not in the next few aeons anyway." "How is Walter going to quench this fundamental illogical passion in us all?"[1]

1. Bobby Rogers to Mabel Dodge, Nov. 12 [1914], Mabel Dodge Luhan: *Movers and Shakers* (New York: Harcourt, Brace; 1936), p. 302.

It was a long time before the social planners were able to formulate a reply to the questions raised by the war. Badly shaken by the events in Europe, they groped uncertainly for answers, contradicting one week what they had said the week before. Not until the third year of the war did they recover their poise. At that point the American declaration of war against Germany made it imperative to find a rationale for the war which would justify American participation in it. At the same time the Russian revolution providentially removed the major obstacle to conceiving of the war as a war for democracy —the fact that Tsarist Russia was fighting on the side of the Allies. These two events, occurring within a few weeks of each other, rescued American radicals from the uncertainty into which the war had cast them. Even then, however, the relief was only temporary; their original doubts returned to haunt them; and by the end of the war they were as uneasy in their minds as they had been at its outset. The war did not destroy American radicalism, but it left it with wounds from which it never entirely recovered.

[II]

From the summer of 1914 to the spring of 1917, confusion held full sway. It left its record in the letters and diaries of the time and in the radical journals of opinion, particularly in *The New Republic*, launched with such enthusiasm in the summer of 1914, only to find itself confronted from the very beginning with a war which called into question the hopes on which it was founded. *The New Republic*, its editor had explained to Randolph Bourne, would be "radical without being socialistic," its "general tendency" "pragmatic rather than doctrinaire."[2] Above all, it was to stand for mastery, the scientific solution of social problems. Walter Lippmann was one of the editors. Herbert Croly, the guiding genius of the enterprise, also believed in the planned society. His book *The Promise of American Life* (1909), in which he argued that the "promise" was not "self-fulfilling," undoubtedly helped to inspire Lippmann's *Drift and Mastery*. A third editor, the economist Walter Weyl, expressed views similar to those of Croly and Lippmann in *The New Democracy* (1914). It would have been difficult to find men able to write more enthusiastically or more persuasively about the possibilities of social control.

The war, alas, intruded, and *The New Republic* was obliged to improvise a foreign policy.[3] Such was their bafflement that the editors could only repeat, again and again, that a policy—some policy—was necessary. The debate over "preparedness" seemed to them to miss the point, because both sides tended "to identify war and peace with more or less armament." Neither arms nor the lack of them would in themselves insure the future peace of the country; the question was what political objectives the country ought to pursue. *The New Republic*

2. Herbert Croly to Randolph Bourne, June 3, 1914, Bourne MSS. In its early days, Bourne frequently contributed to *The New Republic*. See Charles A. Beard to Bourne, May 15, 1914, Bourne MSS.

3. Its efforts have been studied briefly by Eric Goldman: *Rendezvous with Destiny* (New York: Alfred A. Knopf; 1953), pp. 251–3, and more thoroughly by Charles B. Forcey: *The Crossroads of Liberalism* (New York: Oxford University Press; 1961), chapters 7, 8. My own investigation, undertaken quite independently of Forcey's, supports his interpretations and judgments at almost every point, with one exception. Whereas he finds the key to the policies of *The New Republic* during the war in its nationalism, I have been more impressed by its faith in "social control." Accordingly, I have dwelt in detail on the contribution to the war debates made by John Dewey, a figure understandably neglected in Forcey's account.

itself advocated preparedness but argued at the same time that "the essence of preparedness is a definition of foreign policy."[4]

The statement had an authoritative ring; but when it came to defining the policy the definition of which seemed so urgent, *The New Republic* had very little to offer. Should the United States plan to enter the war or should it do everything it could to stay out? *The New Republic* rejected the second alternative without endorsing the first. It advocated preparedness, but for no better reason than that the country might be forced into war against its will. The editors were uncomfortably aware that this position fell short of a policy; it left the most important question of all, the question of war or peace, to the decision of the European powers. That was precisely the effect of the course which the Wilson administration was even then pursuing, a course which *The New Republic* was quick to condemn as a policy of drift. If Wilson was drifting, so was *The New Republic*.

Faced with questions to which their principles supplied no answers, the editors of *The New Republic*, like so many "pragmatic liberals" after them, took refuge in the rhetoric of hard-boiled realism, evidently hoping that the outward appearance of tough-mindedness would conceal the flabbiness of their thought. They took particular comfort in ridiculing the pacifists, for whom they professed a fine disdain. Pacifists talked of the sanctity of treaties, forgetting that "treaties will never acquire sanctity until nations are ready to seal them with their blood."[5] They talked of the importance of international law, forgetting that "pious wishes" meant nothing "without sanctions."[6] Fighting itself was not a sin, *The New Republic*

4. " 'Preparedness' for What?" *The New Republic* [hereafter *NR*], III (June 26, 1915), p. 188; *NR*, V (Nov. 20, 1915), p. 55. See also "Are We Militarists?" *NR*, II (March 20, 1915), pp. 166-7.
5. "Timid Neutrality," *NR*, I (Nov. 14, 1914), p. 7.
6. *NR*, I (Dec. 19, 1914), p. 3.

insisted in the spirit of its hero, Theodore Roosevelt; the great sin was to fight for a "bad cause" or to be afraid to fight for a good one.[7] As for peace, it was more than the "vacuum created by the absence of war," it was "a great construction of infinite complexity."[8]

The trouble with this particular variety of realism was that it was directed not so much against pacifism as against a caricature of it. As one noninterventionist pointed out, all pacifists "deserving of the name" could agree that peace was more than the vacuum left by the absence of war. "The outstanding characteristic of the modern peace movement . . . is the drop from the soaring heights of idealism to the sordid facts of ordinary economic life."[9] *The New Republic* gained its rhetorical successes by attacking the noninterventionist position at its weakest point. As long as the pacifists refused to argue about the substance of foreign policy, proposing instead to reform the machinery by which international affairs were conducted and leaving untouched the sources of imperialistic rivalry which had set off the war in the first place, *The New Republic* had the better of the argument. Crystal Eastman did more to confirm the case against pacifism than to refute it when she replied to *The New Republic* that it was unnecessary for the peace movement to concern itself with questions of policy, because national disputes, like disputes among individuals, were "unavoidable," and the only question was by what means they should be settled. "Quarreling persists among men," she argued, "but duelling has been abolished."[1] In the same vein, Robert Herrick asserted that war was an anachronism. "To speak any longer of the 'arbitrament of arms' is as silly as to speak of a trial by combat or other medieval fan-

7. "Pacifism vs. Passivism," *NR*, I (Dec. 12, 1914), p. 7.
8. "Are We Militarists?" *NR*, II (March 20, 1915), p. 167.
9. Arthur Fisher to *NR*, III (May 15, 1915), p. 43.
1. Crystal Eastman to *NR*, III (July 24, 1915), p. 313.

tasy."[2] Silly or not, however, the war in Europe was a fact, a fact with which the United States had somehow to deal. As *The New Republic* pointed out, the United States was involved in the affairs of Europe in spite of herself. As soon as Americans realized that "with the upsetting of the equilibrium of Europe our own diplomacy is radically altered," they would be able "to discuss the war not in relation to its 'moral' causes, but in relation to its realistic results."[3]

Within a year many of the pacifists had recanted. Herrick declared himself ashamed of "that vague pacifism which I, like so many others, voiced under the first shock of the European war." Now it seemed to him the expression of an "anemic idealism," a "sickliness in our national spirit." Four months in France had convinced him that war was the best cure for this disease, the cure, indeed, for the deep *malaise* of modern civilization, which his novels recorded. "There is no question of the great benefit of this war. . . . There is not a Frenchman who will not tell you of the immense good that has already come to his people, that will come increasingly from this bloody sacrifice. It has united all classes, swept aside the trivial and the base, revealed the nation to itself. . . . A new, a larger, a more vital life has already begun for invaded and unconquered France."[4] Thus Herrick's "religion of life"[5] ended, by a final ironic twist, in a glorification of war.

Since his original pacifism was as muddled as his later defense of war, it is not surprising that it collapsed under the first strain. On one point Herrick was right: the prewar peace movement, of which his own views can be taken as a representative expression, was an anemic affair. But the pacifism of Randolph Bourne, Jane Addams, and a few other people was

2. Robert Herrick to *NR*, I (Dec. 19, 1914), p. 22.
3. *NR*, I (Jan. 23, 1915), p. 8.
4. Herrick: "Recantation of a Pacifist," *NR*, IV (Oct. 30, 1915), pp. 328–9.
5. See above, p. 63.

another matter altogether. *The New Republic* could score points against the former, but the latter raised questions that could not be so easily dismissed. If, as *The New Republic* urged its readers, one searched beneath the machinery of international affairs for the political sources of the war, one discovered that both sides were fighting for war aims so sweeping that nothing short of total defeat would force the other side to accept them; and this fact had important implications for the "realistic results" of the war and for the kind of influence over those results which the United States could reasonably expect to exert. It was not simply that both sides were fighting for imperial spoils. The logic of the war itself, quite apart from the motives with which the various participants had entered it, led the belligerents into progressively more ambitious statements of their objectives. The longer the slaughter went on, the greater the need of the belligerents to convince themselves that their mounting sacrifices would ultimately be redeemed by the complete annihilation of the enemy. The will to victory thus fed upon itself: the more ambitious the war aims, the longer the war was likely to last; the longer the war, the more exalted the ambitions of either side.

The New Republic urged its readers to consider the probable consequences of the war. Very well: the probable consequence of total war was total victory, for one side or the other, and total victory would not only disrupt the balance of power in Europe but leave social injuries which, festering over a period of time, might very likely generate a renewal of the conflict on an even more terrible scale. It was not necessary to be a nonresistant in order to reflect on the futility, not perhaps of war in general, but of the particular war at hand. In August, 1914, at a time when *The New Republic* was still flaying pacifism and fretting over the administration's timidity in refusing to protest the German invasion of Belgium, Colonel

House in a letter to Wilson showed that he had already grasped the "realistic result" of the conflict. "The saddest feature of the situation to me," he wrote, "is that there is no good outcome to look forward to. If the Allies win, it means the domination of Russia on the Continent of Europe; and if Germany wins, it means the unspeakable tyranny of militarism for generations to come."[6]

The only hope in all this was that the two sides were so evenly matched—as the inconclusive character of the fighting seemed to show—that neither side would be able to win a victory. The Allies and the Central Powers might then be forced to conclude a peace which would leave the balance of power essentially unchanged. But what if the United States entered the war? Might not that event revive the Allies' flagging hopes of total victory? Might it not so decisively alter the balance of military force as to enable the Allies to crush Germany, thus opening up central Europe to Russian domination?

The case for nonintervention, in short, could be argued on pragmatic grounds. Eventually *The New Republic* was obliged to admit the force of the argument. By the end of 1915, with the opposing armies locked in a war of trenches and barbed wire which neither side, it seemed, could hope to win unaided, *The New Republic* had begun to back down from its earlier bluster. "At the beginning of a second winter's campaign everything indicates that the subjugation of their enemies will constitute a task beyond the military strength of either group."[7] Accordingly, *The New Republic* began to point out the advantages of an "inconclusive peace" and of complete American neutrality, timid as it might once have appeared. "It is not the

6. House to Wilson, Aug. 22, 1914, in Charles Seymour: *The Intimate Papers of Colonel House* (Boston: Houghton Mifflin; 1926), Vol. I, p. 255.

7. "War at Any Price," *NR*, V (Nov. 27, 1915), p. 84.

verdict of history," wrote Alvin Johnson in July, 1915, "that complete victories are conducive to peace, nor that drawn conflicts are provocative of further war."[8] By November these opinions had become the announced policy of the magazine. "An inconclusive ending to the war and a treaty of compromise and adjustment has [sic] a much better chance of contributing to the ultimate peace of Europe than has the ruthless subjugation of Germany."[9] Previously *The New Republic* had denied that the United States could prevail upon the warring nations to come to terms or could exert any influence at the peace table unless it entered the war itself. Neutral, the editors had argued, the United States would be treated "as a nation of well-meaning people who run no risks."[1] Now *The New Republic* endorsed the view which it had previously dismissed as a sentimental delusion. The United States could influence the outcome after all, even as a neutral. "The American people do not intend to take part in the war," the editors unequivocally announced. Nevertheless, they maintained that the United States could "contribute to the terms of peace" by "keeping alive in the world the light of reason."[2]

The New Republic thus accepted the idea of "peace without victory" (a phrase which first appeared in an editorial of December 23, 1916), but it never quite accepted its full implications. It endorsed American neutrality, but it nevertheless continued to insist that Wilson had made a fundamental mistake at the beginning of the war when he urged Americans to be neutral in thought as well as in deed.[3] It continued to argue

8. Alvin S. Johnson: "An Inconclusive Peace," *NR*, III (July 24, 1915), p. 308.

9. "War at Any Price," *NR*, V (Nov. 27, 1915), p. 85.

1. "Timid Neutrality," *NR*, I (Nov. 14, 1914), p. 8.

2. "Pro-German," *NR*, V (Dec. 4, 1915), p. 108. See also "Playing Germany's Game," in the same issue, pp. 108–10.

3. Walter Lippmann: "Uneasy America," *NR*, V (Dec. 25, 1915), pp. 195–6.

that the administration should have protested the invasion
of Belgium, even though it was no longer clear what purpose
such a protest would have served. Although the editors were
now much closer to Wilson than to Theodore Roosevelt, they
continued for a long time to condemn Wilson and to extol
Roosevelt because Roosevelt had favored a strong stand on
Belgium. So *The New Republic* believed; but on this point, it
turned out, the editors had been badly misinformed. Or rather
they had simply neglected to read what Roosevelt had publicly
said about Belgium in September, 1914: "We have not the
smallest responsibility for what has befallen her."[4] Not until
November, 1914, did Roosevelt argue that the American government should have condemned Germany.[5] *The New Republic* ignored the earlier statement and constructed an elaborate
image of Rooseveltian foresight and forcefulness on the basis
of its own wishful thinking. When the error at last came to
light, the editors admitted that "if at any time" they had "used
the Belgian issue to point a moral against Mr. Wilson and for
Mr. Roosevelt," they had committed an "injustice" which they
deeply regretted. "If this nation 'ignobly shirked' its 'duty' we
were all guilty—Mr. Roosevelt, Mr. Root, Mr. Wilson, and
everyone else who at the time the invasion took place thought
America's first duty was noninterference."[6]

But the question remained: why was it so important to have
protested the violation of Belgium's neutral rights? The invasion of Belgium, it is true, violated international law and
common morality, but *The New Republic* professed to be an

4. Theodore Roosevelt: "The World War: Its Tragedies and Its Lessons,"
Outlook, CVIII (Sept. 23, 1914), p. 173.

5. Theodore Roosevelt: "The International Posse Comitatus, *New York
Times Magazine*, Nov. 8, 1914, p. 1.

6. "Mr. Roosevelt's Afterthought," *NR*, VI (March 25, 1916), p. 204.
Thereafter, *The New Republic* was increasingly pro-Wilson and anti-Roose-
velt.

organ of pragmatic liberalism, it claimed to have cut loose from the legalism and the moralistic abstractions which had so often been the curse of American progressivism, it claimed to weigh political events in the scales of their consequences; and what purpose would have been served by an American protest over Belgium? *The New Republic* returned to the subject again and again, but it never faced this question. It merely condemned, again and again, the idea of noninterference, even after it had accepted the logic of it. It was as if *The New Republic* upheld activism, internationalism, and commitment not because they promised better results than a policy of nonintervention but because they were somehow desirable in themselves, not as policies but as attitudes which it was appropriate for political pragmatists to hold.

The New Republic's attitude toward the war rested less on a critical analysis of the issues involved than on a powerful emotional abhorrence of neutrality in all its forms, at the national and the personal level alike. The fear of neutrality, of political impotence, was the key to the contradictions in which *The New Republic* so often found itself entangled. The effort to distinguish between pacifism and "passivism," as the editors called it, was basic to their enterprise. The so-called pacifists, the editors argued, were really "passivists," because their attitude toward the war was an attitude of fatalistic acquiescence. "Aggressive pacifism," on the other hand, was purposeful and pragmatic. Again, where the passivist was sectarian, rejecting the world because the world was corrupt, the true pacifist tried to use what influence he had in order to improve the world. Passivism represented withdrawal and retreat; pacifism, involvement and commitment.[7] In practice, at the level of policy,

7. See "Pacifism vs. Passivism," *NR*, I (Dec. 12, 1914), pp. 6–7, and "Aggressive Pacifism," *NR*, V (Jan. 15, 1916), pp. 263–5; also *NR*, V (Dec. 11, 1915), p. 131.

the two positions seemed often to be indistinguishable, but *The New Republic* refused to admit this fact. Instead it inveighed interminably against pacifism (passivism) in all its manifestations; one who depended solely on *The New Republic* would have supposed that it was a greater danger than militarism.

It is these endless attacks on the American pacifists, which seemed to have so little to do with the actual policies the magazine was advocating, that suggest so strongly that the editors were committed not so much to any particular set of policies as to the idea of commitment itself. If one can distinguish between interest politics and what a recent sociologist has called "expressive" politics—"political action for the sake of expression rather than for the sake of influencing or controlling the distribution of valued objects"—the politics of *The New Republic* would seem to have verged increasingly toward the latter type.[8]

Since the substance of its own noninterventionism, stripped of its rhetoric, differed so little from that of most pacifists, one infers that the rhetoric may have served a purpose not strictly necessary to the defense of the noninterventionist position. The editors of *The New Republic* seemed to labor under some inner compulsion to demonstrate, over and over again, that it was not a sign of weakness or timidity to wish to stay out of the war. Perhaps a self-conscious and deliberate toughness was a polemical necessity in a country in which the refusal to fight was so often equated with cowardice. Perhaps the editors, as intellectuals—men who appeared to have chosen the contemplative over the active life—occupied a peculiarly vulnerable position in a society that tended to equate contemplation itself

8. For the concept of expressive politics, see Joseph R. Gusfield: *Symbolic Crusade* (Urbana: University of Illinois Press; 1963), p. 19, a study of the prohibition movement. I am grateful to Donald Kirschner for bringing this work to my attention.

with cowardice. But in making such a point of its willingness to fight if necessary, *The New Republic* ran the risk of losing sight altogether of the substance of the debate over the war. The debate itself became almost irrelevant. Political "realism" was not so much an answer to the war as an inner necessity.

[III]

Yet there was an undeniable issue underlying all this, an issue, however, which the hard-boiled rhetoric of *The New Republic* did more to confuse than to clarify. How, without entering the war—for to enter it might destroy the chance of "peace without victory"—could the United States expect to influence the outcome of a struggle which it had played no part in bringing about but in which its interests were unquestionably involved? To put the matter more broadly, how, at a time of political crisis, could men who defined their own responsibility as that of "keeping alive in the world the light of reason" dissociate themselves from policies that were all too obviously unreasonable, without at the same time forfeiting their chance of influence? Events soon gave the question, in its broader form, a new though not entirely unexpected turn. When the United States entered the war, men who advocated an "inconclusive peace" had to explain how they could support a decision which by their own reasoning could only lead to disaster. When the United States embarked upon a venture which could be seen to contain a certain element of madness, men who cherished the "light of reason" were faced with the possibility that they might be forced to dissociate themselves not merely from Europe but from most of their own countrymen. That in turn raised the question of influence in an immediate and painful form: in the act of opposing policies supported by almost everybody else, would the dissenters become a mere remnant, not merely unpopular but politically irrelevant? Or would they become (like the abolitionists of old) the nucleus of a new majority?

That was the deeper question which lurked beneath the debate about the war, the choice between sectarianism or "responsible" opposition from within; but it was not yet, after all, a question many people had to face, not even when the United States entered the war. That the editors of *The New Republic* had begun at least to sense its presence, however, is suggested by the eagerness with which they embraced the war, when it finally came, as an event which put an end to doubt. On January 13, 1917, *The New Republic* was writing that the time was "ripe for a discussion of how and when to end the war."[9] Four weeks later, the editors announced with obvious relief that "the long struggle within Germany" between the militarists and the friends of peace was over and that America's duty was "clear."

> Without any delay diplomatic relations must be broken. The German ships in American harbors should be seized at once and held as hostages. The navy should be mobilized. An anti-submarine fleet should be assembled. Steps should be taken to arm all merchant ships. Plans for financial and economic assistance to the Allies should be set in motion.[1]

The New Republic was all efficiency. Its enthusiasm perhaps reflected an increasing awareness of the dangers of trying any longer to keep alive the "light of reason" at a time when almost everyone else seemed blind to it.

9. *NR*, IX (Jan. 13, 1917), p. 285. See also *NR*, IX (Jan. 20, 1917), pp. 313–15, and *NR*, IX (Jan. 27, 1917), pp. 340–2.
1. Supplement to *NR*, X (Feb. 3, 1917), "Postscript, Thursday Morning, February 1st, 1917."

Having talked for months of the need for peace, *The New Republic* now demanded measures that would almost certainly lead to war. But it was able to reverse itself with a minimum of embarrassment and in such a way as to avoid confronting the implications of its decision to support the government in its break with Germany, because its own view of the world crisis had been undergoing a subtle and almost imperceptive shift. The significance of this change became apparent only when *The New Republic* found itself obliged to fashion an argument for American intervention. Its editorial on the German decision to resume unrestricted submarine warfare—the decision which called forth the brisk recital of emergency measures just quoted—shows what had happened to *The New Republic's* conception of the war and the uses to which its new ideas could be put. The decision to resume submarine warfare, according to *The New Republic*, represented the triumph of the admiralty over the chancellor. Germany was thus seen as divided within, the civilians against the military. The military having won out, Americans had little choice but to go to war, not, however, for the purpose of crushing Germany, but in order to encourage the forces of democracy against the forces of reaction. The qualification enabled *The New Republic* to reconcile its interventionism with the position it had taken earlier. The editors still advocated "peace without victory." But the concept had acquired a new meaning. Whereas an inconclusive peace had formerly been conceived as a negotiated peace between the Allies and the German *government*, it now meant something quite different: a negotiated peace between the Allies and the German *people*. The difference seemed so trivial that it went almost entirely unnoticed. In fact, however, it was fundamental. The earlier view dictated a diplomacy based on the balance of power. The new view dictated a diplomacy of manipulation, the object of which was to bring about a change of government in Germany itself. The consequences of the new diplomacy proved in the end to be far more profound than anyone foresaw.

Among the other assumptions that the war had seemed to call into question was the assumption that the political and cultural awakening, of which American radicals felt themselves a part, was international in scope. The assumption was natural enough when so many of the ideas of the new radicalism derived from Europe. Germany in particular, in the years preceding the war, appeared to be a plentiful source of enlightenment; but even England, which American radicals regarded with a certain impatience, had its socialist and feminist movements, the success of which, there as elsewhere, could be depended upon to put an end to the cultural ascendancy of the middle class. The revolt against the *bourgeoisie*, it seemed, transcended national boundaries. The ties of class were stronger than the ties of patriotism.

Yet when the war came, the dissident movements in each of the belligerent countries cast their lot with the governments that had gone to war. Only in Russia and in America did socialists in any numbers stand by their internationalist principles and oppose the war. Even in Russia, it was the Bolsheviks alone, a small minority of the Social Democratic Party, who opposed the war outright. And in America the united opposition of the Socialist Party reflected not a stronger current of anti-war opinion but the marginal status of the socialist movement as a whole. In England and Germany, particularly in Germany, the socialists represented a real opposition and hence were under correspondingly greater pressure, both from without and from within, to make their opposition "responsible." In America the socialists were merely a dissenting minority of

197 · *The New Republic and the War*

sectarians, not a party at all but a protest group. In Germany they represented a genuine alternative.

The failure of German socialism to hold Prussian imperialism in check greatly troubled American radicals. *The New Republic* might use the occasion to score empty points against the socialist contention that "the interests of capital would make for war and the interests of labor would make for peace," but the "nightmare" remained—"the nightmare of a united Germany."[2] By the summer of 1915, however, this nightmare had begun to be "dispelled." Moderate socialists in Germany, such as Bernstein and Kautsky, began to argue that the German government, if it continued the war, would be fighting not in self-defense but for conquests. *The New Republic* seized on these statements as proof that German socialists were "swinging back into opposition."[3]

Other evidence of political division in Germany came to hand, and although it was equally ephemeral, it was taken up with equal avidity. William C. Bullitt reported that the government itself was divided. The pro-Russian party wished to lure the Tsar from his alliance with England and France and then to crush the Western powers. The pro-Western party hoped to make peace with the West at Russia's expense.[4] It was *The New Republic's* acceptance of this view of German politics that enabled it to interpret the resumption of submarine warfare as a victory for the party which aimed "to make Germany the leader of the East against the West." That interpretation

2. *NR*, III (June 5, 1915), p. 110; *NR*, IV (Aug. 14, 1915), p. 30.
3. Ibid.
4. See William C. Bullitt in Philadelphia *Public Ledger*, Oct. 30, Oct. 31, Nov. 1, 1916, and his "Worse or Better Germany?" *NR*, VIII (Oct. 28, 1916), pp. 321–3. For *The New Republic's* endorsement of this thesis, see *NR*, IX (Dec. 9, 1916), p. 136; *NR*, IX (Dec. 23, 1916), pp. 201–2; and *NR*, X (Feb. 10, 1917), pp. 34–5.

of Germany's action in turn made it possible to argue that the duty of the United States was to join the fight against Germany, not to destroy her but "to force her and lure her back to the civilization in which she belongs."[5]

One objection, however, remained. It was difficult to accept the thesis that the war had become a conflict of democracy against reaction, West against East, when it was the Western powers themselves, not Germany, which had made Tsarist Russia an ally. Germany, *The New Republic* claimed, had become "a rebel nation" and would remain one "as long as she wages offensive war against the western world."[6] But one could argue that the very reverse was the case. As one reader pointed out: "It was Great Britain and France which became traitors to the western world when they allied themselves with the great eastern Powers [Russia and Japan] and it is primarily for the interests of those Powers that this war is now being fought."[7] *The New Republic* itself had taken this position. "Any misgivings we may have entertained about the cause of the Allies," it said in February, 1916, "have always turned upon the contribution that Russia has made to the Alliance. . . . *The New Republic* has argued in favor of an inconclusive peace, largely because it apprehends the consequences on the Eastern frontier of a decisive victory for the Allies. . . . We . . . believe that Englishmen and Frenchmen would eventually regret acquiescence in a course which would tend to weaken Germany as compared to Russia."[8]

The way out of this difficulty was to apply to Russia the same method of analysis which *The New Republic* had applied to Germany; to argue, that is, that American intervention would strengthen the democratic forces in Russia just as it

5. *NR*, X (Feb. 17, 1917), p. 60.
6. Ibid.
7. R. W. France to *NR*, X (March 10, 1917), p. 163.
8. *NR*, VI (Feb. 26, 1916), pp. 103-4.

would strengthen them in Germany. But the argument that seemed so plausible in the case of Germany, with its large and vigorous socialist movement, was much less convincing when applied to Russia. It seemed unlikely that a country in which opposition was not even tolerated was on the verge of revolution, let alone a liberal parliamentary revolution. Writing of Russia in September, 1915, *The New Republic* had professed to see "straws" in the "wind of discontent," but in the succeeding months this hope appeared to fade.[9] Then in March, 1917, the Tsarist government unexpectedly collapsed, a liberal regime took power, and the argument that had seemed so tenuous before acquired immediate and tangible substance. "It is now as certain as anything human can be," said *The New Republic*, "that the war which started as a clash of empires in the Balkans will dissolve into democratic revolution the world over."[1]

It remained only to show that the war would encourage democracy at home as well as abroad. Many liberals feared that war would not only put an end to domestic reform but generate a pervasive spirit of intolerance and repression. President Wilson, on the eve of asking Congress to declare war, told Frank Cobb of the New York *World* that war "would mean that we should lose our heads along with the rest and stop weighing right and wrong." It required illiberalism at home to fight it abroad, for "to fight," Wilson said, "you must be brutal and ruthless, and the spirit of ruthless brutality will enter into the very fibre of our national life, infecting Congress, the courts, the policeman on the beat, the man in the streets."[2] The perceptiveness of this analysis, indeed its moral grandeur,

9. *NR*, IV (Sept. 25, 1915), p. 193.
1. *NR*, X (April 7, 1917), p. 280.
2. Frank Cobb: *Cobb of "The World"* (New York: E. P. Dutton; 1924), pp. 269-70.

is the more remarkable for its having come from the one man who of all others had the best reason for wishing to shut his eyes to the prospect ahead, the man charged with initiating the very machinery of hate the workings of which he foresaw so clearly. By contrast, those whose duty it was to reflect on events rather than to initiate them, and who from their relative detachment from the pressure of decision might have been expected to bring to public debate a measure of skepticism and restraint (thus "keeping alive the light of reason"), could see in "the great decision" to go to war, as *The New Republic* called it, only the promise of a brilliant future. They were not able to match Wilson's sense of the war (however fleeting it proved to be) as a tragic necessity, a lesser evil. *The New Republic* in particular was now so eager to get behind the President that it managed to keep several steps ahead of him, anticipating the reasoning by which Wilson himself, suspending his own reservations, soon defended the war as a war to make the world safe for democracy and to end war. Colonel House now found it difficult "to keep them in line because of the President's slowness of action."[3]

Wilson was initially reluctant not only to go to war but to rationalize the war as a war for democracy. According to the diary of Robert Lansing, one of the most conservative members of the Cabinet, it was Lansing himself, not Wilson, who first thought of the idea and suggested it be used in the President's war message. Lansing "felt strongly that to go to war solely because American ships had been sunk and Americans killed would cause debate." The "sounder basis" on which to build support of the war was to stress "the duty of this and every other democratic nation to suppress an autocratic government like the German because of its atrocious character." Such an

3. House MS Diary, March 9, 1917.

indictment of Germany, Lansing argued, "would appeal to every liberty-loving man the world over."[4]

Wilson, according to Lansing, did not immediately commit himself to this reasoning. All he said was: "Perhaps." But he incorporated in the draft of his war message not only the famous statement about making the world safe for democracy but a more specific statement to the effect that the United States could not negotiate with Germany until she had a government that could be trusted. It was a doubly ironic reversal of roles that this last phrase, apparently inserted on the advice of the conservative Lansing, was taken out at the insistence of the liberal House (subsequently to reappear, however, as a main theme of the Wilsonian diplomacy). House had no difficulty in persuading the President that "it looked too much like inciting revolution." But as an indication of the general confusion in which so much of the discussion of American war aims was conducted—and which an account of the discussion ignores at its peril—in the very same conversation House told Wilson "that he should state that the United States would not join a league of nations of which an autocracy was a member."[5]

In any case, the manipulative motive behind Lansing's suggestion—a suggestion, by the way, of which he later repented—is perfectly clear. (More typical of Lansing and of the conservative position in general was his later reflection that "the German people will never change their code of morals" and that "the surer and better way," therefore, "would be to take away from Germany the chief sources of her present military power."[6]) Wilson's adoption of this suggestion, however, probably reflected not so much a cynical intention to get public

4. Lansing MS Diary, March 20, 1917 (memorandum of a Cabinet meeting of that day), Robert Lansing MSS, Library of Congress.

5. House MS Diary, April 2, 1917.

6. Lansing MS Diary, Oct. 24, 1917.

opinion behind any slogan that could be used to justify the war effort as an awareness of the problem that unavoidably confronted all the powers engaged in the war—the fatal gap between the sacrifices they were now called upon to make and the original objects for which they had gone to war. Officially, the United States had broken with Germany over the issue of neutral rights, but it was perfectly obvious (quite apart from the fact that Germany was not the only violator of American rights) that the mere defense of neutral rights could not justify such slaughter as the United States was now embarked upon. It was in the same spirit that *The New Republic* early took the position that the United States was entering the war not "because we are lawyers upholding a precedent, but because our own existence and the world's order depend on the defeat of that anarchy which the Germans misname the 'freedom of the seas.' "[7] The "war for democracy" was above all an example of that escalation of war aims, noted above, which was one of the most terrible features of the war.

The war liberals (or "realists," as they now called themselves), brushing aside the fear that war would breed not liberalism but intolerance, now began to argue that a national emergency of such scope would unify the country behind a program of socialized democracy, binding up the wounds that had rent the body politic and putting an end to years of aimless drift. Already the editors of *The New Republic* had discerned signs of a "new temper and a new intelligence in our national life"; but it was John Dewey, appropriately enough, who formulated the classic defense of the war as an agency of socialization.[8] In August, 1917, Dewey predicted in *The New Republic* that the war would see "the beginnings of a public

7. *NR*, X (Feb. 10, 1917), pp. 33-4.
8. *NR*, X (Feb. 3, 1917), p. 4.

control which [would] cross nationalistic boundaries and interests," the beginnings of an international community based on a new sense of solidarity among all peoples.[9] A year later he spelled out the argument in greater detail. The war would lead not only to a new international consciousness but, more specifically, to a "more conscious and extensive use of science for communal purposes" and to a greater degree of public control over private enterprise ("the creation of instrumentalities for enforcing the public interest in all the agencies of modern production and exchange"). Above all, the war, in Dewey's opinion, offered an instance of what Jane Addams was later to call "education by the current event." It drove home the lesson, as no amount of sermonizing could ever have done, that all the parts of modern society were mutually interdependent. It promoted the sense of social cohesion which had so long been missing from American life and from the life of the rest of the world as well.[1]

In the meantime, however, the political climate became more oppressive every day. The administration suppressed radical papers, connived at the persecution of the People's Council and other radical organizations, refused to allow American socialists to attend a conference on peace terms in Stockholm, refused to allow any discussion of peace terms whatever. George Creel's Committee on Public Information announced in May, 1917, that "speculation about possible peace" was a "topic which may possess elements of danger, as peace

9. John Dewey: "What America Will Fight For," *NR*, XII (Aug. 18, 1917), p. 69. Dewey's articles on the war were later reprinted in his *Characters and Events* (New York: Henry Holt; 1929), this one in Vol. II, p. 565.

1. Dewey: "What Are We Fighting For?" *Independent*, XCIV (June 22, 1918), pp. 474, 481; *Characters and Events*, Vol. II, pp. 552, 556. For Jane Addams's phrase, see *The Second Twenty Years at Hull-House* (New York: Macmillan; 1930), chapter 12.

reports may be of enemy origin, put out to weaken the combination against Germany."[2] The President himself denounced
the German "peace intrigue" and called for war to the limit—
and "woe be to the man or group of men that seeks to stand in
our way."[3] On all sides people shouted for war and yet more
war, demanding that everything which interfered with it
should be indefinitely suspended. "Every democratic movement," said a former anti-imperialist, "every social, moral and
political cause whatever should be side-tracked or modified if
their promotion interferes in the slightest degree—directly or
indirectly—with the great opportunity for service in 'winning
the war.'"[4] The very thought of peace had become an act of
disloyalty.

Dewey at first waved all these things away with a gesture
of impatience. He was "not . . . specially concerned" that
"liberty of thought and speech" would "seriously suffer . . . in
any lasting way." All that troubled him was that "conscription
of thought" was not the most efficient means of promoting
"social solidarity," since it gave rise to resentment among its
victims.[5] That was in September, 1917. Two months later, however, Dewey had to admit that what he had written in September seemed "strangely remote and pallid." The increase in
"bigotry" had been such that "years might have passed." As he
wrote, the government was on the verge of suppressing the
socialist press. "The appeal is no longer to reason; it is to the
event."[6] Now, if not before, one might have concluded that the
hopes on which American progressives had based their support

2. New York *Evening Post*, May 28, 1917.

3. *The New York Times*, June 15, 1917, p. 4 (Flag Day speech).

4. Erving Winslow to *Survey*, XXXIX (Dec. 8, 1917), p. 301.

5. Dewey: "Conscription of Thought," *NR*, XII (Sept. 1, 1917), p. 129;
Characters and Events, Vol. II, pp. 568–9.

6. Dewey: "In Explanation of Our Lapse," *NR*, XIII (Nov. 3, 1917), p. 17;
Characters and Events, Vol. II, p. 571.

of the war had one after the other collapsed. Surveying the ruin, one might understandably have decided that the time had come for a reassessment of the strategy of making peace by waging total war. But the war liberals continued to resist the conclusion to which events seemed ever more clearly to point.

[IV]

To add to their troubles, the supporters of the war were coming under increasingly articulate attack from the Left. A few skeptics had maintained all along that American entry would prolong the war rather than shorten it. "It will make Germany desperate," said Amos Pinchot in March, 1917, "close the fist of the militarist government upon the people, and hold down the democratic impulses that stand for peace. . . . It will solidify the British Government's determination not to make peace until a decisive victory is won, and to offer no terms in the meantime that will not impel Germany to fight on to the bitter end."[7] Jane Addams took the same position.

The most formidable challenge to the pragmatic defense of the war came from Randolph Bourne. As early as August, 1917, Bourne had announced "the collapse of American strategy," the will to victory, as it seemed to him, having superseded the wish for an inconclusive peace.[8] He had early come to the gloomiest conclusions about the outcome of the war— economic disorganization abroad, a repressive state socialism at home—and now he proceeded to inquire into the amazing optimism of American progressives in the face of what seemed

7. Amos Pinchot to New York *Evening Post*, March 27, 1917.
8. Bourne: "The Collapse of American Strategy," *Seven Arts*, II (Aug., 1917), pp. 409–24, reprinted in Randolph Bourne: *Untimely Papers* (New York: B. W. Huebsch; 1919), pp 61–89.

to him an unmitigated and overwhelming disaster. The fault,
he thought, lay not so much with pragmatism itself—he liked
to think that William James would not have accepted the war
"so easily and complacently"—as with John Dewey's corruption of pragmatism, which had encountered in the war a
"power too big for it."[9] What the war seemed to show was that
although Dewey's instrumentalism worked well enough in a
rational setting, in which there already existed a strong will to
orderly progress, it was inadequate to an emergency such as
war. Bourne decided that it was no accident that Dewey's
philosophy—to which he himself had once subscribed—had
won its greatest successes in the school. It was "precisely the
school . . . that is of all our institutions the most malleable" and
the most rationally motivated.[1] The school was a laboratory in
which experiments in social control could successfully be conducted because the technicians, as in any laboratory, could
themselves determine the conditions of their experiments. But
when a technique derived from education was applied to
society and politics, transferred from a rational and controllable
environment to an environment in which reason seemed powerless to arrest the drift of events, it revealed itself as utterly
useless to the occasion. The very fact that the country had not
made education its "national enterprise" but had chosen war
instead—had chosen it, Bourne thought, out of "a dread of intellectual suspense"—disposed of the assumption that whole
societies could be educated in the path of social reform.[2] It

9. Bourne: "Twilight of Idols," *Seven Arts*, II (Oct., 1917), pp. 688-9;
Untimely Papers, p. 116.
1. Bourne: "Twilight of Idols," *Seven Arts*, II, p. 691; *Untimely Papers*,
p. 120.
2. Ibid. For the idea of war as a relief from indecision, see "The War
and the Intellectuals," *Seven Arts*, II (June, 1917), p. 143; *Untimely Papers*,
p. 40.

showed that "nations," unlike schools, "are not rational entities."[3] It suggested also—although Bourne himself was only beginning to explore this line of thought—that the pragmatists in their enthusiasm for social planning had been fatally indifferent to questions of power. In the school, power belonged (in some cases anyway) to the social planners; but American society as a whole was controlled, insofar as it was controlled at all, by the "socially significant classes," as Bourne now began to call them.[4] That being the case, nothing short of the overthrow of these classes, it seemed, would clear the way for social change.

This analysis, it should be noted, carried with it by implication an attack on the theory of progressive education as well as on the progressive defense of the war. It pointed up the fallacy of Dewey's equation of the school with "life" by suggesting that the school's chief characteristic was (or ought to have been) precisely its remoteness from life.

The logic of his attack on pragmatism drove Bourne to try to formulate an alternative theory of society to set up against the doctrines of the social planners. Eventually he embarked on a full-scale study of the modern state, on which he was working when he died. Bourne at his best was a polemicist, not a philosopher (nor yet a writer of genteel essays for the *Atlantic*); and the fragment that he left, although it has been praised as a "close analysis and scathing indictment" of the state, is inferior to his earlier polemics.[5] Anger suited him better than philosophical detachment, and his best intuitions about the state sprang not from sustained reflection on the subject

3. *Untimely Papers*, p. 121.

4. "Unfinished Fragment on the State," *Untimely Papers*, pp. 140–230, *passim*.

5. Ernest S. Bates: "Randolph Bourne," *Dictionary of American Biography*, Vol. II, p. 486.

but from his immediate appreciation of the fact which in the last year of his life bore down on every detail of his existence: that the war, whatever else might be said about it, represented "an absolute, coercive social situation."[6] The war presented itself to Bourne as an implacable force, unamenable to rational control, for the very reason that, having been unable at the outset to accept it (for whatever reasons peculiar to his own chemistry), he found himself engaged in a prolonged and essentially futile resistance to the demands it made on the ordinary citizen. He saw the war as one of its victims. The social planners, on the other hand, in the act of supporting the war managed to retain their tenuous connections with the administration, the trappings if not the substance of power. For them the war was a bustle of activity: trips to Washington, consultations with government officials. For men such as these, war held no terrors. On the contrary, it brought a gratifying, if temporary, inflation of the ego.

One who resisted the war knew no such consolations. The act of resistance led only to the discovery of one's powerlessness to influence the outcome. But it was this experience alone which enabled one to make some sort of peace with the sense of impotence which had afflicted so many intellectuals of that generation; and in the act of acknowledging it, to transcend it. One sensed that a lonely protest which carried the ring of truth might in the long run count for more than the self-justification of men who were determined at all costs to hold on to their influence—only to find, in the end, that the influence itself was an illusion.

Bourne, then, saw the war from "below the battle," from the point of view of young men called on to serve their country in a cause that had no intelligible relation to the idea of serv-

6. Bourne: "A War Diary," *Seven Arts*, II (Sept., 1917), p. 539; *Untimely Papers*, p. 97.

ice.[7] From his peculiar vantage point, it was possible to see something that eluded the editors of *The New Republic* and their contributors. It was possible to see that young men did not submit to the draft because they believed in a League of Nations or a war to end war or even because they hated the Hun. They submitted because they had no meaningful alternative— "conscientious objection," an isolated gesture devoid of political content, appeared as meaningless as death on the battlefield. These observations led Bourne to the important conclusion that the conditions of modern society had made patriotism "superfluous"—a conclusion that paralleled and supported Edward A. Ross's analysis of the superfluity, under modern conditions, of the social sense in general.[8] The great mass of people, Bourne discovered, cared nothing about the war; yet the war went on. Men served because they could not avoid serving. The power of the state rested on "coercion from above . . . rather than patriotism from below"; it rested on acquiescence rather than cooperation. The pragmatists argued that the call to arms would inspire people with a new social idealism; but if Bourne's observations were correct, that assumption rested on a radical misunderstanding of the nature of modern warfare.[9]

What struck Bourne wherever he turned was the general purposelessness not only of the war but of all the activities of the state, to which people submitted so apathetically. Purposelessness seemed to him as complete at the top of the social structure as at the bottom. If men submitted to the state for no other reason than that they had no choice, the decisions of the state themselves seemed dictated by a similar submission to necessity. The whole business of war seemed "automatic." "War determines its own end—victory, and government crushes

7. See "Below the Battle," *Seven Arts*, II (July, 1917), pp. 270–7, *passim*; *Untimely Papers*, pp. 47–60.

8. See above, p. 176.

9. "A War Diary," *Untimely Papers*, pp. 93–4.

out automatically all forces that deflect, or threaten to deflect, energy from the path of organization to that end."[1] Thus it was useless for Dewey to urge "the merely good, the merely conscientious," to give up their opposition to the war and instead "to connect conscience with the forces that are moving in another direction."[2] The point was that there *were* no forces moving in another direction, there was no such thing as "a peculiar kind of democratic and antiseptic war." There was only war itself. All governments at war acted automatically, "the most democratic as well as the most autocratic." "War is the health of the state." The pacifists had opposed the war because they knew that a democratic war was an illusion. "For once the babes and the sucklings seem to have been wiser than the children of light."[3]

The war liberals did not so much reply to these arguments as dismiss them. The war spirit admittedly was a fact, but they rejected out of hand the possibility that the war spirit was a product of the war itself. Dewey dismissed that argument as simply "lazy." Rather, the "explanation of our lapse," as Dewey referred to the mounting hysteria, lay in a combination of historical circumstances peculiar to America and having nothing to do with the war: America's remoteness from Europe, its historical isolation, its heterogeneous population. These things generated uncertainty about the degree of unity with which the country had gone to war and inspired compensatory efforts to enforce an excessive unanimity of opinion. But many of these excesses, Dewey thought, could also be traced to the simple fact that Americans lacked familiarity with war; a fact, as Dewey

1. Ibid., p. 101.
2. Dewey: "Conscience and Compulsion," *NR*, XI (July 14, 1917), p. 298; *Characters and Events*, Vol. II, p. 580.
3. Bourne: "A War Diary," *Untimely Papers*, p. 101, and "The State," in which the phrase "War is the health of the state" is a recurrent refrain.

hastened to point out, which was not entirely to their discredit. "In many ways we have been tumbling all over ourselves and getting in our own way since war was declared. The exhibition, even if awkward, is not altogether unlovely. The amusement aroused by the display is tinctured with affection as for all the riotous gambolings of youth."[4] Thus did Dewey end the article in which he himself had admitted that "the appeal is no longer to reason; it is to the event."

That admission is only one of many signs that the war liberals knew more about the temper of public opinion than they cared to take into their calculations. *The New Republic*, even while it insisted on the democratic character of the struggle, worried endlessly about the state of public feeling, fearing that the demand for vengeance would undermine the hope of a negotiated peace with the democratic forces in Germany. Ray Stannard Baker, a man close to the President and one of the most ardent of the war liberals, went to a dinner at the Harvard Club and was appalled to hear the mayor of New York recite a list of alleged German atrocities in Belgium and declare that he would not be satisfied until similar atrocities had been committed on German soil. "He wanted reprisals and he was savage about it. The applause he received," Baker added, "showed that this doctrine of hatred is growing enormously."[5] Such were the "riotous gambolings of youth."

The best evidence of the war liberals' mounting uneasiness —their uneasiness about the war, their inability to answer the pacifists to their own satisfaction—is the compulsiveness with which they returned again and again to the attack. As always,

4. Dewey: "In Explanation of Our Lapse," *NR*, XIII (Nov. 3, 1917), p. 18; *Characters and Events*, Vol. II, p. 574.
5. Ray Stannard Baker: *Woodrow Wilson: Life and Letters* (Garden City: Doubleday, Page; 1927–39), Vol. VII, p. 528, quoting from his own notebook of Feb. 5, 1918.

they ignored the pragmatic arguments raised by the pacifists and then went on to condemn the pacifists for their refusal to argue pragmatically. They equated pacifism with conscientious objection and then dismissed it as a form of "self-conceit."[6] In their more candid moments, however, they openly confessed that they had not begun to answer the real objections to the war. Dewey admitted that Jane Addams was not a "passivist"; but all pacifists, he added weakly, were not like Jane Addams.[7] If that was the case, however, it was surely more important to reply to Jane Addams than to the conscientious objectors; but Dewey made no effort to do so. He merely denounced, once again, the futility of conscientious objection, the futility of opposition, the futility of drift.

Yet his arguments for activism and engagement revealed a deep and pervasive fatalism of their own. The essence of the argument for war, when stripped of everything else, was simply that the war was a historical necessity. The naïveté of the pacifists, according to Dewey, lay in their inability to see that it took two to keep the peace, just as it took two to make a war. The United States had gone to war because the Germans had not cooperated in keeping the peace, and it was silly to argue as if the United States had had any choice in the matter. "It was a poor judge of politics who did not know from the very day of the Lusitania message—or at all events from that of the Sussex message—that the entrance of the United States into the war depended upon the actions of Germany."[8] In his eagerness to establish his own hard-headed approach to politics, Dewey unwittingly put his finger on the weakness of the Wilsonian strategy which he and so many other "realists" endorsed. The

6. Dewey: *Characters and Events*, Vol. II, p. 580.
7. Dewey: "The Future of Pacifism," *NR*, XI (July 28, 1917), p. 358; *Characters and Events*, Vol. II, pp. 582-3.
8. Ibid., p. 581.

weakness of Wilson's diplomacy in the prewar period was precisely its passivity. When Wilson threatened reprisals after the sinking of the *Sussex* (May, 1916) and thereby forced the German government to give up its submarine attacks on Allied shipping, he appeared to have scored a diplomatic triumph; but by committing the country to war if the attacks were renewed, he had in truth handed over to Germany the decision for war or peace—a decision that a more realistic statesmanship would have reserved to itself. As so often happened, the "tough-minded" liberals had mistaken the rhetoric of realism for its substance. There was a certain irony therefore in Dewey's argument that the pacifists had unrealistically opposed a war "which was already all but universal."[9] The last defense of the activists, it appeared, was that they alone knew how to submit gracefully to the inevitable. So much for mastery.

[V]

In the end the war liberals accepted practically the entire pacifist indictment of the war. But they never admitted that the pacifists had been right in the first place. Instead they blamed their defeat on Woodrow Wilson's betrayal of liberalism. Having deified Wilson in the effort to convince themselves that he was amenable to liberal influence, after the war they turned violently against him. Randolph Bourne had predicted that the "gay debauch" of the war would create "its own anti-toxin of ruin and disillusionment."[1] His prediction was borne out in full and sooner than he had expected.

No sooner was the general shape of the peace terms ap-

9. Ibid., p. 584.
1. Bourne: "Twilight of Idols," *Untimely Papers*, p. 117.

parent than the realists deserted the administration in droves.[2] Their rejection of the peace was as unreasoning as their acceptance of the war. Faced with the same question which had faced the country in 1917, the question of withdrawal from Europe or full participation in its affairs, they now adduced against the treaty and the League the same arguments which the pacifists had once used against the decision to go to war. Dewey's article of March, 1920, in which he pictured the country as faced with the dilemma that "isolation is impossible and participation perilous," could have been the work of a pacifist writing three years before. Dewey now maintained that the foreign policies of Great Britain and France were without question "non-democratic" and that the United States had an obligation, therefore, "not to engage too much or too readily with them until there is assurance that we shall not make themselves and ourselves worse, rather than better, by what is called sharing the common burdens of the world."[3] This reasoning would have been more appropriate to the outset of the war than to its close. By 1920 one could at least have taken comfort from the growing opposition in Britain and France to the terms of the treaty and to imperialism in general, whereas in 1917 those countries were united behind the demand for a victor's peace. At that time, however, Dewey had publicly betrayed no suspicion of the Allied cause. Not until the very end did he acknowledge what others had been saying from the

2. Not all the war liberals, of course, rejected the treaty. Many, if not most, of them stood by Wilson to the end. Most of those who did, however, were old-style liberals rather than new radicals, though some of the latter (like Newton D. Baker) also remained loyal. They felt defensive about it, however, whereas the old-style liberals did not. For these latter, indeed, Wilsonian "internationalism" eventually became a variety of imperialism as unapologetic as any that had preceded it.

3. Dewey: "Our National Dilemma," *NR*, XXII (March 24, 1920), p. 118; *Characters and Events*, Vol. II, p. 619.

beginning, that the Allies were fighting not for democracy so much as for national self-aggrandizement.

Had the pacifists, then, been right from the first? Dewey admitted that "the consistent pacifist has much to urge now in his own justification."[4] Nevertheless, he still insisted that the pacifists had been wrong in the main and the realists right. The great crusade had failed not because the United States had entered the war but because she had not used her influence as a belligerent to force the Allies to abandon their imperialistic war aims. Not only the pacifists but the policymakers themselves had underestimated the uses of physical force in international politics. The realists alone, he implied, had understood that idealism was not enough to force the Allies to the American way of thinking. But he did not explain how a country was supposed to have used "force to the limit" against its own allies.[5]

It was the realists, surely, who did not understand the role of force. During the war they had repeatedly called for a revision of war aims. (For that matter, so had the pacifists.) But they had tied the demand for democratic war aims to the demand for Germany's democratization in such a way as to undermine them both. They saw the revision of war aims as a manipulative device for prying the German people from their government. They reasoned that if the Allies were to renounce "annexations and indemnities," the German people would make peace rather than continue the war for the sake of spoils. Rather than continue the war, they would overthrow their rulers and make peace with the Allies. The democratization of war aims, in the liberal strategy, was a device not for bringing

4. Dewey: "The Discrediting of Idealism," *NR*, XX (Oct. 8, 1919), p. 285; *Characters and Events*, Vol. II, p. 630.

5. Ibid., p. 631.

about an immediate and general discussion of peace terms (as it was in the pacifist strategy) but for engineering the fall of "German autocracy," a government with which, in the liberal view, negotiations were out of the question.

What this strategy ignored was precisely the question of force. The Kaiser's government fell at the end of the war, but its fall did not thereby bring about an inconclusive peace. The Allies proceeded to inflict on the new government the same terms with which they had threatened the old. They were able to do so because no force opposed them. The German army was the only force that might have stood in their way, and the German army had collapsed. Only when the army collapsed did the Kaiser fall. The American liberals underestimated the loyalty of the German people to their government, a loyalty so strong that only military defeat called it into question. They were the victims of their own propaganda: having convinced themselves that the imperial government was an inhuman autocracy, they assumed that this truth would be equally obvious to the Germans. They were also the victims of their belief in the educative influence of propaganda. The strategy of democratizing Germany by advertising the war as a war for democracy was a particularly striking example of the manipulative approach to politics, and its failure might have served once and for all to show the limits of the concept of social engineering, especially when applied to the relations between sovereign states. But even as they confessed that "the defeat of idealistic aims," in Dewey's words, had been "enormous," the social planners continued to uphold the strategy which had led to that defeat.[6] The strategy itself, they contended, had been sound. The fault lay with Wilson's failure to carry it out.

Deserting Wilson, therefore, the war liberals now advocated withdrawal from Europe at the very moment when the argu-

6. Ibid., p. 630.

ments for participation had become almost irrefutable. Even if one conceded that the war had ended disastrously, with Germany prostrate and the Allies blindly and perversely exacting from the new republic (which they themselves had called into being) retribution for the sins of the old monarchy; even if one conceded that Europe was in ruins, the new boundaries as arbitrary as the old, the landscape devastated, the people starving; even if one conceded that the League of Nations had proved to be not the foundation of a new world order but a holy alliance of reactionary powers thrown up in the face of social revolution—even if one conceded all this and more, it did not follow that the United States should therefore retire into its former seclusion, resolutely turning its back on the chaos and misery abroad. Yet those who had insisted on America's duty to Europe in 1917 were only too eager to leave Europe to her fate in 1919, when her condition was if anything more desperate than ever.

Overnight the advocates of political realism adopted the style of passionate sectarianism. Even Walter Lippmann cast off his habitual reserve and denounced the treaty as a monstrous injustice. Writing to his friend Newton D. Baker in June, 1919, he accused Wilson of having broken almost every promise he had ever made. Wilson and the other peacemakers had set up over the Saar Valley a regime which was "humanly intolerable," had transferred German territory to Poland, Denmark, and Italy, and had forced separatism on Austria; all in violation of "the most solemn assurances." Not content with that, they had disarmed Germany, saddled her with impossible reparations ("the most drastic kind of interference in the internal life of Germany"), and then excluded her from the League of Nations. As for the League itself, it represented nothing more than a means of preserving the territorial and political *status quo* and of encouraging France in her imperial delusions. "It's a very dark moment," Lippmann wrote. The prospect of war and revolution was "appalling," and "the responsibility resting upon the men who commit the American people to detailed participation" in the settlement was "simply enormous."[7]

Baker agreed that the terms of peace were unsatisfactory; but what was the alternative? If Wilson had left the conference, there would have been "no disinterested moderating force present at all." If the conference should break up in disagreement—it was then in the final stages of securing Germany's agreement to the treaty—Europe would be plunged into further turmoil. New revolutions would break out, "indefinitely postponing relief measures and perhaps creating new and terrible areas of distress before any sort of settlement could be made." "I certainly have not a compromising temper," Baker declared, ". . . but clearly we can't wait to start all over again; too many people would die in the meantime." Moreover, the larger situation might yet be retrieved. Democracy was still a "rising tide"; wrongs committed in the past might be redressed "when the tempest has abated"; the League, "wisely administered and sympathetically supported," would engender a spirit of accommodation. This last was too optimistic, but it was difficult to escape the main force of Baker's argument, that conditions in Europe would not wait upon a renegotiation of the treaty of peace. "The thing I can't get out of my imagination," Baker declared, "is some pictures I saw of starving babies in Budapest hospitals, who were plainly dying. If I could once feel that they and others like them were fed, I think I would be more willing to debate at length for conditions which more nearly respond to our ideals."[8]

7. Lippmann to Baker, June 9, 1919, Newton D. Baker MSS, Library of Congress.
8. Baker to Lippmann, June 13, 1919, Newton D. Baker MSS.

Those who had once wept over the German atrocities in Belgium, most of which had never even taken place, were now deaf to such appeals. Turning to Colonel House, Lippmann poured out his disappointment. He had "hoped up to the very last for a Treaty which would in a measure redeem our promises to the world" and which "would not open the suspicion that the Covenant is a new Holy Alliance." The outcome of the peace conference had "shaken the faith of millions of men in the integrity of those who now rule the world." The best that could happen now was that Wilson would admit his failure. "The world can endure honest disappointment, and no one can complain of a failure confessed. . . . But I see nothing but pain and disorder and confusion if this first act of honesty is not performed."[9]

In May, 1919, the editors of *The New Republic*, "after much searching of heart and prolonged discussion," decided "to write ourselves out from under the Treaty." "It is a bitter decision to make," wrote Croly to Louis D. Brandeis, "because it is practically a confession of failure, so far as our work during the last few years is concerned." But the decision had been unanimous; everyone agreed that "the League is not powerful enough to redeem the treaty."[1] Only six weeks before, when *The Nation* had expressed just such opinions as these, *The New Republic* pointed out that its rival stood side by side with the most reactionary members of the United States Senate.[2] It must have cost the editors an effort to swallow their words.

Whether *The New Republic* looked back or looked ahead,

9. Lippmann to House, July 19, 1919, Edward M. House MSS, Yale University Library.

1. Croly to Brandeis, May 13, 1919, Louis D. Brandeis MSS, University of Louisville Law Library; "Peace at Any Price," *NR*, XIX (May 24, 1919), pp. 100–2.

2. "The Nation Attacks the Covenant," *NR*, XVIII (April 5, 1919), p. 298.

the view was dark. If the past was a record of failure, the future was blacker still, for in rejecting the treaty *The New Republic* severed its last links to the administration and thereby condemned itself, so it appeared, to political impotence. The new arrangement may have suited Walter Weyl, who had long chafed under Croly's reluctance to offend the administration, but there is evidence that Croly found his isolation uncongenial.[3] He spent the remaining ten years of his life looking in vain for another statesman to whom he could attach himself and his magazine. As for Lippmann, he parted company with *The New Republic*, struck out on his own, and by sheer persistence eventually raised himself into a kind of political institution in his own right, an unofficial embodiment of the national purpose. Such influence as he came to wield, however, he owed not to his intimacy with men in power but to his independence of them. His later successes as a free-lance columnist underscored his earlier failures as an editor of a journal which had deliberately sought to work in closest harmony with the government, even at the expense of its editorial independence. The editors of *The New Republic*, after breaking with Roosevelt, had gone to extreme lengths to establish their devotion to Wilson, without effecting in the slightest, it would seem, the policies he pursued. They had conferred every week with Colonel House so that they "might write intelligently," as House explained in his diary, "and not conflict with the purposes of the government."[4] Croly had urged House to

3. For Weyl's growing impatience with *The New Republic,* see his MS diary (in the possession of the family, and quoted by permission of Nathaniel Weyl), July 25, Aug. 10, Aug. 17, 1918. "The paper," he thought, "should be more of a fighting organ."

4. House MS Diary, July 26, 1917. For the weekly visits, see also the following entries: Jan. 15, 1917 ("Walter Lippmann and Croly came for information for this week's issue of the New Republic. I gave them enough food for thought to keep them on the right road."); Jan. 22, 1917 ("Lippmann and Croly came for their weekly talk to get information in order to

"let us know whether or not we are misinterpreting what the President is trying to do." He and Lippmann, he once said, "are more interested in doing what little we can to back the President up in his work than in anything else we have ever tried to do through the New Republic."[5] Yet the advice of *The New Republic*, in small matters as in large, was consistently ignored. When Croly urged the administration to sponsor a lecture tour by Norman Angell, one of *The New Republic*'s English contributors—it would be "of great assistance," he thought, "to the general propaganda for the kind of war for which the American people are fighting"—Wilson told House that Angell's presence in the country would only be "embarrassing to the Administration." He did not want people to get the impression that Englishmen wanted an early peace. "This is a line," he added, "which I am afraid the 'New Republic' generally are going to take, i.e. that of 'the smothered opposition to the war which exists in England.' "[6] Later, when Lippmann tendered advice about propaganda, Wilson was "very much puzzled as to who sent Lippmann over to inquire into matters of propaganda." "I have found his judgment most unsound," the President continued, "and therefore entirely unserviceable, in matters of that sort because he, in common with the men of The New Republic, has ideas about the war and its purposes which are highly unorthodox from my point of view."[7] The rewards of loyalty were meager indeed.

---

write intelligently in the New Republic."); Jan. 30, Feb. 5, April 17, Sept. 21, 1917; Feb. 14, 1918 ("Croly came to discuss the President's foreign policy so as to be certain the New Republic properly understood it.").

5. Croly to House, Dec. 26, 1916, quoted in Charles Budd Forcey: "Intellectuals in Crisis: Croly, Weyl, Lippmann and the New Republic" (unpublished Ph.D. dissertation, University of Wisconsin, 1954), pp. 552–3.

6. Croly to House, April 17, 1917, and Wilson to House, April 20, 1917, House MSS.

7. Wilson to House, Aug. 31, 1918, Woodrow Wilson MSS, 2nd series, Library of Congress.

[VI]

When one looks back over the entire record of the realists'
response to the war, it is difficult to avoid the conclusion that
they acted throughout from motives of which they were not entirely aware. Having gradually worked out, in the first two and
a half years of the war, a case for nonintervention which was
logically convincing but which they were clearly uneasy in
holding, they proceeded with evident relief to throw it over at
the first opportunity. In the spring of 1917 they argued for
intervention, but as soon as it became clear that the original
objections to intervention had not been entirely overcome, their
former doubts began to return. In an effort to drive away these
doubts, they convinced themselves that the war would end
in a worldwide upsurge of democracy. Even then they could
not get rid of the nagging suspicion that these hopes were
merely "a sugar coating," in Dewey's phrase, "for the bitter
core of violence and greed."[8] And when the war ended not in
democracy but in a victor's peace, the pragmatic liberals rejected Wilsonian internationalism as eagerly as they had embraced it, with an air of giving up a position that had long
since become untenable. In the years that followed, most of
the new radicals who had supported the war publicly repented
of their sins. But these confessions, though they may have been
good for the souls of those who made them, left unanswered
the question of why they had supported the war in the first
place.

Presumably the answer was the one suggested by Randolph
Bourne, that the intellectuals had gone to war out of "an
unanalyzable feeling that this was a war in which we had to

8. Twice, on widely separated occasions, he raised this doubt; see *Characters and Events*, Vol. II, pp. 565, 630.

be.'"[9] Logic may have dictated nonintervention, but something deeper than logic dictated war. The thirst for action, the craving for involvement, the longing to commit themselves to the onward march of events—these things dictated war. The realists feared isolation not only for America but for themselves. Accordingly, they went to war and invented the reasons for it afterward.

Long after the war was over, some of the war liberals tried to invent a retrospective rationale for their support of the war. Walter Lippmann argued that it had been necessary to go to war in order to prevent Germany from upsetting the world balance of power.[1] It was a plausible argument, but it was not the one Lippmann gave in 1917. On the contrary, practically everything he wrote about the war at the time shows that, like other radicals, he feared an Allied victory almost as much as a German one. Moreover, his criticism of the treaty indicates that his support of the war rested not on considerations of the balance of power but on Wilson's implicit "promises" that the war would have a democratizing influence on world politics. On another occasion Lippmann explicitly said: "We are conducting the war on the assumption that there is a distinction between the German government and the German people."[2] That statement does not sound like the hard-boiled *Realpolitik* which Lippmann later claimed to have professed all along.

The First World War was the great adventure for which a generation of Americans had long been preparing themselves. Even the editors of *The New Republic* in their paneled offices— men deeply committed to the life of the intellect—quickened to the distant sound of battle. How much more insistent was the

9. Bourne: "A War Diary," *Untimely Papers*, p. 96.

1. Walter Lippmann: *U. S. Foreign Policy: Shield of the Republic* (Boston: Little, Brown; 1943), pp. 33-7.

2. Memorandum for Newton D. Baker, n.d. [Aug., 1917], entitled "Reply to the Pope's Proposal," Baker MSS.

war's appeal to men with a more pronounced enthusiasm for public excitements! For men such as these, the war was more than a historical event, it was a collective fantasy. That the war was in some sense the fulfillment of a dark and unacknowledged wish becomes clear when one turns from *The New Republic* and its friends to men caught up more completely in the daily rush of events. The "unconscious" character of the war emerges with particular clarity from the history of the curious friendship, to which we must now turn, between Lincoln Colcord, a liberal journalist, and Colonel House; a friendship based on a shared vision of the future in which dreams of the cooperative commonwealth were mixed with dreams of death and destruction.

7 / Lincoln Colcord and Colonel House: *Dreams of Terror and Utopia*

[I]

LINCOLN COLCORD WAS BORN IN 1883, BUT HIS ORIGINS EVOKE a much earlier period of American history. He was the son of a sea captain, and his family had been seafarers in Maine for five generations. He was born at sea, off Cape Horn, during one of his father's voyages. For the first ten years of his life he traveled with his father up and down the China coast. His formal schooling, begun late, ended when he left the University of Maine in his junior year. After that he worked intermittently as a civil engineer in the Maine woods, wrote a few stories and poems, married, and settled down at the family seat of Searsport on the Maine coast, apparently to a life of uninterrupted domesticity.

Nothing in Colcord's early life seems to contain any suggestion of what was to follow: his sudden emergence, in 1916, as the highly prized Washington correspondent of the Philadelphia *Public Ledger*; his intimacy with people close to the center of national power; his political radicalism. Such a career seemed hardly to follow from a boyhood spent at sea and in the New England wilderness. Colcord's tastes ran to literature, history, horticulture, and nautical subjects, and his tempera-

ment seemed to thrive on solitary reflection.[1] He once wrote to
Colonel House of his fondness for Searsport.

> It's not a bad place, much like many others, but the secret of our
> love for it lies in what I have just said—we know it intimately.
> This is the lesson I get from Thoreau. Love your own pond. All
> are beautiful. Be contented where you are. Content!—a lost word
> in our America. This restless ambition—I cannot feel the truth
> of it. I cannot follow there. I am quite willing to be out of touch
> with my times. I would live as if the times were out of touch
> with me.[2]

Yet within a few months of writing these lines Colcord
(like his sister Joanna, who had become a social worker) was
completely caught up in the current of political reform. He who
spoke so proudly of being out of touch with his times had
been captivated by a political emotion the essence of which was
precisely the sense of oneself as part of a larger movement of
humanity, the sense of having given oneself up to what Colcord
once called "the majority spirit of service." Solitude was at an
end. Colcord now belonged to a self-conscious group of reformers; and "spreading through our group," his publisher
H. B. Brougham declared, the spirit of reform was "giving
rise to a new school of statesmanship."

> If I do not mistake it has in it, also, the germs of a new age of
> social customs, art, and literature [Brougham went on]. What-
> ever our faith summons us to do will become possible, and with
> us shall be the responsibility for bringing this nation into its full
> stature. . . . Simultaneously with the organization of its capabili-
> ties of labor the imagination of the people will be set free. As their
> political and industrial will is expressed in new decisions their
> life will be invigorated and be reflected in a sincerer drama, in

1. See his long correspondence with George Kennan on the subject of
flowers and gardening, in the George Kennan MSS, Library of Congress.
2. Colcord to House, June 23, 1916, Edward M. House MSS, Yale University Library.

books that regard its issues with courage and frankness and in music and painting that may express with originality and daring the aspirations that rise from vital national consciousness.

Nor shall the "spirit of women" be forgotten in this age of emancipation. "Our vision will become darkness if this should be forgotten."[3]

The letter that contained these exalted opinions, it is interesting to note, began simply as a declaration of friendship, Brougham having taken a great liking to his new reporter.[4] "It is a friendship, Colcord, such as few men know." But no sooner had he said that than Brougham went on to speak of the new spirit "spreading through our group." For some progressives every emotion, it appears, had been subtly politicized. Friendship, once an ideal in itself, could thrive now only in the context of larger expectations. The private and the public blended imperceptibly together, the one taking on the color of the other. Private pursuits came to seem sterile and unproductive unless invested with political meaning; while politics, on the other hand, came more and more to serve not as a forum for the resolution of competing interests, but as a screen on which men's inner ambitions and secret fears were most vividly projected. The politics of the conflict of interest, when it did not actually give way altogether, came to be increasingly overlaid with the politics of fantasy.

3. H. B. Brougham to Colcord, July 28, 1918, Lincoln Colcord MSS. These papers are in the possession of Mrs. Lincoln Colcord, and are quoted here with her permission and with the permission of Brooks Colcord.

4. To Colonel House, who had sponsored Colcord's appointment to the staff of the *Public Ledger*, Brougham wrote that although "Colcord is still new in this business," "if he is a cub he is a lion's cub, and waxing powerful. . . . Since he came here I have watched his course with an amazed admiration which I find it difficult to conceal. He is a man of hungry and indomitable energy, and facts are his prey, which he devours and assimilates with a veritable rapacity after the truth." (Brougham to House, July 19, 1917, House MSS.)

The career of Lincoln Colcord, no less than that of his publisher—a career in which political opinions were suffused with the kind of passion formerly associated with poetry and religion—was an omen of the age of total politics, in which men turn to the realm of power in search of satisfactions that once belonged to the realm of love and beauty. In another time, one imagines, Colcord would have cultivated the inner life. His tastes and habits of mind mark him as a survivor, even in his own time, of an earlier New England tradition with which, in fact, he liked to identify himself. He admired Thoreau, and sometimes he reminds one too of Hawthorne, not only in his sense of the dark undercurrent of life but in his increasingly ambiguous relation to men in power; in the 1930's, for instance, Colcord attempted to secure a patronage appointment for himself, as a deserving Democrat, from an administration whose policies he shortly came to abhor.[5] His friendship with Colonel House was likewise shot through with contradictions—an almost uncritical adulation on the one hand and on the other a quickness to condemn which exceeded the bounds of a reasonable skepticism about the motives of powerful men. Both, however, were aspects of the passionate commitment to politics so characteristic of men of this kind—the investing of politics with absolute values, the confusion of ultimate and immediate ends.

What was true of Colcord was true to a much more remarkable degree of Colonel Edward M. House. The tendencies that in Colcord (as in most radicals) were but dimly shadowed forth, in House achieved a kind of perfection. In House's case the confusion between the private and the public, between poetry and politics, became at times almost complete. House's public career, as he himself did not hesitate to point out, had the quality of proceeding according to a preconceived scenario

5. See Colcord to Franklin Roosevelt, March 22, 1933, House MSS.

or script, actor and author merged in one identity. No doubt House exaggerated the continuity and coherence of his career and the degree to which he himself had predetermined its course; but that is the point. He found it increasingly difficult to distinguish what was happening from what he had predicted was to happen. Indeed, the more reality diverged from his predictions, the more House convinced himself that his predictions were being borne out in every detail.

According to House's own account, his career as president-maker and adviser *extraordinaire*—astonishing enough on its face—had all been carefully plotted out beforehand. Having reached what he considered a dead end in the politics of his own state (Texas), where he had played an important advisory role in the progressive administration of Governor Hogg, he resolved to embark, he later explained, upon a more ambitious course in national politics. His health was too precarious to permit him to seek office himself, however, so he determined to attach himself to some leading figure of the times and through him to institute the reforms necessary to save the country from anarchy. Almost any public figure would do for his purpose, providing he could be elected President. Obviously some would do better than others; but that all would prove susceptible to his influence House never seemed to doubt. His vision of human nature was of something infinitely malleable, assuming one knew the secret of its malleability. Flattery, persuasion, appearing to yield to the better judgment of his superiors—whatever means were necessary to gain his ends, House was determined to employ.

As for the ends themselves—but here the clarity of House's design broke down. The ends toward which his efforts were presumably directed receded always from view. The means were all the ends in sight. Ostensibly the object of his ambition was to save the country from civil war, to save it from being torn apart by the struggle of class against class. Left to themselves, House argued, the plutocracy would persist in their reckless expropriation of natural and human resources, until the people would be forced in desperation to take up arms against them; and in the ensuing struggle civilization itself might perish. It was imperative, therefore, that the industrial order be reformed before it brought about its own destruction.

Such was the ostensible moral of *Philip Dru: Administrator,* the utopian novel published anonymously by House in 1912— his most coherent formulation of the problem at hand. Like so many utopian fantasies of this period, however, the novel relishes the scenes of violent national emergency against which it purports to be a warning. In *Philip Dru,* the action of which is set in the 1920's and 1930's, the dreaded civil war has come to pass. The country divides along sectional lines, democratic West against plutocratic East, and Philip Dru, a young West Point graduate who has renounced the army for a career as social critic, leads the forces of progress in a single decisive battle in which the forces of privilege go down to defeat. "A master mind had at last risen in the Republic."[6] Proclaiming himself "Administrator of the Republic," he assumes dictatorial powers and puts through a comprehensive program of reforms. In the manner of Napoleon—to whom he is several times implicitly compared—he crowns his domestic triumphs with foreign conquest. "In spite of repeated warnings from the United States, Mexico and the Central American Republics had obstinately continued their old time habit of revolutions without just cause."[7] Philip Dru marches into Mexico, overthrows a corrupt and reactionary regime, and eventually brings

6. Edward M. House: *Philip Dru: Administrator; A Story of Tomorrow, 1920-1935* (New York: B. W. Huebsch; 1912), p. 148.
7. Ibid., p. 280.

the whole of North America under the sway of the United States. Then, somewhat abruptly, he lays down his duties and sails out to the Pacific with his bride and devoted follower, Gloria Strawn. "Where were they bound? Would they return? These were the questions asked by all, but to which none could give answers."[8]

The mystery of his disappearance is only one of the implausible elements in the career of Philip Dru. One would expect a retiring dictator, at the very least, to leave instructions as to his succession; but House is not interested in such details, much less in the question of how the country, after the seven-year reign of Philip Dru, finds its way back to constitutional government. He makes only the most perfunctory attempts to explain either the origins or the consequences of the civil war, and what explanations he does offer betray an astonishing lack of political sophistication on the part of a man who spent most of his life in politics, and who, indeed, in many of his judgments about the First World War, showed himself to be more astute than most of his contemporaries. What is striking, in *Philip Dru*, is not House's belief in a "conspiracy" to overthrow popular government. Many progressives believed in the existence of an "invisible government," if not in a conspiracy; and there was plenty of evidence to bear them out. Amos Pinchot collected some of it in his *History of the Progressive Party*, which showed how the Morgan interests had been able to use Theodore Roosevelt's party of protest to advance their own designs.[9] In *Philip Dru* the "interests" also use an unsuspecting demagogue as the agent of their sinister plans, but the aura that surrounds these events belongs to the time of McKinley rather

8. Ibid., p. 299.
9. Amos R. E. Pinchot: *History of the Progressive Party 1912–1916*, ed. Helene Maxwell Hooker (New York: New York University Press; 1958).

than Roosevelt and George Perkins. Ignoring the evidence of his own time, House constructed a "conspiracy" which reminds one of nothing so much as the "front-porch campaign" waged by Marc Hanna on behalf of McKinley in 1896; except that Hanna's famous campaign fund, collected from businessmen frightened by the prospect of Bryan's victory, becomes in the novel a secret "corruption fund" raised by means of a blind pool. This "corruption fund," together with a plan to pack the Supreme Court, is the entire substance of House's "conspiracy"; yet "when the story was published it was clear to every far-sighted person that a crisis had come and that revolution was imminent."[1]

The disparity between cause and effect, in the matter of the civil war, is one indication that House's imagination ran to melodrama more than to history and politics. There is also the matter of the reforms laid down by dictator Dru. The "master mind" promulgates a new code of laws, a graduated income tax, a federal incorporation act, an act prohibiting holding companies and providing for government representation on the boards of directors of public utility companies, universal suffrage, a short ballot, and "burial reform," together with a law depriving the courts of their power to pass on the constitutionality of acts of Congress. Only the last of these could be described as a radical measure. The "revolution" is as pallid as the "conspiracy." Both episodes show House's political imagination to have been of the most conventional sort. He identified the imperfections of American society not with exploitation but with corruption, and he saw the remedy as a series of purely political reforms which would have left untouched the social and economic injustices so obvious to other reformers of his day. He conceived of urban poverty in terms

1. House: *Philip Dru*, p. 105.

of the widows and orphans of party platform rhetoric, when the real horror of the slums, as Jane Addams and others pointed out, was the dehumanizing of the poor themselves; so that the worst form of exploitation proved on investigation to be not the exploitation of labor by capital but the exploitation of immigrant children, in sweatshops, by their own parents. Such ironies were lost on Colonel House; his social sympathies were restricted, to say the least. He thought of Latin Americans as people sunk in the habit of revolution "without just cause." As for Negroes, "we lifted the yoke from the black man's neck, but we went too fast in our zeal for his welfare."[2]

The anomaly of *Philip Dru* is that a man of such completely conventional opinions as House should nevertheless have imagined himself as a revolutionary despot, an enemy of respectable society. When Philip Dru gives voice to his heretical views on the state of the nation, Gloria murmurs in horrified admiration: "A history professor I had once lost his position for talking like that."[3] Colonel House himself would never have committed the kind of indiscretion that might have cost him his job. Quite the reverse; he usually said what he thought people wanted to hear. Yet his daydreams were dreams of subversion and civil strife. They seem to reflect, not merely a shy and rather timid individual's wish for martial glory, but, beyond that, a fierce resentment against the society in which men like himself could rise to eminence and power. Along with other prominent men of his time—Theodore Roosevelt, for example—Colonel House nourished a deep suspicion that American society, having lost what Roosevelt called the martial virtues, might succumb to hardier races. That House should have shared these fears is not in itself surprising. What is

2. Ibid., p. 284.
3. Ibid., p. 11.

surprising is that he should have identified himself, in his fantasies, not with the forces of order but with the forces of destruction.

[II]

House and Colcord seem to have met in 1916, possibly somewhat earlier. In that year House recommended Colcord to the Philadelphia *Public Ledger*, where Colcord remained until 1918, after which he went to work for Oswald Garrison Villard on *The Nation*. In 1916 the *Public Ledger*, under the direction of Brougham and John J. Spurgeon, was momentarily a paper of liberal views. In fact, House had hopes of making it into a semi-official organ of the Wilson administration, along with the New York *World* and *The New Republic*, on which he had similar designs. More than that, he hoped through his numerous friendships with young progressive journalists to provide himself with access to the public, in order not so much to air the views of the administration as to air his own particular interpretation of what the administration was doing. For although his opinions not infrequently diverged from the President's and diverged markedly from those of other advisers in Washington (a fact he was at least intermittently aware of), House did not hesitate to represent himself to reporters as the authentic voice of Wilsonian democracy. And his acquaintances were not reluctant to believe him. Not only did House charm them with his attentions, which formed so striking a contrast to the coldness with which they were received by the President himself, but he also convinced them by subtle inference that his own political ideas were more advanced than Wilson's, and that he himself, in fact, was the chief force impelling Wilson in a progressive direction.

To insure publicity for his views, then, House collected

about him a circle of able and energetic young newspapermen
—Colcord and William C. Bullitt of the *Public Ledger*, Frank
Cobb and Herbert Bayard Swope of the New York *World*,
David Lawrence of the New York *Evening Post*, Walter Lippmann of *The New Republic*. Together, they constituted a personal following, all of them devoted to the Colonel, all of them
convinced that he represented the pinnacle of political wisdom
and convinced, moreover, that his views were those of the
administration as a whole. It was through their innocent efforts,
in part, that the liberal public was so long deceived about the
real direction of Wilsonian foreign policy. If Herbert Croly
could privately predict in June, 1917, that the war would not
last the winter, and if he could assure Colonel House as late
as September, 1917, of his expectation "that a really vital peace
discussion . . . will be taking place during the coming Fall,"
his optimism, which was by no means unusual, owed something to *The New Republic's* easy access to the Colonel.[4] In
his innumerable talks with his friends, House succeeded in
"giving them the right steer," as he liked to put it.[5] But in
giving people the right steer—that is, in convincing them of
what, after all, liberals wanted most to believe—he experienced
the additional pleasure of hearing himself lavishly praised.
That was at least as important as the satisfaction of seeing his
opinions in print. Thus, when Frederic C. Howe came to vent
his fear that the war would lead to a "hate campaign," House
"gave him an insight into my thoughts" and duly noted in his
diary that it "seemed to please him much, for upon leaving he
said quite fervently, 'I pray your life may be spared to do the
things you have in mind.' "[6] That House should so often have

4. Alice [Stone Blackwell] to Jane Addams, June 13, 1917, Addams MSS;
Croly to House, Sept. 7, 1917, House MSS.

5. See, e.g., his remark after a talk with Lawrence: "I gave him the right
steer, and he wrote the article as it appeared." House MS Diary, Feb. 1, 1918.

6. House MS Diary, May 11, 1917.

felt impelled to record such tributes indicates the degree to which all his personal relations seem in one way or another to have turned on a pattern of mutual flattery. The surface of his friendships was rarely broken by the critical exchange of opposing opinions. When such exchanges took place—as eventually happened in the case of Colcord—House tended to waver in his affections. Such were the habits of a man whose gift, it was said, was "the gift of agreeing with everybody."[7]

Few people outside the Wilson administration, in the critical year 1917, were in such constant contact with House as Lincoln Colcord. Colcord saw House at least two or three times a week. At one point he seems to have made daily visits.[8] Nor were these visits perfunctory. Often they ended in an invitation to lunch or dinner and an evening of conversation. At other times, when House was in New York, they took the form of walks through the city, "usually up and down Park Ave. between 53rd Street and Grand Central; when the Colonel has more time, they swing off to Madison Ave. and Fifth Ave. They usually last a half or three quarters of an hour, beginning at eleven thirty."[9] In addition, there was a constant exchange of letters. And although the main advantage of the relationship, for House, lay in his rather calculated effort to make out of Colcord a mouthpiece for his views, it is clear also that there was, for a time at least, a deeper bond as well, made firmer still by Colcord's unconcealed admiration. On at least one occasion House confided to Colcord opinions which were not only not intended for publication but which, as he told Colcord, he had confided to no one else.

House was by temperament secretive and duplicitous. Yet

7. *Liberator*, I (Dec., 1918), p. 5.

8. House MS Diary, May 22, 1917: "Lincoln Colcord made his usual daily visit to discuss articles for the Public Ledger."

9. Colcord MS Diary, April 14, [1917].

one gets the impression that he came as close to opening his mind to Colcord as to anybody. The unguarded character of some of his observations suggests that in the presence of a sympathetic audience House could, on occasion, throw off his habitual caution; even as on other occasions, pretending to be in full accord with Colcord's opinions, he said things that were directly contradicted by things he had said to other people. Most of the time he spoke in accents that seemed to Colcord deeply prophetic. These conversations appealed to Colcord's sense of the apocalyptic, so characteristic of the new radicalism as a whole. It was this habit of mind that enabled so many of the new radicals to reconcile progressivism with support of the First World War. The war was the cataclysm from which the brave new world would arise.

Not that House and Colcord did not have certain immediate misgivings about America's entering the war. In February, 1917, Colcord, anticipating President Wilson's famous conversation with Frank Cobb, told Colonel House that his "only real objection" to our entering the war was the "thought of our passing into a state of emotion and unreason." "When I thought of another great nation passing into a state of emotion, losing the ability to see straight, beginning to hate and be hated, forsaking its sound basis of logic and reason, I must confess that I had my doubts."[1] But the consideration that finally overrode such doubts was the one Colcord had set down in an article two months before: "It is unthinkable that all Europe is to fall into the lap of reactionaries; that out of the present conflict is not to emerge a new and more liberal order of internationalism, whereby vital matters may be settled without resort to arms."[2]

1. Colcord MS Diary, Feb. 24, 1917.
2. Colcord: "The United States as a Sea Power," *New Republic*, IX (Dec. 30, 1916), p. 241.

That a reactionary Europe was unthinkable was implicit also in the position taken by Colonel House. Sensing, correctly enough, that Europe was passing through some momentous and fundamental transformation, House, like most American progressives, assumed that whatever was happening could lead only to upheavals that in the long run would prove constructive in nature. (As Colcord once wrote to President Wilson: "Ultimately, of course, there can be no disaster in revolution."[3]) Nor was House blind to the immediate advantages of the revolution that the European countries seemed to be undergoing. Revolutionary energies might be manipulated so as to hasten the downfall of the German monarchy and the end of the war. As early as June, 1915, House had urged the President to exonerate the German people of any responsibility for the sinking of the Lusitania, "stating that we were fighting for their deliverance as well as the deliverance of Europe."[4]

Now, in the spring of 1917, he agreed with Colcord that Wilson's war message ought to be interpreted to mean that peace with "the German Government as constituted at present" was impossible; in other words, that the Allies ought to encourage the German people to overthrow their government by promising lenient terms of peace—"peace without victory"— if they did so.[5] By May, 1917, House was recommending such a strategy to Wilson, who replied that it "chimed exactly" with his own thoughts.[6]

In June, however, Wilson issued a ringing call to war that seemed to preclude not only peace with the German government but any discussion of peace terms whatsoever. This

3. Colcord to Wilson, Dec. 8, 1917, Colcord MSS.
4. House to Wilson, June 3, 1915, in Charles Seymour: *Intimate Papers of Colonel House* (Boston: Houghton Mifflin; 1926), Vol. II, p. 466n.
5. Colcord MS Diary, April 5, 1917.
6. Seymour: *Intimate Papers*, Vol. III, pp. 132-3.

Flag Day speech was for most radicals the first intimation
that in the general enthusiasm for the war Wilson's peace
without victory might be lost sight of, that Wilson might lose
sight of it himself. At the same time, men like Lincoln
Colcord found it difficult to believe that they had lost the
power to influence men and events. Nor did anyone do more
to sustain the illusion of power than Colonel House, who of
course shared it himself. When Colcord asked him "if he
had not noticed a trace of imperialism, a certain appeal to
emotionalism, a false note, in the President's Flag Day Speech,"
House nodded, but he denied that there was "any danger of
the President's turning imperialist or losing some of his former
liberalism." "You know as well as I do that no such thing
is possible."[7]

In fact, however, Colonel House had no reservations about
the Flag Day speech at all. He fully approved of it. At least
that is what he told the President.[8] Although he had fretted
because Wilson did not consult him about the text in advance,
and although the speech when finally delivered would seem
to have confirmed his fear that the President might speak
"too casually and without sufficient consideration," in his diary
he pronounced it "great." The President, he thought, had
finally made "a proper indictment of Germany."[9]

House in truth steered a tortuous course. When he talked
to radicals, he represented himself as prodding a reluctant
President into a discussion of peace terms in the midst of
war, even at the risk of offending the Allies. Yet in April,
1917, just after the United States entered the war, it was
Wilson, not House, who wanted to force a discussion of peace

7. Colcord MS Diary, June 25, 1917.
8. House to Wilson, June 14, 1917, Seymour: *Intimate Papers*, Vol. III,
p. 137.
9. House MS Diary, June 14, 1917. For his earlier misgivings, see the
entry for June 13, 1917.

THE NEW RADICALISM IN AMERICA (1889-1963) · 240

terms with the British. He thought "it would be a pity to have Balfour go home without a discussion of the subject." House, however, "argued against discussing peace terms with the Allies."[1] "Differences would be certain to arise and the problem now was to beat Germany and not discuss peace."[2]

Two months later the roles were reversed. House began to see the necessity of persuading the British that a decisive defeat of Germany might be impossible to achieve.[3] He went so far as to suggest an exchange of views between the *Berliner Tageblatt* and the New York *World,* designed to disclose any agreement that might subsequently become the basis of negotiations between Germany and the Allies. Wilson, rejecting the idea, repeated the very arguments made to him in April by House. "England and France *have not the same views with regard to peace that we have* by any means." When the war was over, Wilson thought, we could "force them to our way of thinking, because by that time they will, among other things, be financially in our hands; but we cannot force them now, and any attempt to speak for them or to speak our common mind would bring on disagreements which would inevitably come to the surface in public and rob the whole thing of its effect."[4] House had counseled more effectively, perhaps, than he knew; the position first outlined so persuasively by himself, that nothing must be allowed to interfere with the Allied unity on which military victory depended, was to remain Wilson's position throughout the rest of the war, in spite of all attempts to persuade him that the Allies would never again be so likely to listen to American advice and to end the war short of total victory.

1. House MS Diary, April 26, 1917.
2. House MS Diary, April 22, 1917.
3. House MS Diary, May 13, 1917.
4. Wilson to House, July 21, 1917, Ray Stannard Baker MSS, Library of Congress.

His liberal friends knew nothing of the Colonel's earlier opposition to talk of peace. In "liberal circles," as Colcord wrote from Washington in September, House's opinions continued to be "held in the highest regard."[5] The more the progressives became conscious of the rising demand for total victory, at home as well as abroad, the more they looked to Colonel House as the man who stood between the President's original program and the triumph of reaction. House himself came increasingly to share this view of the role he was destined, it seemed, to play. He began to imagine himself as the tribune of the people, engaged with the representatives of organized imperialism in a battle to the death. He caught glimpses of Armageddon: the old order collapsing, the new democracy rising on its ruins, himself in the center, his possession of the most intimate secrets of the corruption of the old regime the key to power in the new.

In June, 1917, he unburdened himself to Colcord of an extraordinary series of recollections and prophecies.[6] It was in this conversation that he assured Colcord that Wilson's Flag Day speech did not imply a retreat from progressivism. After lunch the talk turned to *Philip Dru,* which Colcord had read, it turned out, with enthusiasm. It struck him now as a "strange coincidence" that House had written the book before he even knew Wilson and "long before the present world-crisis had been dreamed of." Yet the book seemed to have predicted just such events as were now unfolding.

House agreed that it was "strange enough."

"I feel queerly about it sometimes [he went on]. It is an actual fact that I didn't know the President then, so couldn't have had him in mind. I was simply putting down how the job ought to be done. I remember Houston's telling me I was all wrong; that the

5. Philadelphia *Public Ledger,* Sept. 28, 1917.
6. Colcord MS Diary, June 25, 1917.

job of readjustment ought to be accomplished through the existing machinery of government. I asked him how you could reform the political system through the political system—said that that would be a job for a century at least. I wanted quick action, so created an imaginative circumstance whereby my hero could become temporarily a benevolent dictator."

"Well," said the Colonel deliberately, "it wouldn't have been the same, of course, or so good, but I could have made a go of it some way with any Democratic President."

"Champ Clark, for instance?" I suggested.

"Yes, Champ Clark. I would rather have worked with Champ Clark than Bryan; Bryan is so opinionated. But I resolved to tackle it with someone. I had left state politics for good and all, and resolved to enter national politics. I had even made up my mind to try it with a Republican President, if he wasn't too reactionary. I don't think I have told you that I had Roosevelt in mind one time, and went to the trouble of getting a personal estimate of his mind?"

But when he went to see Roosevelt, House explained, he was distressed to find that Roosevelt monopolized the conversation and paid no attention to House's advice about how Roosevelt might "break down the solid South." "So I didn't bother with Roosevelt any more. I saw that I could never work with him."

Warming to his subject, the Colonel's imagination leaped from past to future.

"Do you know what I have made up my mind to do? I will tell you something now that I have never told anyone, not even Miss Denman [House's secretary] or Mrs. House. If I see that the Peace conference is going wrong, if I become convinced that liberalism is not coming through and that there is no hope of its coming through, I have made up my mind to throw my whole life and career into the balance, to tell what I know, to have all the cards out on the table, to kick up a rumpus that will ring from end to end of the world—in short, to turn on the crowd I have been playing with, and appeal to the peoples of the world. I know that such a course would sacrifice all my connections and friendships, would ruin my reputation with those whom I work with to-day, and would spoil my present and future efficiency; but nevertheless I have decided that it must be done. I feel that I have been living my life for that crisis, for that demand. I mean to concentrate my whole life on that moment. The people do not know me; I have almost forcibly kept myself out of the public eye, with a definite purpose of playing the game of diplomacy on its own ground. But I know how bad and incapable the diplomats are. I will turn socialist, even anarchist, overnight. The people will hear from me then. I have never been able to tackle the official side of public life; my health has not permitted it. I could have done it well. I have simply been unable to think of it. But I can do this thing that I have just told you—and then close the page."

Colcord sat for some time looking at him in silence.

I am willing to confess [he wrote that night] that I was overcome by the greatness of his conception. After a while I managed to tell him imperfectly what I felt. This is the man whom the people do not know.

"I hope it will not need to happen sir," I said. "But perhaps it might be the best way, too. I would like to be with you on such a program. You don't realize, perhaps, that you could not possibly fail—that your triumph would be complete and absolute, and that you would appear before the people as the great religious figure of the times."

"Don't be too sure," he said. "I'm not cynical when I say that the gang is strong."

"And if you don't have to do it," I said reflectively, "if the conference results in liberalism, that will be through you, too. You are the greatest potential power in the world to-day."

"Perhaps I'll always be potential," he said, I thought rather wistfully. I had never heard him speak of his health in this way before. More than once he has told me of his scorn of office, of his inability to speak in public, etc., as the real reason why he has not gone into the active field of politics. This is a deeper reason—it slipped out unawares.

The sentimentality that ran through so much of the progressive world view, a counterpoint to the high seriousness which the new radicals brought to experience, is never more apparent than at such moments as these, when the "quest for adventure" that Jane Addams and others invested with such complicated and subtle meaning seemed finally to dissolve into the clichés which the phrase itself so readily calls to mind. The unsung hero, "the man whom the people do not know," whose good deeds cannot be publicly avowed; the man who cunningly plays "the gang's" game, only to turn on the adversary at the last moment with terrible vengeance—these were the dreams drawn from boys' fiction and popular romance; drawn also, in many of their details, from the romance of city life which the journalism of the day had done so much to popularize. The idea of Armageddon as an exposé owed something to the muckrakers; and Colcord's vision of Colonel House as "the great religious figure of the times" breathed the atmosphere of the yellow press, in which all values had so long been systematically cheapened and debased. The spirit of the city room presides over the entire scene. Note the self-consciousness with which House spins out his plans and with which Colcord writes them down. This consciousness of oneself as a leading figure in the biggest news story of all time, this sense of how it will look in print when the story finally breaks, is the note that reverberates throughout the conversation. In the modern world, so comparatively uncomplicated an emotion as ambition is an anachronism. In a world which manifests itself through the mass media, ambition is more likely to take the form of a kind of voyeurism directed in upon oneself, a longing to see oneself as one appears to the world, immortalized in the glare of publicity. One's own life, even when it promises to realize the adventures which for so long seemed to happen only to others, comes to be lived vicariously. The self becomes as an other to itself.

A terrible violence pervades these fantasies; yet these were not men baffled and frustrated by poverty or prejudice and wishing to revenge themselves on all the oppressors ranged against them, but members of the comfortable middle class, men who shared (or at least had the illusion of sharing) in the highest decisions of state. By any measure one might choose to apply, the world had showered its favors with unusual generosity on Colonel House; yet his monologue culminates in a vision of destruction. He longs to drag down the world about his shoulders, "to kick up a rumpus that will ring from end to end of the world."

[III]

Most disturbing of all, to one who reads over these records half a century later, is that into the fabric of these fantasies there should have been woven more than a single thread of historical truth. The fact is that the world was coming more and more to resemble what Colcord and House imagined it to be. The world indeed was "plunging on to revolution," in Colcord's memorable phrase. The secrets, moreover, of the old regime, symbolized by the secret treaties, were about to be exposed for all to see, exactly as House imagined. Yet the part in which he cast himself, in his daydreams, bore less and less resemblance to the one he played in life. Heroes appeared, men who turned on "the gang" and published the evidence of its iniquity. But it was not House but Lenin who published the secret treaties; House, meanwhile, was drawn into a tangled web of bargains and compromises. Not House but Woodrow Wilson attempted at Versailles to appeal to the peoples of the world over the heads of their leaders, while House behind his back engaged in old-style intrigue and secret diplomacy, undertaking negotiations which on more than one occasion undermined the President's position.[7]

House by then had lost the confidence of people like Lincoln Colcord. In fact, Colcord now tended to imagine acts of perfidy and betrayal which had not even taken place. In March, 1919, he accused the Allied leaders of having decided to invade Bolshevik Russia with an army of 200,000 men—a report, as House hastened to assure him, in which there was "absolutely no truth."[8] By that time the failure of the Versailles conference either to recognize and support the revolution, in accordance with Wilsonian principles, or to take effective steps to suppress it, had confirmed Colcord's sense of the impotence of the old order. In 1917, however, it was still possible for him to imagine that Colonel House would "dominate the conference, and have things measurably his own way." "There will not be a diplomat or statesman in Europe," Colcord thought then, "who can match him when the peace conference comes."[9]

Throughout the year, Colcord continued to express reservations about Wilson's incipient imperialism and House continued to quiet them. The President, he explained, by his own

7. See Paul Birdsall: *Versailles Twenty Years After* (New York: Reynal and Hitchcock; 1941), *passim*; and for an account of House's devious negotiations with the Allies on the subject of Russia at the peace conference—one of the best examples of his duplicity—Christopher Lasch: *The American Liberals and the Russian Revolution* (New York: Columbia University Press; 1962), pp. 176–98. On the "new diplomacy," see Arno J. Mayer: *Political Origins of the New Diplomacy* (New Haven: Yale University Press; 1959), especially pp. 368–93.

8. Colcord to House, March 8, 1919, Louis D. Brandeis MSS, University of Louisville Law Library; House to Colcord, April 3, 1919, House MSS.

9. Colcord MS Diary, Aug. 25, [1917].

admission had a "one-track mind." And as he reminded Colcord, he, House, knew "the President's mind better than anyone in the world," so that he could speak with authority on the subject.

> I have noticed the difference between us so often in talking with him; I can go from one thing to another without any trouble— in fact, I like to, I enjoy it, it rests my mind. Not so with him; he sets his teeth in a subject and will not be turned aside. He has done exactly that this summer—set his teeth in the subject of organization for war.

"And forgotten the international situation," Colcord complained. "That is what I have told you all summer but you did not think it was important." The Flag Day speech and the refusal to allow American socialists to attend the conference at Stockholm to discuss peace terms had "paved the way for a failure on this issue."

To these misgivings House gave his usual reply: "I don't believe it will be a failure. I think I have said just the right things to him, and that he will come around."[1]

Late in August, 1917, Wilson, in reply to a papal appeal for peace, announced that it was impossible for the Allies to "take the word of the present rulers of Germany as a guarantee of anything that is to endure."[2] The note reinforced Colcord's doubts about the President; it seemed to him to put too much emphasis on "the German-autocracy phase" of the question. House agreed. "Wilson's emotions," he said, led him to make too much of that. "But when I thought it all over, and took into account the necessity for appealing to the sup-

---

1. Colcord MS Diary, Aug. 18, [1917].
2. Ray Stannard Baker and William E. Dodd: *The Public Papers of Woodrow Wilson* (New York, 1927), Vol. III, p. 96.

port of the Allies, I decided to make no objection. The liberalism is all there, and they will discover it soon enough. The tail wags the dog."[3]

For Colcord, the Bolshevik revolution in November, 1917, posed the decisive test of the administration's good faith. The failure to aid the revolution, followed by the decision to intervene in Siberia, convinced him that Wilson had gone over to the reactionaries. Colonel House found it impossible any longer to reassure him about Wilson's liberalism—or rather his susceptibility to House's influence. As early as January, 1918, House found that it was "no longer a pleasure to talk with him." When Colcord stayed for any time in Washington, House complained, "he loses his perspective hopelessly. . . . He is always filled with some point of view which he has gathered in the incessant merry-go-round at Washington."[4] By 1919 Colcord was "well aware of the friendly but nevertheless severe discount which attaches itself in your estimation to any statement of mine."[5]

In a more belligerent mood he served notice that "if the guns are turned on the mob, the trouble will begin." "I am sure you appreciate," he wrote to House, "that if that time comes, I and the group of young men whose language I am now speaking will have to be over there on the side on which the guns are turned. I hope, too, that you will not feel that I am speaking wildly."[6]

One of the last extended conversations between Colcord and House took place in July, 1918, shortly before Wilson announced his support of the Allied expedition to Siberia.[7]

3. Colcord MS Diary, Aug. 29, 1917.
4. House MS Diary, Jan. 27, 1918.
5. Colcord to House, March 8, 1919, Brandeis MSS.
6. Colcord to House, Jan. 25, 1918, Colcord MSS.
7. Colcord MS Diary, July 17, 1918.

Colcord seems to have gone out of his way to adopt the provocative tone which had become such an irritation to House.

"Would you like to see Lloyd George tipped over?" I asked.

He glanced at me keenly, but made no answer. He had expressed himself to me on that score plenty of times in the past, however, even so late as after his return from the Versailles Council last fall.

"If you really want the present government to fall, I can't understand why you actively support it," I went on. "Actions speak louder than words."

"The government will fall when the opposition is ready," he said. "That is England's own business."

"But in the meantime," I persisted, "you are not leaving it to England. You are playing politics in England very powerfully, and on the wrong side. . . ."

"You exaggerate the importance of the whole matter," he repeated. "As for American labor, they don't know which side they are on, anyway." [Colcord had observed that the American labor movement seemed to be growing more and more reactionary.] "They can be liberalized at any time. These things that they are saying now can be changed at a word from the White House."

"Do you think so?" I commented, completely disheartened by the whole conversation.

The conversation indeed was discouraging enough; but what is so interesting is the form Colcord's discouragement assumed. His talk of taking his place on the other side of the guns was of a piece with Colonel House's picture of himself leading a world revolution against "the gang." The two men, in opposition as in friendship, shared the vision of a revolutionary apocalypse, at once noble and appalling. "The world is plunging on to revolution," wrote Colcord to William Bullitt. ". . . It will be a tragic but splendid time, lit by the lurid light of chaos."[8] The state of the world in 1918 justified

8. Colcord to Bullitt, Nov. 5, 1918, William C. Bullitt MSS, Yale University Library.

the prediction; but the vision of destruction appears so frequently in Colcord's letters, and he took such obvious literary relish in portraying it, that one is left with the feeling that his words express not so much a fear as a wish—a wish that many people, in a time of violence, have probably entertained in their darker moments.

8 / The Education of
Lincoln Steffens

[I]

THE 1920's, IT IS SAID, WERE A TIME OF "DISILLUSIONMENT." Progressivism had failed. The war for democracy had ended in the debacle of Versailles; idealism gave way to "normalcy." Defeated, intellectuals turned away from reform. Following H. L. Mencken, they now ridiculed "the people," whom they had once idolized. Many of them fled to Europe. Others cultivated the personal life, transferring their search for salvation from society to the individual. Still others turned to Communism. In the general confusion, only one thing was certain: the old ideals, the old standards, were dead, and liberal democracy was part of the wreckage.

Such is the standard picture of the twenties; but it is a gross distortion, a caricature, of the period. It has the unfortunate effect, moreover, of isolating the twenties from the rest of American history, of making them seem a mere interval between two periods of reform, and thus of obscuring the continuity between the twenties and the "progressive era" on the one hand and the period of the New Deal on the other. The idea of historical "periods" is misleading in itself. It exercises a subtle tyranny over the historical imagination. Essentially a verbal and pedagogical convenience, it tends to become a principle of historical interpretation as well; and as such it leads people to think of history not as the development of social organisms far too complicated to be depicted in simple linear terms but as a succession of neatly defined epochs, happily corresponding, moreover, to the divisions of the calendar, each century, each decade even, having its own distinctive "spirit of the age." Thus the *Zeitgeist* of the twenties, it is assumed, must have been "disillusionment," just as that of the thirties was reform.

The picture of the twenties as "disillusioned" derives from such books as Frederick Lewis Allen's *Only Yesterday,* a popular account written in 1931 under the misapprehension that the "twenties" had ended decisively in the year 1929, the year of the great depression. Books like Allen's, which did so much to influence subsequent interpretation of the twenties, derived in turn from the writings of "disillusioned" contemporaries. The image of the twenties as a period of "tired radicalism" finds its justification, it would seem, in the works of the tired radicals themselves and in the larger literature of disenchantment of which they were a part. Fitzgerald's men and women mourned the loss of innocence; Hemingway's could no longer bear to hear such words as "sacred, glorious, and sacrifice and the expression in vain."[1] Walter Lippmann wrote of the "vast dissolution of ancient habits which the emancipators believed would restore our birthright of happiness." The emancipators, he decided, "did not see very clearly beyond the evils against which they were rebelling."[2] Other liberals agreed with this verdict: prewar progressivism had been superficial, timid, and moralistic, bent on reforming men rather than conditions. John Chamberlain

1. Ernest Hemingway: *A Farewell to Arms* (New York: Modern Library; 1932), p. 196.
2. Walter Lippmann: *A Preface to Morals* (New York: Macmillan; 1929), p. 6. Note, however, that Lippmann had said exactly the same thing in *Drift and Mastery,* written fifteen years earlier; see above, pp. 112-13.

spoke for a whole generation, it seemed, in making his *Farewell to Reform*. But the most sustained and thoroughgoing indictment of progressivism was to be found in *The Autobiography of Lincoln Steffens*, which traced in great detail, step by step, Steffens's progress—typical, it seemed, of his time —from reform to revolution; and it was this famous book, hailed from the moment of its publication as a minor classic of American letters, which more than any other set the style for writing about the decline of the progressive movement in the aftermath of the "great crusade." When historians attribute the decline of progressivism to its own shortcomings, to its naïve belief in the power of moral exhortation and to its confidence that special interests could be expected to act in the general interest, they are echoing the argument that Steffens advanced so persuasively in 1931, in explanation of his own conversion from liberalism to Communism.

I propose in the course of this chapter, among other things, to examine Steffens's autobiography in detail, comparing his own account of his life with the version that emerges from his letters and his contemporary writings; but I should explain in advance that it is a mistake, in my opinion, to take the literature of disillusionment at its face value. The radicals and bohemians of the twenties claimed to have lost their illusions about the world, but if their own earlier testimony is to be believed, they had never had any illusions to begin with—not, at any rate, the particular illusions they later claimed to have lost. Certainly they had never been progressives in the sense in which they later used the term. On the contrary, men like Lippmann, John Dewey, Brand Whitlock, Fremont Older, Frederic C. Howe, and Lincoln Steffens had attacked progressivism all along as a variety of "puritanism." If progressivism meant uplift, the new radicals had opposed it from the beginning, and they added very little in the twenties to the indictment which they had drawn up at the height of the so-called "progressive era." If, on the other hand, progressivism meant social control, if it meant the scientific approach to politics, if it referred, more broadly still, to the "pragmatic" habit of mind, then the new radicals were progressives; and they did not cease to be progressives even after they had repudiated "progressivism." Part of the difficulty that surrounds the subject of "disillusionment" lies in the ambiguity of the term "progressivism" (or "liberalism"), which contemporaries used indiscriminately to refer to quite different things. The progressivism of the politicians, from the La Follettes and the Borahs down to the local reformers in their "annual contest with the saloon" (in Randolph Bourne's contemptuous phrase), was very different from the progressivism of the intellectuals. The progressive intellectuals disowned the progressivism of the politicians, not in the twenties, but from the moment it became a political fashion during the Roosevelt administration. They disowned it as they disowned every other manifestation of the culture of the middle class.

But in that case, one may ask, why did they reject it all over again in the twenties? It is difficult to understand this second disillusionment unless one remembers the extent to which disillusionment, for many American intellectuals, had early become an end in itself. One of the dogmas of the new radicalism was that appearances were illusory. Behind the political façade was the "invisible government." Beneath the smiling surface of American life was the "submerged tenth." Beneath the moral man was the inner, uncivilized man. Muckraking, history, social work, psychological theory, all seemed to lead to the same conclusion: that reality was precisely what cultured people, respectable people, sought to keep hidden. Disillusionment, therefore—the loss of the illusion that the world actually worked as the official guardians of the social order, parents, preachers, and teachers, pretended it worked—was the necessary beginning of wisdom.

It also tended to become, as I have suggested earlier, a style or attitude, deliberately adopted, in which a certain type of rebellion expressed itself as a matter of convention. One reason why the twenties seem particularly disillusioned is that the convention had become by that time so general that it was taken up by people whose rebellion went no further than an impatience with parental restraint. But if that was so, it was precisely because older men had already established the pattern, long before the war, the peace, and the excitements of the 1920's. The muckrakers, among others, had already made it clear that a hard-boiled skepticism about the canting morality of the middle class was indispensable equipment for aspiring young rebels; and none of the muckrakers had taken more delight in turning official morality upside down than Lincoln Steffens, whose very first book contained the statement that "the Fourth of July oration is the 'front' of graft" and that "there is no patriotism in it, but treason."[3] The man who could turn out such epigrams was already well advanced toward "disillusionment." Yet so pervasive was the myth of disillusionment in the twenties that Steffens himself succumbed to it; he spoke of himself, at times, as a man whose illusions had survived intact right down to the end of the war. That he knew better, the *Autobiography* itself makes clear in many places; in spite of which, however, historians persist in reading it as a study of disenchantment and, beyond that, of the way in which a burning sense of injustice drove so many liberals in the postwar years into the regrettable but essentially humanitarian heresy of Communism. Our understanding of the process by which radicals are made remains

3. Lincoln Steffens: *The Shame of the Cities* (New York: Hill & Wang; 1957 [New York, 1904]), p. 8.

astonishingly sentimental and crude, and our picture of the cultural history of the twenties and thirties, accordingly, seldom rises above the level of a cliché. Thus in Arthur Miller's recent play *After the Fall,* as a reviewer has noted, "all of the ex-Communists . . . are merely 'fighting injustice,' while the friend who commits suicide is 'a decent broken man that never wanted anything more but the good of the world.' "[4] And Richard Rovere has written that "the typical intellectual of the thirties was a man so shocked by social injustice and the ghastly spectacle of fascism that his brain was easily addled by anyone who proposed a quick and drastic remedy."[5] It is time we began to understand radicals like Lincoln Steffens not as men driven by a vague humanitarian idealism but as men *predisposed* to rebellion as the result of an early estrangement from the culture of their own class; as the result, in particular, of the impossibility of pursuing within the framework of established convention the kind of careers they were bent on pursuing. The intellectuals of the early twentieth century were predisposed to rebellion by the very fact of being intellectuals in a society that had not yet learned to define the intellectual's place. Under such ·conditions intellectuals were outsiders by necessity: a new class, not yet absorbed into the cultural consensus.

[II]

In his *Autobiography* and in a number of letters written while he was working on it, Steffens accused the muckrakers

4. Robert Brustein: "Arthur Miller's Mea Culpa," *New Republic,* CL (Feb. 8, 1964), p. 28.

5. Richard H. Rovere: *The American Establishment and Other Reports, Opinions, and Speculations* (New York: Harcourt, Brace & World; 1962), p. 175.

of substituting mere exposure for analysis, and he accused himself of having shared their illusion that the people would elect good men to office once the bad men were exposed. It was only after the experience of the war and two revolutions, the Mexican and the Russian, that he had been able to see, he said, that muckraking had been a "great mistake," that it had only "improved the graft system" and "protracted the age of folly."[6]

Yet *The Shame of the Cities*, published in 1904—the book which won Steffens a reputation as a muckraker—was actually one of the first attacks on muckraking. It contained passages of earnest moralizing, of the kind which Steffens later came to associate with progressivism in general, but it also contained attacks on progressivism which showed that Steffens was already "disillusioned" with reform. "Reform with us is usually revolt, not government, and is soon over. Our people do not seek, they avoid self-government, and 'reforms' are spasmodic efforts to punish bad rulers and get somebody that will give us good government or something that will make it." This kind of reform, Steffens already saw, would "result only in the perfection of the corrupt system."[7] Nor was it enough simply to expose evils. Steffens insisted several times in *The Shame of the Cities* that he was exposing nothing that was not already common knowledge. The people knew all about Minneapolis, St. Louis, Pittsburgh, and the rest. The people were "not innocent." That was "the only 'news' in all the journalism of these articles," and even that, Steffens added, was probably news only to himself. He had set out initially, he said, to show

6. Steffens to Marie Howe, Dec. 28, 1919, in Ella Winter and Granville Hicks, eds.: *The Letters of Lincoln Steffens* (New York: Harcourt, Brace; 1938), Vol. I, p. 519; Steffens: "A Muckraker's Memories," in Ella Winter and Herbert Shapiro, eds.: *The World of Lincoln Steffens* (New York: Hill & Wang; 1962), p. 257, hereafter cited as *World*.

7. *Shame of the Cities*, pp. 137, 40.

how the people were "deceived and betrayed" but had found instead that they willingly tolerated the corruption that openly flourished all about them.[8] Already Steffens was using to good effect the autobiographical device around which, twenty-five years later, he built the account of his "life of unlearning." Already he was exaggerating his innocence for literary effect.

But not only for literary effect; he wanted to show also that he had arrived at his mature ideas by a process of scientific experimentation. The pose of disillusionment was essential to the pose of detachment. If it could be shown that he had clung to his preconceived assumptions about the world until the facts of the matter left him no choice but to give them up, he could not be accused of having bent the facts to suit his wishes. Like all the new radicals, Steffens was fascinated by science, but the degree of his fascination was unusual, as was the thoroughness with which he tried to reduce historical phenomena to natural laws. He seems, like Edward A. Ross, to have had a horror of the subjective and the delusional, for he went to great lengths, returning to the subject again and again, to prove that his own wishes ran counter to his political and social discoveries. Thus he wrote to Brand Whitlock in 1924 that he had abandoned liberalism, after a long struggle, as a form of wishful thinking. He had come to realize that liberal ideas —all ideas of right and wrong, good and bad—were no more than cultivated human wishes. As a result of his discovery, he had given up wishing altogether in favor of scientific research into the natural laws of history.[9]

Steffens claimed that his faith in the scientific method was itself a recent discovery, the product of experiences that over-

8. Ibid., p. 9. See also p. 101, and *The Autobiography of Lincoln Steffens* (New York: Harcourt, Brace; 1931), Vol. I, p. 374; Vol. II, p. 564.

9. Steffens to Brand Whitlock, Jan. 28, 1925, Lincoln Steffens MSS, Columbia University Library. See also Winter and Hicks: *Letters of Lincoln Steffens*, Vol. II, pp. 683–5.

turned his earlier ideas. In fact, however, it antedated those experiences. Long before he became a muckraker, much less a revolutionist, Steffens began what was to be a lifetime's search for a "science of ethics." As a young student in Europe in 1892, he wrote to his father that he was working on an essay that would "revolutionize Ethics and carry it far from the field of rationalistic speculation into that of a real science."[1] The essay did not materialize, but Steffens never wavered from his early conviction that human behavior could be analyzed with the precision of a natural science—a conviction that he derived not from "life" but from the lecture rooms of the German universities. Thus his investigations as a muckraker, far from revolving around the moralism that he later read back into them, reflected a deliberate search for a scientific law of political corruption—the "typical stages of corruption," as he put it in *The Shame of the Cities*.[2] Just so, much later, he reinterpreted the Book of Moses as the account of a "typical revolution" and tried to convince his friends that the excesses of the Russian revolution were "due, not to the misconduct of the Bolsheviki, but to the laws which govern all revolutions."[3]

Steffens's early career, if one disregards the pattern he himself wished to impose on it, reveals the elements one finds in the careers of so many intellectuals of his time—not only the cult of science but the whole pattern of rebellion associated with the rise of the new radicalism. His letters, together with what information one can reliably gather from the early portions of the *Autobiography*, tell a familiar story: the restlessness and uncertainty born of having actively to choose a career, instead of accepting it as given; the mounting disgust with

1. May 25, 1892, *Letters*, Vol. I, p. 77; see also *Autobiography*, Vol. I, pp. 127, 164.

2. *Shame of the Cities*, p. 136.

3. "Moses in Red" (1926) in *World*, p. 77; Steffens to Ella Winter, June 13, 1922, in *Letters*, Vol. II, p. 590.

cultural "advantages" one nevertheless continued dutifully to pursue; the sense of unworthiness; the longing for experience. Steffens inherited opportunities that his parents had not enjoyed. His father had worked by day and sent himself through commercial college by night; migrated from Illinois to California, traveling by horseback through a West that was still wild; and beginning as a bookkeeper in Sacramento, had risen to affluence as a merchant. In this way he accumulated the fortune that sent his son to Berkeley and then to the universities of Europe, where he dabbled in philosophy and aesthetics, traveled, acquired a taste for expensive clothes, and met a well-to-do young woman named Josephine Bontecou whom he secretly married. Here was the painful contrast, felt by so many of Steffens's contemporaries, between the pioneer generation and their overeducated children, the latter blessed with advantages which only delayed their entrance into "life." And as if to drive home the point, a letter from his father awaited Steffens on his return to America at the age of twenty-six, a letter which, more than thirty years later, he could still remember "word-perfect":

My dear son: When you finished school you wanted to go to college. I sent you to Berkeley. When you got through there, you did not care to go into my business; so I sold out. You preferred to continue your studies in Berlin. I let you. After Berlin it was Heidelberg; after that Leipzig. And after the German universities you wanted to study at the French universities in Paris. I consented, and after a year with the French, you had to have a half a year of the British Museum in London. All right. You had that too.

By now you must know about all there is to know of the theory of life, but there's a practical side as well. It's worth knowing. I suggest that you learn it, and the way to study it, I think, is to stay in New York and hustle.

Enclosed please find one hundred dollars, which should keep
you till you can find a job and support yourself.[4]

It was not much consolation to be told later that his parents
would scarcely have taken such a position had they known
of his marriage. The rebuke must all too closely have coincided
with Steffens's own accumulated self-contempt. Like Jane
Addams, Steffens was trapped in "the snare of preparation,"
and he did not need his father to tell him so. He had pursued
culture with the same dutiful and overearnest zeal which
drove Jane Addams, in these same years, from one cathedral to
another; only to find that there was nothing in it which held
his interest. "Classical music is a bore," he wrote to his sister;
eventually he came to enjoy it, but only after a struggle.[5] He
approached art, moreover, with an inhibiting uncertainty
about the reliability of his own opinions, afraid, as always, of
giving himself away as a "sucker." (Without Ruskin, he wrote
home, "I don't know what I should do, for I was without any
sound taste and must have been led by popular verdict or,
worse still, by my natural and unsound taste.")[6] It is hardly
any wonder that he came home at last, vaguely intending to go
into business or teach, with a heavy sense of failure which it
needed only his father's letter to bring to a head.

Stranded in New York with a wife and no money except
what he could bring himself to take from her mother, Steffens
found a job on the New York *Evening Post* and plunged into
the teeming life of the city with the same exhilaration with
which Jane Addams had discovered the west side of Chicago.

4. *Autobiography*, Vol. I, p. 169. Though he claimed to have remembered
his father's words verbatim, the letter as it appears in the *Autobiography*
bears strong traces of Steffens's mature style, a fact which suggests that
he may have put into his father's mouth his own self-condemnation.
5. Steffens to Lou Steffens, Nov. 16, 1889, *Letters*, Vol. I, p. 25.
6. Steffens to Laura Steffens, Aug. 18, 1889, *Letters*, Vol. I, p. 10.

He reveled in "this American living," "the complex, crude, significant but mixed facts of hard, practical life."[7] Eagerly he sought "the striving, struggling, battling, of the practical world, which far outranks the philosophic heaven."[8] A reporter, he was also a businessman, as he wrote to his father after becoming city editor of the *Commercial Advertiser*, and "not so incompetent as you think in a business way."[9] He intended to prove "that a long course of education need not necessarily unfit a man for business." "Above all," he told his father, "do I want that you should be convinced that you were right in giving me the long training of college and that I am worthy of your long, patient help to a son who did not ever seem worth it all."[1]

The way in which these early experiences influenced his emerging social philosophy is clear. Reality was action, the turmoil and strife of "life as it is lived."[2] There were "strong" men who accepted the hard facts of life as they found them and "weak" men who idealized existence by theorizing about it. The strong men were "insiders," the weak men "suckers." News was inside dope: "what reporters know and don't report."[3] Politics likewise lay mostly hidden behind a polite façade; the real government was an "invisible government."[4] History was not what was taught in books but what strong men were doing behind the scenes. Reality, in short, was in every instance precisely the opposite of what people were taught to believe. "Good people" were really bad people, be-

7. Steffens to Frederick M. Willis, Dec. 19, 1892, Feb. 5, 1893, *Letters*, Vol. I, pp. 87, 90.
8. Steffens to Willis, April 1, 1893, *Letters*, Vol. I, p. 95.
9. Steffens to Joseph Steffens, March 23, 1898, *Letters*, Vol. I, p. 131.
1. Steffens to Joseph Steffens, March 18, 1893, *Letters*, Vol. I, p. 92.
2. *Autobiography*, Vol. I, p. 231.
3. Ibid., Vol. I, pp. 39, 165, 182–3, 199, 223, 274, and *passim*.
4. Ibid., Vol. I, p. 232 and *passim*.

cause their illusions did more harm than the intelligent crimes of the "big bad men."

Steffens claimed that it took him years to learn these things and that he learned them only as a result of his investigations first into the corruption of American cities and then into the Mexican and Russian revolutions. In fact, it seems to have been the other way around: his preconceptions about the nature of politics and society antedated the investigations and to a large extent predetermined their outcome. Thus he made it his practice, in any inquiry, to go directly to the "big men" who ran things.

> Calling with my card at the editorial office, I would ask the office boy: "Say, kid, who is 'it' here?"
>
> "Why," he would answer, "Mr. So-and-so is the editor."
>
> "No, no," I protested, "I don't mean the front, I mean—really."
>
> "Oh, you mean the owner. That's Mr. Blank."
>
> Feigning disgust and disappointment, I would say, "The owner, he's only the rear as the editor is the front. What I mean is, who's running the shebang? Who knows what's what and—who decides?"
>
> "Oh," he would exclaim—whether he was the office boy, a reporter, or an editorial writer—his face lighting up with the intelligence faces habitually conceal—"Oh, the man you are looking for is—Nut Brown."[5]

Given these techniques as a reporter, given also his instinctive admiration for the big men behind the scenes, it is not surprising that Steffens came to the conclusion that it was not the bosses who were to blame for corruption but the people themselves, who put the bosses in power and kept them there because they were too lazy to govern themselves. Steffens's contempt for democratic processes, although not formally

5. Ibid., Vol. I, p. 403.

admitted into his political thought until later, was firmly rooted in experiences that antedated his activities as a muckraker. "The bosses especially attract me," he wrote to his father at the outset of his first trip for *McClure's*.[6] Even earlier, according to the *Autobiography*, he had discovered that he liked the crooks better than the reformers. " 'He's a crook,' I would tell a reporter, 'but he's a great crook,' and I think now that I meant he was a New York crook and therefore a character for us and all other New Yorkers to know intimately and be proud of."[7] Steffens was neither the first nor the last young man from the provinces to celebrate crooks as "characters," in deliberate defiance of the conventional view of things. The gesture was bound up with his plunge, after years of formal schooling, into the turmoil of urban life. "I take it all," he wrote self-consciously to a college friend, "and let the brutal facts resolve themselves into as much truth as my mental digestion is able to find."[8] The more brutal the facts and the more unpalatable, from the point of view of conventional morality, the truths to which they led, the greater the young rebel's delight in discovering them.

Steffens was prepared in advance, in short, to find what he found as a muckraker and published in *The Shame of the Cities* and *The Struggle for Self-Government*: that American politics were ruled by strong "bad" men who remained "invisible" only because "good" people, too weak to govern themselves, preferred not to recognize their existence. That Steffens found what he was looking for does not mean that what he found was untrue. On the contrary, his explanation of political corruption, so far as it went, conformed more closely to the facts than the popular theories which his articles helped to

6. Steffens to Joseph Steffens, May 18, 1902, *Letters*, Vol. I, p. 156.
7. *Autobiography*, Vol. I, pp. 312, 330.
8. Steffens to Willis, Feb. 5, 1893, *Letters*, Vol. I, p. 90.

explode—in particular, the theory that corruption flourished
only where large numbers of immigrants sustained the political
machine in power. (Philadelphia, Steffens pointed out, had few
immigrants but was the worst-governed city in the country.)
It is not the accuracy of his account of political corruption that
is at issue but the accuracy of his account of his own career.
According to Steffens, his career proceeded from one disillusionment to another, experience compelling him constantly to
revise his ideas about it. According to contemporary evidence,
most of the assumptions at which he claimed to have arrived
only after a life of "unlearning" were present almost from the
beginning—byproducts, it would seem, of his early discovery
that the world of intellect and "culture" paled into nothingness
when compared with the world of action.

[III]

In his very first report for *McClure's*, the famous exposé of
the "shamelessness of St. Louis," Steffens had discovered that
"corruption was not merely political," as many reformers had
assumed, but "financial, commercial, social" as well.[9] It was
not enough, therefore, for reformers to turn out the politicians
and put a "businessman's administration" in their place. The
businessmen themselves were corrupt. "In all cities, the better
classes—the business men—are the sources of corruption; but
they are so rarely pursued and caught that we do not fully
realize whence the trouble comes. Thus most cities blame the
politicians and the ignorant and vicious poor."[1]

In *The Shame of the Cities* the implications of these find-
ings were only partially explored, but *The Struggle for Self-*

9. *Shame of the Cities*, p. 9.
1. Ibid., p. 40.

Government, which appeared only two years later, left no doubt about their broader meaning. By 1906 Steffens had already come to realize that political corruption was a *system:* "a regularly established custom of the country, by which our political leaders are hired, by bribery, by the license to loot, and by quiet moral support, to conduct the government of city, State and Nation, not for the common good, but for the special interests of private business." In short, "the highway of corruption is the road to success."[2] Or, as Steffens wrote to his sister a few years later: "Society is made up of legitimate grafters."[3] But when he began to write about national politics in these terms, Steffens found that editors were no longer interested in him. They complained "that I showed up no graft, wrote nothing sensational. That was their criterion: dishonesty, stealing, graft. If an honest senator honestly served a trust that was no disservice to the people; that was not wrong."[4] Everywhere he encountered this "failure of imagination," this inability to see that graft was not so much a crime as a social "process" whereby democracy was transformed into plutocracy, thereby eliminating the need for graft.[5]

Steffens came to the conclusion, therefore, that what was needed, if American society was to be made over, was not a moral awakening but a better appreciation of the nature of American society—not morality but "intelligence." What was needed, as he loved to put it, was "honest crooks"; for an intelligent crook was an "unhappy crook."[6] This paradox, so maddening to orthodox progressives, was another way of saying that society was made up of legitimate grafters. It was

2. *The Struggle for Self-Government* (New York: McClure, Phillips & Co.; 1906), pp. 4-5.
3. Steffens to Dot Hollister, June 26, 1912, *Letters*, Vol. I, p. 303.
4. *Autobiography*, Vol. II, p. 581.
5. Ibid., Vol. II, pp. 449, 445-6.
6. Ibid., Vol. II, p. 610.

another way of saying that capitalist society was made up of perfectly respectable people engaged in giving and seeking special favors, not illegally but under the approved rules of the system, without the least suspicion that they were doing anything reprehensible. Not the grafters but the system itself was corrupt, in short; but until people realized that the system was corrupt, they would have neither the inclination nor the ability to change it. Hence Steffens's plea for intelligence and his impatience with the reforms which by focusing attention on the crimes of the "big bad men" merely reinforced the self-righteousness of the ordinary citizen.

Once the problem was stated in this way, Steffens's temperamental preference for bad men over good men could be stated more precisely than before. It was not simply that the bad men were "principals" and the good people "heelers" or that the bad men were insiders and the good people suckers. The bad men were admirable above all because they knew what they were doing. The good people, on the other hand, did the same things, or at least condoned them, under the impression that they were doing good. Thus Steffens's indictment of capitalism was also an indictment of the hypocrisy of middle-class morality, and he turned to the bad men for the same reason other intellectuals turned to the working class, because they were outcasts from respectable society. The more he became convinced that there was no virtue in the virtuous, the more Steffens tended to identify himself with the crooks. The former suspected him of being a good man, but the latter accepted him as one of themselves and allowed him to address them "as one honest crook to another."[7]

A curious incident in his personal history, recounted rather obliquely in the *Autobiography*, helps to explain how Steffens arrived at this characteristic formulation of the social problem.

7. Ibid., Vol. II, pp. 486, 563, and *passim*.

Like similar incidents in the lives of other radicals, it had something of the character of a religious crisis—it was followed by a
period of intense interest in Christianity, during which Steffens
re-read the New Testament as a revolutionary manifesto—and
something of the character of a self-psychoanalysis, brief but
painful.[8] In 1903 Steffens gave Ray Stannard Baker, then his
colleague at *McClure's*, both the idea and the title for an exposé
of monopolistic practices in the building industry. When
Baker's article appeared prominently in the September, 1903,
issue of *McClure's*, Steffens's wife Josephine reproached him
for giving away his ideas. Steffens replied that the authorship
of the article was unimportant and that in any case Baker knew
that the original idea had come from him. "Nonsense," she
said, "Baker will never remember," and she proved her point
by getting Baker to describe how he had come to write the
piece. He did so without reference to Steffens. "She won,
smiled, and I felt—yellow; whether with jealousy of Baker
or humiliation at the defeat by my wife, I don't know. It was
an old cause of friction between her and me: my habit of 'telling all I knew' and her insistence upon my 'career.' The incident made me feel mean."[9]

It is easy to see why the subject of Steffens's career was a

8. Steffens did not encounter the theory of psychoanalysis until eight
or nine years later, when he became a regular visitor at Mable Dodge's
"evenings." (He had dabbled in psychology as a student in Paris, however,
and had attended the lectures of Charcot, the teacher of Freud.) Its effect
on him then, he says, was to confirm his objections to middle-class reform
by showing the futility of trying to change men's minds without changing
the conditions under which they lived; but in narrating the episode, he
characteristically attributed to himself an earlier position that he had never
held. "I remember thinking [as he listened to the discussions of Freud and
Jung led by Walter Lippmann] how absurd had been my muckraker's
description of bad men and good men." (*Autobiography*, Vol. II, p. 655.)
What "description" was he referring to? From the start, Steffens had dismissed that approach to politics as hopelessly superficial.

9. *Autobiography*, Vol. II, p. 522.

source of friction between him and his first wife. She was a mirror of his ambition—a quality which, like many ambitious men, he did not want to recognize in himself. The discovery, under his wife's probing, that he wished unconsciously for worldly success seemed to him now to mock his pretensions to moral self-dependence. He too was "one of the righteous"; he too concealed from himself ambitions he was unwilling to acknowledge. It was not the ambition itself that disturbed him so much as the concealment. What humiliated him was the revelation that his wife knew him better than he knew himself; "and all she had to do was to scratch the surface and there it was: envy, jealousy, and all the rest."[1] Ten years later, Steffens had a similar experience which shows quite clearly that his uneasiness on this occasion was bound up with his fear of his wife's power—and not only hers but that of women in general —to bore through his defenses to the secret springs of his being. When Josephine died in 1911, she left him a diary of their marriage which was such an "epoch-making revelation of me to me" that he could bring himself to say of it—in a sentence the ungainliness of which suggests the painfulness of the subject—only that it showed him "what an ass a 'good husband' is in the eyes of an intelligent wife who is thinking of him, who is thinking always of graft or business or—something else; who is always at hand but never at home."[2] Women made him feel like a "blind duffer," Steffens said once; but that was an understatement.[3] They made him feel, much worse, like a good man.

Confronted, then, with his exposed ambition, in the form of his jealousy of Baker, Steffens deliberately put off thinking about it until his "next long, lone railroad journey." Then he tried to face his "yellow streak." He could not, in a single day,

1. Ibid., Vol. II, p. 523.
2. Steffens to Marie Howe, Dec. 23, 1925, *Letters*, Vol. II, p. 722; *Autobiography*, Vol. II, p. 635.
3. Ibid., Vol. II, p. 649.

have probed very deep; but the direction in which his thoughts ran shows how urgent was his need to dissociate himself from reputable, respectable society. He had first to make himself admit that although he did not take bribes, he sometimes went "a bit slow" in something he wrote—"to keep my job, to keep my credit, to hold my readers and 'get by' my editors." That was his crime, then. "I was cheap, like any other good man; I did not come high, like an honest crook; I could be 'got' with my own salary." He could be bribed, in short, as all good people were bribed, without any suspicion of having been bought off; but the act of acknowledging these things, he thought, itself distinguished him from the ordinary unknowing taker of bribes. Self-knowledge rescued him from self-righteousness.

What a relief! What a humiliation and what an advantage! Now I could be as good as I liked and not be a righteous man any more. I could be intelligent; I could do a crooked thing and not be either a cynic or a fool. I would be able to face the men I admired—the men who did bribery and corruption, and knew it —and talk about it with them honestly.

And from that day, Steffens boasts, he was never again mistaken for an honest man.[4]

4. Ibid., Vol. II, p. 524. He completed this therapeutic exercise by writing to Baker in overgenerous praise of the offending article. "I haven't written because, like you, I was in the throes, but, unlike you, I was having troubles with myself. Struck a 'yellow streak,' and it made me sweat burning it out with shame. Ever catch yourself at mean thinking? I guess not. I envy you your perfect honesty.

"Of course you know what a crash your article made among the lies and the self-righteousness of the hypocrites. The triumph was the greatest a man can have with the pen: you made both sides see themselves as they are. All you have to do now is to rub it in. I verily believe we all will accomplish something yet."

The rest of the letter has an unconscious humor. "I'm to do the states this year, as you know, beginning here with Missouri. . . . It's bad for the

No doubt this was too easy, too convenient a resolution of the suspicions inadvertently raised by his wife; but whatever the limits of Steffens's self-scrutiny, the incident shows once again how closely the radical impulse was allied with the effort of introspection. It was for that reason that the new radicals wrote most freely and convincingly in the autobiographical vein: what they had to say about American society was inseparable from the record of their own re-education or "disillusionment." The problem of society was a problem preeminently of consciousness or, in Steffens's phrase, intelligence—a problem, at bottom, not of politics or economics but of psychology and culture. Stated in psychological terms, the problem, as Steffens had come to see it, was that good people could not admit to themselves that they were doing bad things. The very violence with which they reacted to Steffens's ideas showed at once how great was their need to deceive themselves and how disastrous were the psychological consequences of the deception. When Steffens tried to convince Theodore Roosevelt that the patronage system was a form of "legitimate" bribery and that Roosevelt, under the rules of the system, "had to" give bribes, Roosevelt "was appalled, almost speechless; his balled fists and wrenching arms wanted to express him."[5] Roosevelt's fury was the rage of the righteous man, and it could only confirm Steffens in his thesis that American society suffered from an excess of "unconscious guilt."[6]

If the problem was psychological, it was also cultural, since the source of guilt, Steffens thought, was the disparity between middle-class ideals and the political and economic demands

magazine to duplicate as we did in Chicago and New York, but perhaps you could come along right after me personally and let the articles be separated by a couple of months." "We must pull together," he finishes. (Steffens to Baker, Nov. 8, 1903, *Letters,* Vol. I, p. 159.)

5. *Autobiography*, Vol. II, p. 578.
6. Ibid., Vol. II, p. 612.

of an industrial society. The reason good people could not admit to themselves that they were doing bad things was that their political ideas did not know the distinction between the goodness of the actor or agent and the evil of the system which *compelled* him to do wrong. Having "tried out on a few individuals the healing effect of the sight of themselves as honest men doing dishonest things, as law-abiding citizens breaking the law," Steffens was convinced of the efficacy of this kind of therapy; but he was also convinced that a thoroughgoing social reformation would have to wait upon the overthrow of the whole system of ideas which enabled an entire people systematically to delude themselves about their way of life.[7] As early as 1908, Steffens had committed himself to "a long, patient game": "before I die," he wrote to his sister, "I believe I can help to bring about an essential change in the American mind." He urged his brother-in-law, a wealthy rancher, to play the game "according to the rules" if he had to, but to "acknowledge that the rules are wrong and should be revised radically."[8] Later he formulated the matter more broadly: if society was ever to be reformed, the old culture, the culture of the middle class, would have to give way completely. The "intellectual culture" would have to give way to the "scientific culture," as he came to call it.[9] The "historical, experimental method of 'seeing'" would have to take the place of the "logical" method.[1] Intelligence, in short, would have to replace virtue as the acknowledged aim of social life.[2]

7. Ibid.
8. Steffens to Laura Suggett, Sept. 23, 1908, *Letters*, Vol. I, p. 202.
9. E.g., *Autobiography*, Vol. II, p. 796.
1. Steffens to Ella Winter, Nov. 18, 1932, *Letters*, Vol. II, p. 934.
2. Cf. Edward A. Ross, in the introduction to *Sin and Society* (Boston: Houghton Mifflin; 1907), p. vii: "This book deals with sin, but it does not entreat the sinner to mend his ways. It seeks to influence no one in his conduct. It does seek to influence men *in their attitude toward the conduct of others*. Its exhortation is not *Be good* but *Be rational*."

Through all the vicissitudes that marked the course of world politics in the last twenty-five years of his life, this conviction, reiterated again and again, remained the bedrock of Steffens's political philosophy. "Our old culture is finished, we all have got to turn to welcome the new culture, which covers everything—the arts, science, business, life."[3] And although Steffens several times changed his mind about the means of bringing about the social transformation he hoped to see, he never changed his mind about the nature of the transformation itself. When he welcomed the Russian revolution, it was because he saw the revolution as the "experimental" method in action. When he acclaimed the "new capitalism" of the 1920's, it was for the same reason: the managers, he thought—practical men interested not in profits but in the most efficient method of organizing production—had expropriated the capitalists, and "either way," the Russian or the American, "the race is saved."[4] "Mass production is here," he wrote in 1930, "mass distribution is coming. Trusts, combinations, mergers, are steps toward the organization of all industry, all business into one unit, which will eventually be the sole government. We shall have no political government. And probably no stockholders. No middle class." With or without a revolution, men would become "free, or democratic, or safe, but not by wishing," he added in the old vein. "We have to get rid of our old moral culture and learn the new culture, already here in science and in big business: what I call our experimental culture."[5]

The depression eventually killed Steffens's enthusiasm for the new capitalism, but not for technocracy, which still seemed to him a harbinger of the new approach to social problems. Meanwhile he continued to argue for the Russian revolution,

3. Steffens to Joseph R. Boldt, Jr., Sept. 10, 1935, *Letters*, Vol. II, p. 1007.
4. Steffens to Jo Davidson, Feb. 18, 1929, *Letters*, Vol. II, p. 829.
5. Steffens to Alfred Harcourt, April 24, 1930, *Letters*, Vol. II, pp. 869–70.

long after most of his friends had deserted it, because he assumed that Communists and technocrats (in spite of their noisy disagreements) were working for the same thing. "Doing the job," he thought, "is the Communist virtue."[6] Beyond that, there was the prospect that mass employment, in America as in Russia, would bring mass leisure and thereby "free taste and beauty."[7] Just as he himself had begun life "looking for the good and found nothing but the beautiful," so the new society, having got rid of the impulse to judge, would liberate the impulse to enjoy. The "scientific culture" presented itself to Steffens not as a drab and regimented anti-utopia but as a realm of unexpected beauty. "Science," he once said, "is a song."[8]

[IV]

At the same time, Steffens had to concede that the new society was "hard, dull, level, moral," as he put it after coming out of Soviet Russia in 1919. Revolutionaries were "righteous." "I admire them tremendously, but I don't like to be with them." He had seen the future and it "worked"; but he preferred to live in the present. "We are not going to like the Rule of Labor," he predicted. After the "hard morality of Moscow," Paris, even the Paris of the peace conference, struck him like a fresh breeze of spring. "The joy of life, of which we hear so little, is the best of life."[9]

6. Steffens to Ella Winter, Dec. 24, [1932], *Letters*, Vol. II, p. 944.
7. Steffens to Ella Winter, April 2, 1933, *Letters*, Vol. II, p. 956.
8. Steffens to Hutchins Hapgood, Feb. 7, 1926; Steffens to Ella Winter, [Dec. 16, 1919], *Letters*, Vol. II, p. 731; Vol. I, p. 504.
9. Steffens to Marie Howe, Nov. 23, 1919, *Letters*, Vol. I, p. 493; to Matthew Schmidt, July 20, 1926, Vol. II, p. 758; to Marie Howe, April 3, 1919, Vol. I, p. 463; to Laura Suggett, June 18, 1919, Vol. I, p. 471.

Not only Paris but his courtship of Ella Winter inspired these reflections, heightening the contrast with Soviet Russia. Miss Winter was a student at the London School of Economics who had come to the Versailles conference as an assistant to Felix Frankfurter. She was twenty-one or two, Steffens fifty-three; "but I felt something," he wrote later, "which I smothered by likening her to a boy."[1] He called her Peter, took her up and down Paris, and explained to her, with his irrepressible gaiety, why the peace conference could not possibly succeed. A courtship, their relationship was also the relation between teacher and protégée. She called herself a radical, but "she 'saw through' nothing," and Steffens delighted in undermining her illusions.[2] The Bolsheviks, he told her, would succeed and the liberals would fail, because the Bolsheviks alone approached politics as a science. Even at this idyllic season of his life, Steffens's thoughts turned to Russia. The joy of life was the best of life, but the Rule of Labor was drawing near.

Ella Winter proved to be a willing pupil—too willing, perhaps. She gladly imbibed Steffens's ideas, but she did not imbibe his humor. He was a skeptic, she an enthusiast. He loved her for precisely that reason; her enthusiasm evoked the unquenchable idealism of youth, of which, in his later years, Steffens spoke with increasing warmth. Yet it was a quality, however admirable, that his own temperament lacked altogether. Nothing is more instructive than the way in which Steffens's ideas, when Ella Winter expressed them, lost the irony that had always subtly qualified his generalizations and became dogmatic assertions of revealed truth. That historical events were "revelations" was a favorite idea of his; but in her hands the same idea seemed suddenly to acquire a new and

1. *Autobiography*, Vol. II, p. 812.
2. Ibid.

slightly sinister meaning. To him, it meant that human judgment was fallible, it meant that no judgment could long withstand the test of historical fact. To her, it seemed to mean that the Russian revolution had revealed, once and for all, the proper form of social organization. Steffens had come out of Russia at once elated and oppressed. Ella Winter, who made her own pilgrimage to Russia in 1930, felt no such misgivings. She even accepted the claims of a Soviet psychiatrist who told her that "inferiority complexes have more or less vanished." Thirty years later she could still maintain that Communism "did not seem to create our Western conflict between individual and social ethics and behavior."[3]

Steffens and Miss Winter were married in 1924. From then until his death in 1936, Steffens grew progressively more enthusiastic about the Soviet Union—partly, it may be, as a result of his new wife's influence—at a time when other liberals and socialists were coming back from Russia with reports of misery and repression on a vast scale. He accepted the reports as true; he had no wish to minimize the cost of revolution; but he insisted that the cost had to be paid and that the reign of terror and violence was a phase through which all revolutions necessarily passed. It was pointless to deplore it; the terror was historically inevitable. The trouble with liberal critics of the revolution was that they expected the revolution to conform to their own wishes, their own preconceived theories of "right and wrong."

When you see the Russian Revolution [Steffens wrote to Gilbert E. Roe in 1924] you observe that it goes against your theories and mine, wherefore you "give it up"; it is all wrong. Emma [Goldman] did that. I, having seen two revolutions, the Mexican and the Russian, got from their perverse courses the notion that,

3. Ella Winter: *And Not to Yield* (New York: Harcourt, Brace & World; 1963), p. 163.

not the revolutions, but my theories were somehow wrong. I read up other revolutions. I found that they all took the same course. I inferred thence that a revolution, like a storm, is subject to natural laws and forces, which produce always the same effects.

And upon this conviction I cast out, not the revolution, but my old manner of thinking, ceased to be a liberal and have since been watching events as if they were divine (or natural) revelations.[4]

The anti-Communists, Steffens believed, had closed their minds to the assault of historical evidence. Charles Edward Russell, whose autobiography Steffens reviewed in 1933, seemed a case in point. A former muckraker, Russell had become a socialist before the war and had then been read out of the Socialist Party in 1917 on account of his vigorous support of the war. In the twenties and thirties he became a leading opponent of the Bolshevik regime and a leading defender (although he still claimed to be a radical) of the *status quo* in America. Through it all, his theories about the benevolence of man and the possibility of orderly progress had survived intact. Russell, for Steffens, was an example of the true believer, for whom political commitments (in Russell's case, a passionate commitment to liberal democracy) take the place of political analysis. Russell had once confessed to him, in effect, that he had joined the Socialist Party because he was tired of thinking. "I had to have something to believe."[5] The conversation stuck in Steffens's memory as a terrible warning; in his review of Russell's memoirs he mentioned it again. Russell, he said, had proceeded all his life not "from question to question but from answer to answer. He had—he had to have—always a cause to fight for. He had to know, so he always knew 'what to do about it.' That was one way he saved himself and his mind.

4. Steffens to Gilbert E. Roe, April 16, 1925, *Letters*, Vol. II, p. 693.
5. *Autobiography*, Vol. II, p. 632.

And the other," Steffens added, "the most persistent mental trick he has, most methodically, most humorously exposed in this tragic book, is his willful determination to see that he, I, we, the world, always won—something. He thinks, for instance, that city governments are better than when we began to show them up. I think he thinks so on the same evidence that makes me think we only improved the graft system."[6]

Steffens, unlike Russell, was willing to change his mind when events made his ideas obsolete; yet the irony of his career is that his open-mindedness, carried to an extreme, produced something of the same effect as Russell's dogmatism. It is true that he never became a dedicated Communist. "It was my job" as an " 'intellectual,' " he once said, "to doubt," and he annoyed the Soviet leaders by "being able to state their case and yet staying out of the Communist Party."[7] Toward the end of his life, however, he became increasingly uncritical of the Soviet Union. He also made close friendships among American Communists, in cooperation with whom he and Ella Winter tried to organize the migratory agricultural workers of California. These activities drew down on Steffens and his family the wrath of their neighbors in Carmel, California, who subjected them to a campaign of systematic abuse. The local paper, for instance, charged them with failure to bring up their son in a "civilized" manner.[8] The combination of this vilification and his enthusiasm for the revolution brought Steffens to the point of migrating to Russia. Late in 1935 he received an offer from the Soviet government to live in the Crimea and "report events without authority."[9] His letters, particularly the ones in his unpublished papers, seem to show that he intended to

6. Review of Russell's *Bare Hands and Stone Walls*, in *World*, p. 257.
7. Steffens to Dot Hollister, March 16, 1921, *Letters*, Vol. II, p. 565; to Upton Sinclair, May 19, 1926, Vol. II, p. 744.
8. Ella Winter: *And Not to Yield*, pp. 206–7.
9. Steffens to Sam Darcy, Jan. 4, 1936, *Letters*, Vol. II, p. 1012.

279 · *The Education of Lincoln Steffens*

accept it. His brother-in-law, Allen Suggett, was planning to visit the Crimea and to settle there if he liked it, and he urged Steffens to sell his house and go to Russia to stay; there would be more security for his family in Russia than in California.[1] Steffens agreed that California had become "a dumb, respectable, vigilante state."[2] In February, 1936, he wrote to his friend Sam Darcy, district organizer of the Communist Party in California, that he and his family intended to apply for a passport to Russia—which shows that he contemplated at least another visit—but his health gave way and he was unable to leave his bed.[3] Letters from Russia urged him to come, but his condition was such that he could not proceed.[4] A few weeks later he died.

The proposed trip to the Soviet Union, together with Steffens's general leftward swing, have to be considered against the background, not only of his personal difficulties in California, but against the general crisis of Western life in the mid-thirties. The depression seemed to have paralyzed the democracies of Western Europe and North America, thereby bearing out the contention, long maintained by people such as Steffens, that liberal democracy could not survive the rigors of the twentieth century. Only the Fascists and the Communists seemed to be getting things done. The United States itself, under Franklin Roosevelt, seemed to be moving, if not toward outright Fascism, toward a modified state capitalism. That did not necessarily mean that one had a moral obligation to choose between Communism and an American variety of statism. One could have rejected all such alternatives. But given the feeling that one had to choose, Steffens's choice of Communism in

1. Allen Suggett to Steffens, Jan. 4, [1936], Steffens MSS.
2. Steffens to Frederic C. Howe, March 11, 1936, *Letters*, Vol. II, p. 1016.
3. Steffens to Sam Darcy, Feb. 25, 1936, Steffens MSS.
4. Steffens to Suggett, May 26, 1936, Steffens MSS.

the thirties was no more reprehensible or misguided than the anti-Communist liberals' choice of the "free world" in the forties and fifties.

If anything, Steffens's choice—or more accurately, the manner in which he made it—was morally more attractive than the choice made by the anti-Communist liberals in the aftermath of the Second World War. They announced their decision with loud protestations of self-righteousness, coupled with strident attacks on younger liberals who did not share their all-encompassing hatred of the Soviet Union; Steffens based his turn to the Left on a strong sense of his own fallibility. In the generational struggle that developed within the liberal community as a result of the cold war, the older generation insisted again and again, in a manner that struck younger liberals as completely arbitrary, on its own superior wisdom and experience; in its eyes, those who could not bring themselves to see the cold war as a clear-cut struggle between Truth and Error were simply repeating the mistakes of the thirties (in spite of the fact that the international situation had appreciably altered in the meantime).[5] Steffens, on the other hand, believed that the younger generation could see things that eluded his own. This confidence in youth became the dominant note of his later writings. However sentimental, however misplaced his confidence, it accounted for much of the serenity and charm of the last phase of his life. It rescued Steffens from the bitterness that afflicted so many of the disappointed liberals of his time. Above all, it saved him from intolerance and dogmatism, to which so many of them eventually succumbed. Even in the act of embracing a dogmatic and intolerant ideology—if he can be said to have "embraced" it—he

5. An important exception to this pattern was Dwight Macdonald, whose choice of the West is discussed in some detail below, pp. 327 ff. For the more vehement anti-Communist Left, see below, pp. 299 ff.

281 · *The Education of Lincoln Steffens*

himself came more and more to embody the liberal virtues of tolerance and intellectual modesty which some of the later defenders of liberalism so conspicuously lacked.

Having discovered that he himself had no desire to live in the Soviet Union—and as late as 1930 he was repeating his wish not to go back—Steffens did not reconsider the revolution, he reconsidered himself. He wrote first *Moses in Red* (1926) and then the *Autobiography* (1931), to show that "all that was or is or ever will be wrong with [the world] is my—our thinking about it."[6] The Book of Moses, he thought, furnished a parallel not merely with the Russian revolution but with his own inability wholly to accept it. Moses, having led his people out of Egypt, was struck down by God as he was about to enter the Promised Land. Why? Because Moses was not fit to live in the new society. "Moses would have been disappointed. The Russian revolutionists and the other revolutionists who have gone through hell dreaming of heaven only to wake up on earth—they and their anguish have shown us in our day that Moses would have been brokenhearted if he had lived on and gone over thither."[7] The future, then as now, belonged to the young; the older generation had lived too long in Egypt to adapt themselves to the austere virtue of the Promised Land. "The slaves of Egypt," Steffens explained to Marie Howe, "could not learn [God's] new ideas of law and conduct, nor take and hold and create the Land of Promise." And "in our day" God would have had "to put La Follette and,—me out of the way to save mankind, because we also were reared,—in opposition, but none the less,—in Egypt."[8] "We were ruined; we could recognize salvation, but could not be saved."[9]

6. *Autobiography*, Vol. II, p. 873.
7. *World*, p. 150.
8. Steffens to Marie Howe, Nov. 15, 1924, *Letters*, Vol. II, p. 669.
9. *Autobiography*, Vol. II, p. 799.

The *Autobiography*, following close after *Moses in Red*, was among other things a celebration of youth. Its composition coincided with the birth and infancy of Steffens's son Pete, whom Steffens doted on and avidly studied. His observations convinced him that children, uncorrupted by the wisdom of the grown-up world, were the true revolutionaries and the true scientists. "Why do grown-ups grow up?" asks "Pete" in one of the letters Steffens wrote, in his son's voice, to his mother-in-law. "And why, with all my clear perception of their bunk, why do I aspire to grow up?"[1] The same question echoes through the *Autobiography*, in which learning is seen as a process of getting back to the intuitive understanding of childhood. Children knew, or quickly learned, that "nothing was what it was supposed to be." Still a child, Steffens had discovered that the horse races were fixed, the state legislature was fixed, "the Legislature wasn't what my father, my teachers, and the grown-ups thought; it wasn't even what my histories and other books said." "I had my tragedy of disillusionment . . . young," only to be filled once again with the illusions of higher education, the illusions of conventional morality, of right and wrong. These, it had taken a lifetime to unlearn.[2]

Watching his son, together with his own "experience in unlearning" (capped by the six years' labor on the *Autobiography*), left Steffens with "a deep faith in the (intellectual) courtesy and a high hope in the inborn capability of our successors—youth."[3] It is not surprising therefore to find him identifying himself, in 1934, with the young Communists "out in the field." He had written a review attacking Max Eastman's *Artists in Uniform*; Eastman in reply accused Steffens of having become a Stalinist tool and of abetting the Stalinists' cam-

1. Steffens to Mrs. A. Winter, Aug. 19, 1925, *Letters*, Vol. II, p. 707.
2. *Autobiography*, Vol. I, pp. 47, 37.
3. "Becoming a Father at Sixty Is a Liberal Education," in *World*, p. 203.

paign to prevent the formation of a united front against
Fascism by splitting the labor movement.

> I have been watching some Communist leaders of the American
> working class out in the field [Steffens wrote to *The New Re-
> public*, where Eastman's letter had appeared] and I have found
> them to be thoughtful, rather silent men and women, terribly
> overworked but poised in their manifold activities, loyal, uncom-
> promising, daring and very understanding. They do not refuse,
> they labor incessantly but wisely, to achieve a united front. They
> are indeed splitting the trade union movement, but they have not
> gone far enough in that direction; they have not yet chiseled off
> all the old pacifist, liberal, socialist labor leaders whom the big-
> business leaders find "reasonable" and can "do business with."
>   As a mere political observer, I will report to Max Eastman and
> all my other old friends, that out here on the picket lines of the
> actual struggle there are Communist party leaders whom I can
> follow. I can't lead them, Max, but I can follow them with a
> satisfaction I have never felt before in all my professional career.[4]

In the same spirit he explained: "I was not a Communist because that implied leadership and no ex-liberal was fit to lead
people today."[5]

The difficulty was that such modesty led to a sort of dogmatism of its own. It amounted, in Steffens's case, to an abdi-
cation of his own judgment, his own perceptions, his own
feelings. When his feelings told him that the revolution had
somehow failed to bring about a better life, he decided that it
was his feelings, not the revolution, which were at fault. Having lived too long in "Egypt," he was too corrupt to live in the
New Jerusalem. Moreover, he was an intellectual, and the
future—the immediate future, anyway—belonged to men of
action. Others closed their minds to the revolution; Steffens
accepted it, with all its faults, as a "revelation," natural or

4. Steffens to *New Republic*, Aug. 1, 1934, *Letters*, Vol. II, p. 988.
5. *Lincoln Steffens Speaking* (New York: Harcourt, Brace; 1936), p. 210.

divine, of immutable laws that it was beyond the capacity of
mere men to alter.

It cannot be too strongly insisted upon, however, that
Steffens grasped something which eluded the liberal anti-Communists: that the real mission of the Russian revolution, and of
the Mexican revolution too, was the modernization of backward countries. He saw that the underlying issue of the First
World War was the question of which of the European countries was to "bring the backward countries into our system."[6]
He saw too that the Bolsheviks "had respect for our efficiency"
and "envied and planned to imitate our mass production . . .
our big business production, our chain stores and other beginnings of mass distribution."[7] He saw, in short, what others
have discovered only in the 1950's or have yet to discover at all,
that Communism represented a stage in the struggle of backward countries for economic development and national self-
sufficiency. He saw these things with particular clarity in the
case of Mexico; and if his observations on Mexico remain today
the most vivid and convincing of his writings, it is because the
Mexican rather than the Russian revolution has proved (contrary to early expectations, contrary to the expectations of
Steffens himself) to be the prototype of the twentieth-century
revolution.[8] But he also saw these things, though less clearly,
in the case of Soviet Russia, at a time when other liberals could
see in the revolution no more than a struggle for democracy
betrayed.

Unfortunately, Steffens was not content to rest the case for
the revolution on economic grounds alone; he was not content
to argue that the revolution, insofar as it provided a means of

6. *Autobiography*, Vol. II, p. 741.
7. Ibid., Vol. II, p. 837.
8. See the chapters on Mexico in the *Autobiography*, Vol. II, pp. 712-40,
and the brilliant piece of reporting, "The Sunny Side of Mexico" [*Metropoli-
tan*, May, 1915] in *World*, pp. 4-20.

285 · *The Education of Lincoln Steffens*

modernization and national independence, was both necessary
and desirable. He insisted that it was also *inevitable*, ordained
by the inscrutable laws of history. He insisted, moreover, that
it would lead not only to a new form of economic organization
but to a new and better culture. Communism, for Steffens,
represented above all a great advance of the human spirit. In
seeing it so, he was influenced in part by Ella Winter; but the
idea of the "scientific culture" was his own, and he had been
talking about it long before her visit to Russia confirmed what
he had already decided in his own mind. He had long ago
decided that the trouble with American society was not so
much political or economic as cultural—the gap between
middle-class ethics and the realities of industrialism. It followed that nothing short of a cultural revolution—a new way
of thinking—would save what was worth saving of civilization.
It was inevitable, if anything in history can ever be said to be
inevitable, that Steffens should have identified the revolution in
Russia with his own private ambition, conceived while he was
still a student in Europe, at a time when only a handful of
dedicated zealots dreamed of a Communist revolution, to find
and formulate a scientific basis for ethics.

9 / The Anti-Intellectualism

of the Intellectuals

[I]

As the twentieth century wore on, it became more and more difficult in the United States to be a radical and a liberal at the same time. Ella Winter has described how, when she and Steffens landed in America in 1927, they were both surprised to find how much importance the New York intellectuals attached to the distinction "between liberal and radical."[1] In the heyday of the new radicalism, men of advanced social opinions had used the terms "socialism," "radicalism," "liberalism," and "progressivism" with a certain disregard of their various shades of meaning. The distinctions between them mattered less than the vision, common to all, of a "cooperative commonwealth" in which reason would take the place of force. Political salvation, it seemed, lay not in any particular program but in the state of mind with which men approached the solution of social problems. It lay in what Steffens called intelligence. Once crime became conscious, the new radicals assumed, the unreasonableness of the system which made it necessary would be evident to all. Psychology was the key to politics, education the key to social change; the cultural revolution seemed as important as the social revolution, and

1. Ella Winter: *And Not to Yield* (New York: Harcourt, Brace & World; 1963), p. 118.

[286]

men mixed art and politics with the same ease with which they mixed radicalism and reform. After the First World War, political and cultural rebellion tended, for a time at least, to split apart; but more important than that, reform split off from radicalism. The political choice, for intellectuals, increasingly defined itself as a choice between "commitment" and "alienation."

Before the war, the new radicals had assumed that the old order was on the way out, and the war, when it came, only strengthened their belief in its imminent demise. They had assumed, moreover, that the new society which took its place would be one of freedom, spontaneity, and beauty. Both assumptions very soon proved to have been unduly optimistic. The old order not only survived the war, defeating the demand for peace without victory and imposing a "Carthaginian" peace on the Central Powers, but it showed itself far more intransigent than radicals had imagined—more intransigent and at the same time more potent. Imperialism did not melt away in the heat of the great conflagration, as almost everyone had expected; in the West at least it emerged bloodied and scarred but essentially intact. In Russia, on the other hand, the revolution was a fact, a fact the existence of which provided a tangible alternative to imperialism; but the Soviet Union, as each hopeful visitor discovered in turn, was not the promised land of the radicals' dreams. If anything, it was a more repressive society than that of the West. Yet it was a success in its own terms, and as Lincoln Steffens had early foreseen, other backward countries would follow its example as a way of achieving rapid industrialization. The revolution was a fact, then, for all its imperfections; it offered a real alternative to capitalism; and yet the existence of the alternative, for American intellectuals, had an effect precisely the reverse of what had been expected: it narrowed rather than widened the circle of choice. One after the other, American radicals who discovered that the Bolshevik revolution was not their revolution at all—was if anything a gross betrayal of it—found themselves forced either into "choosing the West," as Dwight Macdonald chose it in 1952, or into holding out for still another course (whether in the name of Trotsky or Castro or a native tradition of dissent, real or imagined) at the price of political relevance. In a world divided between Communism and liberalism, American radicalism tended to become increasingly shrill, increasingly desperate, and increasingly bizarre, as it searched for some tenable third position independent of both. Its only hope was the eventual emergence of a genuine alternative, not, finally, in Latin America or Asia or some other part of the world, but in the United States itself. Until that time American radicalism, lacking any reasonable hope of political power, would continue to degenerate into a cult concerned chiefly with preserving the purity of its doctrine and membership. "Alienation" would continue to be an article of faith and the inadequacy of American life an axiom the truth of which it was no longer necessary to demonstrate. Social criticism, like political action, would continue to go by the board. American radicalism would more and more consist of a ritual celebration of radicalism itself, an interminable exposition of the mysteries of the faith.

As for liberalism, it not only survived, it paradoxically thrived in the very circumstances which should have defeated it once and for all. In a world torn between revolution and reaction, it should have been liberalism which faded away—as, indeed, everyone kept predicting it would. Instead, it went from one triumph to another, saved by the unexpected success of the capitalist order in sustaining a decent standard of living; saved, in the last analysis, by the twenty-five years' war, hot and cold, which made that feat possible. Liberals had predicted all along that a reformed capitalism could be made to work, and the "affluent society" of the fifties and sixties, if one could overlook its other defects, appeared to vindicate them. But vindicated or not, they could point to their unquestioned successes at the polls, the great victories of Franklin Roosevelt, Truman, and Kennedy, to prove that the American people were at least willing to elect liberals to power: more, clearly, than they would do for radicals. Whatever the merits of the case, the liberals had the advantage of a measure of popular support.

In each generation, moreover—but especially in the important generation following the Second World War—the ranks of liberalism were refreshed by defectors from the revolutionary camp, ex-liberals turned ex-Communist; and these recruits brought to liberalism the same polemical gifts, the same sense of commitment, and the same intolerance of opposition which they had learned from the Bolsheviks—all of which, so far as its ability to survive was concerned, stood liberalism in good stead. If liberalism became in time the official creed of the intellectual establishment, it was partly because the liberals were able to capture the radicals' reputation for political realism, to present themselves as hard-boiled and "pragmatic," and thus to appeal convincingly to the American intellectual's need to see himself as a "tough-minded" man of the world, not a mere spectator but an active participant in the great events of the day. The rhetoric of the new radicalism, as we have seen, was bound up from the beginning with the cult of the hard-boiled; and the debates of the thirties, forties, and fifties turned not only on substantive issues of policy but also on questions of rhetoric, the outcome depending to a considerable degree on the success with which each side was able to depict the other as sentimental, timid, effeminate, and "utopian." Insofar as liberalism, like other political creeds, is not a program but a language, it survived because liberals were able to adapt the radical style, the radical stance, to their own purposes. It was no accident that the chief architect of the new liberalism, Reinhold Niebuhr, was a disillusioned Marxist whose political "realism" had been forged in the polemical wars which had so long convulsed the literary Left.

[II]

In 1931 *The New Republic* conducted a symposium on the future of liberalism. The magazine had changed hands: Croly and Weyl were dead, Lippmann had taken his talents elsewhere, and the new editors—Edmund Wilson, George Soule, Malcolm Cowley, and others—were men of a more radical bent. The great depression, moreover, was in its second year. "The time has come," said Wilson, "for liberals seriously to reconsider their position."[2]

The debate which followed resolved itself into a triangle. George Soule took the position that liberalism still had a future, provided it was sufficiently "hard-boiled."[3] Wilson argued that liberalism had "bet" on a reformed capitalism and lost, and that intellectuals now had no choice but to align themselves with the proletariat. A third contributor, Benjamin Ginzburg, condemned both Wilson and Soule and argued that the principal

2. Edmund Wilson: "An Appeal to Progressives," *New Republic*, LXV (Jan. 14, 1931), p. 234. Daniel Aaron, in *Writers on the Left* (New York: Harcourt, Brace & World; 1961), pp. 251–3, gives a short summary of this debate; it was through his account that I first learned of it.

3. George Soule: "Hard-Boiled Radicalism," *New Republic*, LXV (Jan. 21, 1931), pp. 261–5.

obligation of the intellectuals was not to any political program but to the intellectual life itself.[4]

Both Wilson and Soule, Ginzburg thought, made the mistake of advocating political solutions to problems that were not political but cultural. Wilson had said that "what we have lost is . . . not merely our way in the economic labyrinth, but our conviction of the value of what we are doing"; but "if we have lost our sense of values," Ginzburg maintained, "we cannot find it by betting on some plan of economic or political action; it is rather by clarifying our sense of values that we ensure intelligent political action."[5] Similarly, Ginzburg found in

4. Ginzburg, born in 1898, graduated from the Columbia University School of Journalism in 1919 and took a Ph.D. in philosophy at Harvard in 1926. He has written on philosophic and scientific subjects and lectured at the New School of Social Research. He published *Adventures of Science* in 1930. Other pieces of his include a review of a collection of philosophical essays (*NR*, LXVII [July 29, 1931], pp. 292–3), in which he attacks John Dewey's version of pragmatism; "Science under Communism" (*NR*, LXIX [Jan. 6, 1932], pp. 207–9); a letter (*NR*, LXIX [Jan. 27, 1932], pp. 296–7) criticizing the editors, in their zeal for "long-range planning," for hiding "the sacrifices that have to be demanded from the present holders of economic privileges" if such planning was to be realized; and another letter (*NR*, LXXXII [Feb. 20, 1935], p. 47) replying to an article by Charles A. Beard on "The Blessed Profit System," in which Ginzburg notes that "the profit motive, denied its outlet in increasing production, has turned cannibalistic, taking a toll from starvation & restriction of production, while the state stands by and plays the priest at the ceremony of human sacrifice."

More recently, Ginzburg served as research director for the Senate Subcommittee on Constitutional Rights and published a second book, *Rededication to Freedom* (New York: Simon and Schuster; 1959), in which he argued that the entire federal security program ought to be dismantled. In a curious introduction, Reinhold Niebuhr—an advocate, it would seem, of precisely the kind of liberal and "pragmatic" compromise over the loyalty issue which it was one of the purposes of Ginzburg's book to undermine—commended the book while cautiously adding that Ginzburg's generalizations were "too sweeping in several instances."

5. Wilson: "An Appeal to Progressives," p. 236; Ginzburg: "Against Messianism," *NR*, LXVI (Feb. 18, 1931), p. 15. All the quotations which follow are from this last article, and from Soule's "Hard-Boiled Radicalism."

Soule's article—given over though it was almost wholly to politics and economics—"an implicit recognition of the underlying cultural and intellectual issues," for Soule had written: "The progressives ought not to be satisfied with the recommendation of specific programs or pieces of economic and social machinery, but should also strive to forge the human values which alone can give these devices validity." The real question, then, as both Wilson and Soule seemed implicitly to admit, was not one of political and economic policies but the deeper question of "the relation of political action to cultural and intellectual values." Whatever the differences between Wilson and Soule, they were both guilty, it seemed to Ginzburg, of approaching political reform as if it were "logically prior to everything else," whereas a "true sense of values" would be "compelled to reverse the perspective" and "instead of staking individual freedom entirely on a realization of political reform," would begin "with the affirmation of moral and intellectual freedom in the present" and make the goal of politics "the extension of the range of freedom in the future." The first point of view led to "messianism, a religion which stakes everything on the hope of the future"; the other, to "a rational critical religion which relies entirely on its sense of values in the present and not upon the turn of events in the future." The latter viewed politics objectively, as a means of realizing and preserving certain values desirable in themselves without "any justification . . . in terms of political dogmas or social policies"; the other, by transforming political action "into a sort of personal salvation," ended up with "a subjective interpretation of reality in its very attempt to be ultra-realistic."

Soule himself, answering Wilson's "appeal to progressives," had accused Wilson of "utopianism," but if Ginzburg's analysis was correct, Marxism was only the more obvious form of political salvationism; and in any case his concept of "messianism" differed critically from Soule's much cruder concept of "utopianism." Soule had accused intellectuals of embracing Marxism not because they really believed that capitalism was about to collapse but because they wished to escape from their political responsibilities. It was this "escape from reality" which Soule condemned as "utopianism of a peculiarly deceptive sort." Communism offered "a heroically appealing way of life," but "unless its faith in the ultimate goal of all this effort is justified, the way of life is merely a way of personal salvation by belief in an imaginary heaven." The test, then, for Soule, was whether the heaven was imaginary or not! The ultimate test of political realism, in other words, was the test of history. History alone would tell whether Wilson had been "justified" in betting on the collapse of capitalism. But it was precisely this appeal to history which Ginzburg believed to be the essence of messianism. Marxism, he noted, "does not rest the demand for the socialization of industry on moral and intellectual grounds, but falls back upon a philosophy of history—the myth of a universal cataclysm which will inevitably bring about the reign of socialism." But the same thing was true of "hard-boiled liberalism." Men like Soule rested the case for liberalism not on moral and intellectual grounds but on the hope that history would ultimately bear them out.

The most striking feature of Ginzburg's argument—one that harks back to Randolph Bourne—was his criticism not of Marxian socialism but of American progressivism.[6] His point was that progressivism too—he was thinking not so much of Soule as of the political philosophy of the early *New Republic*,

6. Cf. Randolph Bourne: *Untimely Papers* (New York: B. W. Huebsch; 1919), p. 135: "Our intellectuals have failed us as value-creators, even as value-emphasizers."

which it was the general purpose of the discussion to review—had succumbed to a myth of historical inevitability, a sort of "inverse messianism" of its own. Seeking to avoid the doctrinaire quality of Marxism, which stood out so clearly "against a background of American ideas and conditions," progressivism had attempted to formulate a social program more in accord with the social conditions that confronted it; but in so doing, Ginzburg thought, it had "attempted far too much to identify itself with the realities of American life, with the masses, to the point of losing touch with the source of its own values." If one recalls the way in which the progressives justified the war, the force of Ginzburg's observation makes itself felt at once, for the "pragmatic" defense of the war boiled down to the assertion that the triumph of democracy was historically inevitable and that the war would only hasten it; and that in any case the war was a fact, which it was futile to oppose. Behind those arguments, I have guessed, lay the intellectuals' fear of losing contact with the main currents of American life, a terrible fear of political isolation. Ginzburg sensed this too. The most important thing about pragmatism, he argued, was, in the last analysis, that it was the political philosophy of the isolated and beleaguered intellectuals.

If we keep in mind the fact that the liberals in America are primarily intellectuals by profession and training, one cannot help wondering whether the preoccupation of intellectuals with political questions is not a pathological reaction to the peculiar cultural conditions existing in America. In no country of the world is there such a tremendous gap between the values recognized by intellectuals and the values that actually govern political and economic realities. And yet in no country is the intellectual so preoccupied with affecting the course of politics to the exclusion of his intellectual interests. The less power he has of determining conditions, the more passionate, it would seem, is his will-o'-the-wisp quest of political influence.

It is here that the philosophy of pragmatism is most revealing. Pragmatism has been wrongly called the philosophy of the practical man. It represents rather the anti-intellectualism of the American intellectual, who is overawed by the practical sweep of American life.

Faced, then, with a cultural crisis—the degeneration of "cultural and intellectual values"—intellectuals put the blame "on the mob, on democracy, on the machine age—anywhere but on themselves." Instead of trying to save culture through politics, Ginzburg argued, intellectuals should first reform culture itself, over which, in any case, they had more power than they had over politics. He was not advocating a retreat to an "ivory tower" or "art for art's sake." He himself was a socialist, and his other writings, such of them as I have been able to dig out of *The New Republic* (he was not, unfortunately, a prolific writer), show him to have been fully as "committed" as the men he attacked. Nor was he an unthinking anti-Communist. He could see that the cultural climate of the Soviet Union was deplorable—not because it was given over to philistinism, nor even because the government exercised iron control over ideas, but because the Russian intellectuals themselves were so pathetically eager to put their talents at the service of history and the state—but he could also see that "the sins of bourgeois liberalism are in many ways far more disheartening." The chief of these sins, it seemed to Ginzburg, was precisely that the intellectual freedom of the West had no "roots in social reality" and lacked the "power to lead to action."[7] Ginzburg was not proposing, in short, that intellectuals turn away from social questions.

He predicted, however, that Edmund Wilson's "Appeal to Progressives" would provoke the rejoinder "that the place of the

7. "Science under Communism," *NR*, LXIX (Jan. 6, 1932), pp. 208–9.

artist is in the studio and not in the social arena." And Paul
Rosenfeld in his article "The Authors and Politics"—a reply
not to Wilson but to the intellectuals who had signed the
manifesto *Culture and the Crisis* (in which they urged support
of the Communist Party ticket in the election of 1932)—took
just such a position.[8] Rosenfeld argued that it was not the
function of the artist "to espouse the cause of 'the world' and to
defend its special interests." The world's interests were those
of "power and booty"; "and it is precisely with the matter of
in whose hands the power, the booty, the property should lie
. . . that the artist has no serious concern whatsoever." The
artist's concern was not with possessions but with the proper
use of them. Rosenfeld did not rule out the possibility that
artists might engage in a kind of social prophecy, but he tended
to associate prophecy with protest against the machine itself,
in the tradition of Ruskin and Morris. Nor did his indictment
of the intellectual bankruptcy of American radicalism cut as
deep as Ginzburg's. Where Ginzburg had been concerned with
the tendency of intellectuals to submit all questions of values
to the verdict of history, Rosenfeld reduced the whole issue
to a matter of taste. The literary radicals wanted merely "a
very generalized access to bourgeois comfort, and what in the
end comes to cars, silk stockings, and radio sets for all." But
unless there was something intrinsically wrong, given the cars,
the stockings, and the radios, with their generalized use, something intrinsically wrong with comfort itself, it is hard to see
why the radicals should have been condemned for wanting
to democratize comfort. That was a sin only if one defined
the issue as a question of art against "philistinism." For Ginz-

8. "The Authors and Politics," *Scribner's*, XCIII (May, 1933), pp. 318–20.
See again, Aaron: *Writers on the Left*, pp. 253–4.

burg, the issue presented itself in a very different light: "rational intellectualism" versus "messianism."

Rosenfeld's line of argument, in spite of its deficiencies, has generally proved more appealing than Ginzburg's to those who reject the messianism both of the Left and of the Center. It was essentially the line taken by the Southern agrarians and by such kindred spirits as Irving Babbitt and T. S. Eliot. *I'll Take My Stand*, the manifesto of the agrarians issued in 1930, attacked industrialism, the "gospel of progress," and by implication, politics itself, since it was unlikely that political action founded on such a program had much chance of success in the twentieth century. Some of the agrarians, to be sure, argued rather half-heartedly for a "program of agrarian restoration,"[9] but most of them seem to have been saying in effect that writers and artists should "take their stand" on an issue which was cultural, not political—resistance to philistinism and the barbarization of taste.[1] The same thing is true of later critics of "mass culture" such as Dwight Macdonald (of whom I shall have more to say), who turned to cultural criticism only when they had become convinced that political resistance to totalitarianism—Communist or democratic—was as futile as resistance to industrialism. Few of them would have gone so far as to say, with Rosenfeld, that the artist had "no serious concern whatsoever" with questions of power and booty, but they would have shared his pessimism concerning the ability of artists to influence the struggle for power.

The reaction, then, to "hard-boiled radicalism," with its exaggerated faith in the efficacy of direct political involvement, often took the form of an exaggerated skepticism about politics.

9. Donald Davidson: "A Mirror for Artists," in Twelve Southerners: *I'll Take My Stand* (New York: Harper Torchbooks; 1962), p. 51.
1. See the passage in Davidson's own essay, *I'll Take My Stand*, pp. 34ff.

It was exactly this reaction that Benjamin Ginzburg was trying to forestall. In attacking "messianism," he was not urging intellectuals to leave politics to the politicians; he was asking them to make a more realistic estimate of their potential political influence. And his own estimate, though superficially more modest than that of the editors of *The New Republic*, since it required intellectuals to admit that they could seldom hope to influence politics directly, was in reality more sanguine than theirs. If Ginzburg was correct, hard-boiled radicalism, whether of the Communist or the liberal variety, represented a surrender to one form or another of historical determinism. Ginzburg's radicalism involved no such abnegation of the will, only a recognition that intellectuals had more influence over politics as *intellectuals* than as political activists in their own right.

In recent years, a few other writers, equally exempt from the suspicion of political indifference, have taken the position outlined by Ginzburg in 1931. C. Wright Mills, shortly before his death in 1962, wrote this warning:

> We cannot create a left by abdicating our roles as intellectuals to become working class agitators or machine politicians, or by play-acting at other forms of direct political action. We can begin to create a left by confronting issues as intellectuals in our work. In our studies of man and society we must become fully comparative on a world-wide scale. . . . We must do so with all the technical resources at our command, and we must do so from viewpoints that are genuinely detached from any nationalist enclosure of mind or nationalist celebration. We must become internationalist again. For us, today, this means that we, personally, must refuse to fight the cold war. That we, personally, must attempt to get in touch with our opposite numbers in all countries, above all those in the Sino-Soviet zone. With them we should make our own separate peace. Then, as intellectuals, and so as public men, we should act and work as if this peace—and

the exchange of values, ideas, and programs of which it consists
—is everybody's peace, or surely ought to be.[2]

What is remarkable, however, is the degree to which voices
such as these have remained isolated and almost unheard in
the debates of the last thirty-five years. It is not the example
of Ginzburg which has appealed to American intellectuals,
or the example, from a somewhat earlier time, of Randolph
Bourne. It is the example of men like Wilson and Soule;
the example, above all, of John Dewey. Political debate
among intellectuals continues to revolve not around the question raised by Ginzburg, the relation of cultural values to
political action, but around the quarrel, increasingly artificial
and abstract, between liberalism and radicalism, two rival myths
of history.

The underlying similarity of these two positions explains
why, in spite of the contempt of liberals for radicals and radicals for liberals, so many men were able so easily to negotiate
the transition from one position to the other. Reinhold Niebuhr
is an example.[3] He began as a pro-war liberal in 1917, but
soon regretted his support of the war and his liberalism in

2. From an unfinished work entitled *The New Left*, quoted in Irving
Louis Horowitz: "The Unfinished Writings of C. Wright Mills: The Last
Phase," *Studies on the Left*, III (fall, 1963), p. 10. Unfortunately Mills did
not always follow his own advice; or rather, he interpreted the advice to
mean that intellectual activity was meaningless unless informed by an active
political commitment—a commitment, moreover, to a particular political
position, that of the "new Left." Mills's career, therefore, in spite of his own
warning about the dangers of political "play-acting," became, especially toward the end of his life, a particularly notable example of the habit of mind
which Ginzburg (and presumably Mills himself, in the passage just quoted)
attacked: the habit of politicizing every aspect of life.

3. In the following discussion of Niebuhr, I have relied heavily on
Donald B. Meyer: *The Protestant Search for Political Realism, 1919–1941*
(Berkeley: University of California Press; 1960), particularly chapters 13, 14,
and 16; but Meyer's opinion of Niebuhr's recent writings is much higher
than my own.

general, and after passing through various intermediate stages of political disenchantment emerged in the thirties as a full-fledged Marxist. His theological opinions underwent a similar metamorphosis. Having begun his career in the ministry as a social-gospel liberal, he gradually returned to the orthodoxy of the Pauline and Lutheran traditions, and it was from this perspective, with its emphasis on the fallibility of man and the absurdity of human pretensions, that he launched his campaign against both political and religious liberalism. At the peak of his Marxist phase in the mid-thirties, Niebuhr delivered blow after blow against the utopianism of American liberals (defining utopianism, then, much as Ginzburg had defined it); nor did he fail to see the utopian tendencies of orthodox Marxism itself. But the most instructive aspect of Niebuhr's career was the rapidity with which his realism degenerated, under the pressure of the cold war, into a bland and innocuous liberalism almost indistinguishable—for all its neo-orthodox overtones, and for all Niebuhr's unwillingness to apply the word "liberal" to himself—from the liberalism against which he had initially rebelled.

Like many others, Niebuhr decided, in the late forties, that Soviet totalitarianism was a greater menace than American capitalism; but the effect of defining the choice as a choice between rival systems was to blind him to the possibility that systems as such were neither moral nor immoral and that the choices confronting an American intellectual in the late forties were not questions of ultimate allegiance, not questions of allegiance at all, but questions of tactics and strategy. Niebuhr had all along shown a tendency to exalt political issues beyond their real importance even while attacking the "utopians" for doing so—a tendency to which his preoccupation with the "tragedy" and "irony" of politics bore witness—and in the latter part of his career this habit of rhetorical inflation got completely out of hand. As a result, rhetoric increasingly took the place of social analysis in Niebuhr's writings. In seeing the cold war as a struggle between Marxist "despotism" and the "open society" of the West, Niebuhr was no longer comparing opposing social structures, or even opposing "systems"; he was, in effect, playing off one myth against another.[4] Even during the Stalinist period the distinction between "despotism" and the "open society" was hardly an accurate description of the differences between Russia and America; by the fifties and sixties it had become completely unreal. To speak of the Soviet Union as a monolith, obedient to some mysterious and inflexible law of totalitarianism, made very little sense at a time when the structure of Soviet society was undergoing important and far-reaching changes; to characterize American society as "tolerant and modest" made very little sense at any time in American history. But Niebuhr's thought remained frozen in the polemical patterns of the late forties. Having opted for the "open society," he could no longer appreciate the degree to which American society fell hopelessly short of that ideal. The worst that he could now say about America was that a doctrinaire belief in progress and a penchant for moralizing too often led Americans to "pretend that there is a moral answer to the nuclear dilemma, or a moral way of removing the ambiguity of power and dominion in the community."[5] It was these "utopian" habits of mind, according to Niebuhr, which accounted for the "inflexibility" of American foreign policy and which led him to remark that "it would be tragic, as well as ironic, if the tolerance and modesty which we learned

4. Reinhold Niebuhr: *Nations and Empires* (London: Faber and Faber; 1959), p. 297.
5. Ibid.

or had forced upon us in the peculiar conditions of Western life should become the basis of fanaticism and immodesty in our international relations."[6]

Had he searched for the roots of American inflexibility in the social structure instead of in the national character—or, more accurately, in the myth of the national character—Niebuhr might not have found the situation so ironic. He might then have perceived a certain continuity between American policy abroad and the existence, at home, of what even President Eisenhower did not hesitate to call a "military-industrial complex" of potentially "disastrous" proportions.[7] He might have seen that there was more to American imperialism than a naïve but pardonable wish to spread the gospel of democracy and progress. Tangible interests were also involved, particularly in American relations with Latin America: hard, material, cash interests, the preservation of which depended, not on the spread of democracy at all, but on the maintenance in power of governments the very reverse of democratic. America's rise to world power, according to Niebuhr, represented a new type of imperialism, an imperialism of democratic idealism; but a closer examination of America's rise might have disclosed an old and familiar pattern of exploitation. The whole question of the character of modern imperialism, whether of the Soviet or the American type, was a far more subtle and difficult question than Niebuhr, either in his Marxist phase or in his pragmatic-realist phase, was willing to allow. In the case of the United States, it was by no means clear whether misguided idealism or calculating self-interest best explained the failures of American diplomacy. Neither the

6. Ibid., p. 296. This kind of criticism—more apology than criticism—reminds one of John Dewey's "explanation of our lapse." See above, p. 210.

7. *The New York Times*, Jan. 18, 1961, p. 22.

Marxist view, that democratic idealism was merely the " 'front' of graft" (as Lincoln Steffens would have said) nor the view of the new realists, that the weakness of American diplomacy was precisely the substitution of idealistic objectives for the more limited objectives of national self-interest—neither view seemed wholly adequate as an explanation.

Probably the answer depended on the perspective from which one examined the evidence. If one compared American diplomacy with that of its allies in Western Europe, if one compared Wilson with Clemenceau or Franklin Roosevelt with Churchill or John Foster Dulles with his counterparts in Britain and France, one could cite innumerable occasions on which American idealism—the pursuit of ultimate instead of limited objectives, the tendency to think in terms of morality rather than in terms of power, the disavowal of national advantage in favor of an altruistic internationalism—stood out in sharp contrast to European realism; and one could plausibly argue that American "imperialism" was a function of the very eagerness with which American statesmen had tried to substitute for the old imperial balance of power a new world order based on universal democracy. From the limited perspective of a study of Western Europe alone, the realism of Niebuhr, George F. Kennan, Hans J. Morgenthau, and others made good sense; and it was in fact from a study of recent Western diplomacy that they drew their examples and their evidence. From the point of view of the undeveloped world, however, the realists' picture of the American as an overzealous but genial idealist was absolutely unrecognizable. Here, on the contrary, the old Marxist clichés about predatory capitalism seemed as appropriate as ever. In this larger context the United States was unmistakably a privileged nation aligned with the other "haves" against the "have-nots," fully alive to its interests and determined to defend them to the death. Such at least was the indictment of the undeveloped countries themselves, and as time went on and the nature of American commitments in Latin America and Asia became better understood, the indictment was increasingly difficult to deny.[8]

It is no accident that the "realistic" school of political analysis has been so little concerned with the non-European world. George F. Kennan has argued on many occasions that Europe still holds the key to world politics, and the same bias reveals itself in the large body of scholarship to which the new realism has given rise. The works of Kennan, Charles E. Osgood, Louis J. Halle, Hans J. Morgenthau, and others are all studies of recent *European* diplomacy; and from that perspective, the persistence of imperialistic motives in Western diplomacy is naturally obscured.

It was widely said that Latin America, Cuba in particular, was the "blind spot" of the Kennedy administration, otherwise liberal in its foreign policies. What was not generally appreciated was that Latin America was the blind spot of the new realism as a whole, to which the Kennedy regime was so heavily committed for its ideas about international affairs. Kennedy himself was a good example of the European orientation of contemporary liberalism. His first book was a study of appeasement in England in the 1930's. He never gave comparable attention to the recent history of Africa, Asia, and Latin America. His own brand of cosmopolitanism—actually somewhat parochial, in the broader context—set the tone of his very internationalist-minded administration. It is significant that the one member of that administration who consistently stood

8. For a critique of Kennan, see my article "The Historian as Diplomat," *Nation*, CXCV (Nov. 24, 1962), pp. 348–52; also Staughton Lynd: "How the Cold War Began," *Commentary*, XXX (Nov., 1960), pp. 379–89.

for more radical foreign policies than Kennedy's was Chester Bowles. Bowles, being a long-time student and champion of India, was the one high-ranking member of the administration (subsequently demoted, as it happened) who had some knowledge and awareness of the world outside the West.

The question, in any case—the question of the nature of American imperialism and, beyond that, of the nature of American society itself (was it the "other-directed" democracy of David Riesman or a plutocracy presided over by C. Wright Mills's "power elite"?)—was complicated, and could not be resolved by reference to any single set of generalizations yet devised. What was disturbing about the new realists of the forties and fifties was their willingness prematurely to commit themselves to a view of American society in which the United States appeared unambiguously as the leader of the "free world" and the only alternative, for all its faults, to Soviet "despotism." At best, this view argued a large ignorance of the non-Western world. At worst, it suggested an abstractness of mind as prevalent among the realists as among the liberal "utopians." It is too easy, in the case of Niebuhr himself, to make the obvious point: that the transition from Marxism to pragmatic realism was a transition from one abstraction to another. But in the case of lesser men, whose commitment at once to the Marxism of the thirties and to the cold-war realism of the fifties was far more complete than Niebuhr's, it is difficult to escape the conclusion that both ideologies appealed to intellectuals because they provided unequivocal answers to questions which otherwise would have prevented the kind of total political commitment that American intellectuals seemed so eager to make. What Niebuhr said of the ex-Communists of the far Right, that in "exchanging creeds" they had not varied "the spirit and temper of their approach to life's problems," applied to many of the pragmatic realists as well.[9] If Marxism was a political religion, pragmatism became something of a religion too in the very violence of its reaction from Marxism.

Sidney Hook, an impassioned disciple first of Marx and then of John Dewey, wrote in 1952: "I cannot understand why American intellectuals should be apologetic about the fact that they are limited in their effective historical choice between endorsing a system of total terror and *critically* supporting our own imperfect democratic culture with all its promises and dangers."[1] Ostensibly a plea for political realism, that sentence revealed a utopianism or messianism as thoroughgoing as the utopianism it condemned. To describe the Soviet Union as a "system of total error" was all too obviously to make the same mistake as upholding it as a system of total truth. Hook had simply inverted the Marxist myth, to which he himself, in fact, had once enthusiastically subscribed. Having done so, he was in no position to give to American "culture" the "critical support" he had promised. Support he gave in abundance, but the criticism was not forthcoming. It was no longer necessary; when the adversary was "total evil," the "imperfections" of democracy naturally faded from sight. The only danger was that the "neutralist" intellectuals would persuade the government to follow a policy of "appeasement." Henceforth Hook reserved his criticism for neutralists, just as John Dewey, during the First World War, had reserved his harshest abuse not for the militarists but for the pacifists. "You are prepared to surrender the world to the Communists," Hook declared in a debate with Stuart Hughes on nuclear deterrence—this from the man who defined the "cardinal attribute of the life of

9. Reinhold Niebuhr: "Liberals and the Marxist Heresy," in George B. Huszar, ed.: *The Intellectuals: A Controversial Portrait* (Glencoe: The Free Press; 1960), p. 304.

1. Sidney Hook: "From Alienation to Critical Integrity: The Vocation of American Intellectuals," in *The Intellectuals*, p. 528.

thought" as "the capacity to discriminate, to make relevant distinctions."[2] In 1962, long after the rise of China and the revival of France had disrupted both the Russian and the American alliance systems, and long after most liberals, even the most orthodox, had admitted that the rhetoric and policies of the cold war were no longer relevant to world politics, Sidney Hook was still preaching a "pragmatism" that was the very antithesis of pragmatic, making a religion out of the defense of the "free world." The novel *Fail-Safe*, a popular fantasy of accidental nuclear war, stirred him to write a fervent defense of American military policy interlarded with elaborate and dismal forebodings about the probable effect of the book. "If the influence of *Fail-Safe* grows and the hysteria it germinates affects public policy and American defense efforts are curtailed, the Communists will become progressively emboldened. They will adopt more and more intransigent attitudes at the disarmament negotiation sessions in the expectation that the growth in hysterical fear about accidental war in Western countries will make their representatives 'more reasonable' in granting concessions." As for the book itself: "There is something repugnant to moral sensibility, something that transcends the limits of legitimate political criticism in impugning the patriotism and *bona fides* of men who have faithfully served the cause of freedom."[3] Hook's "critical support" of American culture was hard to distinguish from unconditional acceptance.

2. Ibid., p. 531. For Hook's attack on Hughes, see the symposium, "Western Values and Total War," *Commentary*, XXXII (Oct., 1961), p. 287.

3. Quoted in *New York Review of Books*, II (April 2, 1964), p. 18. It was possible, of course, to attack *Fail-Safe*, and other such popular fantasies, on their artistic merits. It was possible to argue that by raising false issues instead of real ones they had a bad effect on the public. (See Ithiel de Sola Pool: "Fantasy and Reality," *New Leader*, XLVII [Aug. 31, 1964], pp. 28–30.) But Hook's argument, that such novels undermined the national will to resist and thereby "emboldened" the Communists, went far beyond these considerations.

[III]

Sidney Hook carried to an extreme the political fashions of the fifties and sixties: the cult of the hard-boiled, the cant about "freedom" and the "free world." In somewhat milder form, the new "realism" swept through the liberal press (which abruptly extricated itself from its recent involvement with the Marxist "heresy"), captured the academies, and finally, under Kennedy, achieved the status of a national consensus or style—to use two of the favorite words of the neo-liberals. The most representative spokesman of the new liberal orthodoxy was Arthur Schlesinger, Jr., whose dual career as a historian and as a Democratic polemicist, adviser, and speechwriter testified to the enthusiasm of the new liberals for active political commitments. Schlesinger's writings both as a scholar and as a publicist showed the degree to which realism had become inseparable, in the popular liberal mind, from what Schlesinger called the "tough-minded" tradition of American pragmatism.

Too young to have been involved in the polemical battles of the 1930's, Schlesinger came to politics without a previous commitment to Marxism. He was deeply impressed, however, by the example of Reinhold Niebuhr, whose works, he once said, revealed to those of his own generation "a new dimension of experience—the dimension of anxiety, guilt and corruption."[4] He was influenced also, he tells us, by the pragmatism of Dewey and James; but in capturing the Jamesian concept of "tough-mindedness" for the neo-liberal position in politics, Schlesinger was putting the idea to uses which James at least could hardly have sanctioned. James, when he distinguished between the tough- and the tender-minded, was attempting

4. Arthur M. Schlesinger, Jr.: *The Vital Center* (Boston: Houghton Mifflin; 1962 [Boston, 1949]), p. xxiii.

to distinguish between two philosophic traditions, the rationalistic and the empirical. But those distinctions did not necessarily coincide with political differences of opinion over the issues of the cold war. Not all empiricists favored the policy of containment; not all rationalists opposed it. It was exactly the purpose of Schlesinger's writings, however, to show that the Jamesian distinction coincided with his own distinction between the pragmatic and utopian traditions in American liberalism, and that both these distinctions, moreover, coincided with the distinction, in contemporary politics, between the hard-boiled anti-Communist Left and the fuzzy-minded apostles of unilateral disarmament and other fanciful solutions to the hard problems of the day.[5] Both as a historian and as a propagandist, Schlesinger tended to raise political issues to the level

5. Thus: "From the beginning of the republic, there have been two strains, related but distinct, in American progressivism. One strain may be called pragmatic: that is, it accepts, without approving, the given structure of society and strives to change it by action from within. The other may be called utopian: that is, it rejects the given structure of society, root and branch, and strives to change it by exhortation and example from without. The one springs from the political commitments of eighteenth-century America. Its philosophers were Locke and Hume; its early exemplars, Franklin and Jefferson. The other springs from the religious commitments of seventeenth-century America. Its philosophers were the Levellers and the millennarians; its early exemplars, George Fox and Jonathan Edwards. . . .

"William James divided them into the 'tough-minded'—empiricist, pluralistic, skeptical—and the 'tender-minded'—rationalistic (going by principles), monistic, dogmatic."

This historical division, Schlesinger goes on to explain, was "inherent in the polemics of the Fifties," as, indeed, it had been inherent in American politics all along. It expressed itself "in the divergence between those intellectuals, like Galbraith and Rostow, who worked with Stevenson and Kennedy and the Democratic Advisory Council and those, like David Riesman and Paul Goodman, who explicitly renounced pragmatism and proclaimed the necessity of utopianism." It expressed itself, finally, in the politics of the 1960's: "The left-wing critique of the Kennedy Administration in the United States today, is, in great part, a new expression of the old complaint by those who find satisfaction in large gestures of rejection against those who find satisfaction in small measures of improvement." ("The Administration and the Left," *New Statesman* [London], LXV [Feb. 8, 1963], p. 185.)

of philosophical issues and to see in every public controversy the opposition of fundamental principles. The habit of inflating political issues in this way was of course the essence of the messianism which both pragmatism and neo-orthodoxy seemingly condemned. Schlesinger did not so much use those ideas, from which he claimed to have derived his own, as appropriate them. In this way he gave the old liberalism a new appeal by dressing it up in the fashionable garb of philosophical pragmatism and religious orthodoxy.

Plus ça change, plus c'est la même chose. Just as the hardboiled radicals of the 1930's had sneered at the shallow idealism of the progressive era, so the realists of the fifties and sixties sneered at the utopian radicalism of the thirties. Each generation claimed to be tougher and more disillusioned than the last. But the central feature of the new radicalism, the assumption that cultural reform could be achieved through political action, survived each change of fashion. If anything, it became more explicit than before. Thus Schlesinger announced in the midfifties that the chief task of modern liberalism would be not the redistribution of wealth but the improvement of the quality of the national life. Liberals and radicals had been calling for the improvement of American culture for half a century, but they had seldom committed themselves so openly to a purely political solution of the problem. Schlesinger demanded a "'qualitative liberalism' dedicated to bettering the quality of people's lives and opportunities." The new liberalism, he said in 1956, would concern itself with education, medical care, urban planning, "the bettering of our mass media and the elevation of our popular culture—in short, with the *quality* of civilization to which our nation aspires."[6]

John F. Kennedy's New Frontier could be interpreted as a

6. Arthur Schlesinger, Jr.: "The Future of Liberalism: The Challenge of Abundance," *Reporter*, XIV (May 3, 1956), p. 9.

fulfillment of these hopes. That liberal intellectuals unhesitatingly took it as such indicates the degree to which the concept of culture had degenerated over the years, even as it retained its former importance in liberal thought. The cult of the Kennedys showed that culture had become practically synonymous with chic. There was much to be said in praise of Kennedy, especially during his last year in office: the test-ban treaty; the earnest plea, at American University, for a relaxation of the cold war; the civil-rights legislation. Liberals were not content, however, to praise Kennedy's achievements. They were also infatuated with his "style." To be sure, Kennedy had a certain flair. He was, after all, an exceptionally attractive man. But looking at the Kennedy administration from a distance, one could not avoid the suspicion that what liberals called his style consisted largely of a Harvard education, a certain amount of conscientious concert-going, and a feeling, never very precise, that the arts ought somehow to be officially encouraged. The desperate gratitude with which intellectuals welcomed even these few crumbs from the presidential table was disheartening. "What was . . . moving," said Richard Rovere, ". . . was the admiration for excellence that led Kennedy to surround himself . . . with the best people our present civilization has to offer."[7] Murray Kempton was surely closer to the truth when he wrote that the special quality of Kennedy's "style"—it seemed to Kempton a source of strength—was a "proportion of indifference." "Mr. Kennedy would not have thought himself deficient in duty if he did not think about music from one day to the next; but, when State occasions demanded, he expected the music to be as worthy of a decent ear as the food was of a refined palate."[8]

7. R[ichard] H. R[overe]: "Letter from Washington," *New Yorker,* XXXIX (Nov. 30, 1963), p. 53.
8. *Spectator* [London], Feb. 7, 1964, p. 168.

Most intellectuals, however, wanted to believe that Kennedy cared deeply and thought profoundly about the cultural life of the nation. Rovere's eulogy of the dead President, a fine specimen of the jargon of the New Frontier, came back again and again to the same point: Kennedy had "brought to the Presidency a genuinely distinctive style." He surrounded himself with people of "large, bold aims and a large expansive view of life."

> There was not a reformer among them, as far as anyone could tell. Pragmatism—often of the grubbiest kind—was rampant. "Facts" were often valued beyond their worth. "Ideology" was held in contempt—too much so, perhaps—and was described as a prime source of mischief in the world. But if there were no do-gooders around, and no planners, and not even, really, very much in the way of plans, there were large thoughts and large intentions and very long looks into the future.

Kennedy himself was "interested in and amused by and critical of everything in American life." He was "the first modern President who gave one a sense of caring—and of believing that a President ought to care—about the whole quality and tone of American life." He cared about the aesthetics of motels, he cared about the "ugliness and vulgarity and intellectual impoverishment" of urban life, he cared about the quality of American education. "He proposed to have, in time, an impact on American taste. He proposed to impress upon the country—to make it, if he could, share—his own respect for excellence of various kinds." Rovere admitted that Kennedy himself "did not respond much to painting or music, or even to literature"; rather he dutifully "looked at paintings he didn't enjoy, and listened to music he didn't much care for, because people who he thought were excellent people had told him they were excellent things." (Kempton's Kennedy, with his "proper proportion of indifference," was quite unrecognizable here.) Rovere was not sure but what "this sort of thing," in anybody but a President, might have been "the opposite of admirable," and he conceded that there was something a little fatuous in Kennedy's idea "that he might do something to advance American civilization." What was important, however, was Kennedy's "style." What was important was that Kennedy admired "excellence" and surrounded himself with excellent people. "He made thinking respectable in Washington."

The most interesting thing about the cult of the New Frontier was what it revealed about the changing conception not only of culture but of intellectual life in general. The downgrading of Kennedy's political skill and the upgrading of his vigor and restlessness of mind was intended to show not simply that Kennedy had surrounded himself with intellectuals but that he *was* an intellectual; and the tributes to his keen mind and discriminating taste can thus be taken as a flattering self-portrait of the intellectual as a cultivated aristocrat and man of the world. As a reflection of the intellectuals' own self-image, the portrait of Kennedy as an intellectual provides a full measure of the degree to which the idea of the intellectual life had become bound up with images of worldly success and prestige. What the intellectuals admired in Kennedy was his youth, his good looks, his cultivation, his cosmopolitanism, his savoir faire, his taste, his respect for "excellence," his wealth itself—what all of his admirers, in short, presumably admired; but the intellectuals not only admired these things, they associated them with *intellect*. It was the sum of them which made Kennedy, in their eyes, an intellectual; that, together with the quality of his mind—"detached, consecutive, and explicit," as Arthur Schlesinger called it.[9]

The intellectuals' self-image, it will be seen, had come to coincide with the popular stereotype of the intellectual. The

9. Quoted in Rovere: *New Yorker*, XXXIX, p. 53.

popular stereotype, contrary to a widespread impression among intellectuals themselves, was not unfavorable. By the 1960's it was a well-documented fact that the intellectual professions stood high in the sociologists' hierarchy of social prestige.[1] Although the content of the image of the intellectual cannot be documented with such precision, one can summarize it approximately: the intellectual was typically a graduate of an Ivy League college; he wore Ivy League clothes with the same casual authority with which he talked about books, wine, and women; he had traveled widely, mostly in Europe; he lived in a modern house filled with Danish furniture; his boys had long hair instead of crew cuts; his political opinions, like his other tastes, were vaguely unconventional and advanced; he was always questioning things the rest of us took for granted. In short, he was "sophisticated." The older images of the intellectual as absentminded professor, or again as wild-eyed, long-haired political agitator, were no longer current. The new intellectual was a bright young man, not a bumbling academic; and even when he appeared as an agitator, he retained his Harvard accent and his club tie. The picture could be reversed, as it was in the days of McCarthy; if admiration turned to envy, then the very attributes that once seemed admirable turned sinister. The intellectual's cosmopolitanism became un-American, his sophistication snobbery, his accent affectation, his clothes and his manner the badge, obscurely, of sexual deviation. But the point about the "anti-intellectual" image of the intellectual is that it agreed with the picture of the intellectual as a young executive; it merely put a different construction on the same evidence. Even as a subversive, the intellectual was still an Ivy League aristocrat, an Alger Hiss. As many com-

1. See Richard Centers: "Social Class, Occupation, and Imputed Belief," *American Journal of Sociology*, LVIII (May, 1953), pp. 543–55; Seymour Martin Lipset: *Political Man* (Garden City: Doubleday; 1960), chapter 10.

mentators pointed out at the time, the villainy of the intellectual, in the "anti-intellectual" mind, consisted precisely in his Eastern clothes and his Eastern accent; McCarthyism was a form of populism (using the term in its broadest sense), based on envy.

What is surprising is that the intellectuals in condemning McCarthyism did not question the essential accuracy of the popular image of themselves; they merely objected to the ugliness and unseemliness of organized envy. Peter Viereck's well-known attack on McCarthy as a neo-populist—an attack carefully coupled with attacks on the "shame" of the intellectuals who had sold out to Communism in the thirties—was also a defense of the elite against the mob.[2] So were some of the essays in *The New American Right*, a selection of scholarly studies published at the height of the McCarthyite terror.[3] And when the terror had subsided, it was the discovery that they had, after all, exaggerated the contempt in which their class was popularly held which convinced the intellectuals that the world had once more been made safe for intellect. The sociological data which showed that intellectuals enjoyed an unexpectedly high degree of social status was pointed to as proof that intellectual *values* were held in high esteem. The confusion, in the mind of the intellectuals, between intellect itself and the interests of the intellectuals as a class had become almost complete, though the two things, in truth, had never been more hopelessly at odds.

2. "In America the suddenly enthroned lower classes cannot prove to themselves psychologically that they are now upper-class unless they can indict for pro-proletariat subversion those whom they know in their hearts to be America's real intellectual and social aristocracy." (Peter Viereck: "The New American Radicals," *Reporter*, XI [Dec. 30, 1954], p. 41.) See also Viereck's *Shame and Glory of the Intellectuals* (Boston: Beacon Press; 1953).

3. Daniel Bell, ed.: *The New American Right* (New York: Criterion Books; 1955).

The liberalism of the fifties and sixties, with its unconcealed elitism and its adulation of wealth, power, and "style," was firmly rooted in a social fact of prime importance: the rise of the intellectuals to the status of a privileged class, fully integrated into the social organism. If the new radicalism represented the world view of the intellectuals emergent, the liberalism of the Eisenhower-Kennedy era was the ideology of a mature class jealous of its recognized position in the social order. As Edward A. Ross had predicted, the "mandarinate" had made itself economically indispensable to modern society.[4] The post-industrial order created an unprecedented demand for experts, technicians, and managers. Both business and government, under the pressure of technological revolution, expanding population, and the indefinitely prolonged emergency of the cold war, became increasingly dependent on a vast apparatus of systematized data intelligible only to trained specialists; and the universities, accordingly, became themselves industries for the mass-production of experts. Some of the larger universities, moreover, were directly implicated in the national defense and in the whole "military-industrial complex" by virtue of their role in developing and perfecting new instruments of warfare. To the extent to which they came to depend for support on the government and on the private foundations, they lost their character as centers of independent learning and critical thought and were swallowed up in the network of the "national purpose"; but the compensatory advantages of wealth, power, and prestige exerted an almost irresistible attraction, and the competition for government contracts, accordingly, waxed as fierce among institutions of higher learning as it did among the great private corporations. It gave rise in time—particularly in the case of the great technical schools such as M.I.T. and

4. See above, pp. 173-4.

the California Institute of Technology—to a new academic type, the academic entrepreneur or "statesman," indistinguishable both in his social function (to lobby for patronage) and in his style of life (expense-account affluence) from his counterpart in industry. Such types more and more dominated the higher reaches of academic life; the lower reaches were staffed, increasingly, with high-grade technicians. Often they went on to Washington, not as career bureaucrats but as temporary advisors and "coordinators," and their presence there caused other intellectuals to marvel at the remarkable renaissance of ideas in the capital city—as if ideas were even remotely the business, much less the pleasure, of the new academic statesmen.[5]

Neither the academic statesmen nor the academic technicians were any longer intellectuals at all, if intellectuals were defined as people who derive pleasure and profit from playing with ideas.[6] They were intellectuals only by Reinhold Niebuhr's definition of intellectuals as "the more articulate members of the community," and the technicians did not qualify even under a definition as broad as that.[7] Intellectuals in the classic sense, in the new society, were to be found chiefly in the borderland between academic life and liberal journalism. Even there they led a precarious existence. If the universities tended to function as a national resource, merging imperceptibly with industry and government, journalism tended to degenerate into public relations, advertising, and propaganda. The daily press and the mass magazines, once the media of muckraking,

5. See Christopher Rand: "Center of a New World," *New Yorker*, XL (April 11, 1964), pp. 43–90; XL (April 18, 1964), pp. 57–107.

6. On the playfulness of intellect, see Richard Hofstadter: *Anti-intellectualism in American Life* (New York: Alfred A. Knopf; 1963), p. 30.

7. Niebuhr: "Liberals and the Marxist Heresy," in Huszar, ed.: *The Intellectuals*, p. 302.

had long since been assimilated into the national consensus, partly because of their economic dependence on corporate wealth, partly because of the decline of competition within the newspaper industry itself (in particular because of the monopolization of news-gathering by the great news services), partly perhaps because the sheer impenetrability of the modern state made informed criticism of its activities increasingly difficult. The mass media, like the universities, took on the character of semi-official institutions devoted not so much to criticism and analysis as to the diffusion of official attitudes. Even the larger literary magazines acquired an institutional tone, not because they were subjected to governmental control (any more than most newspapers were subject to direct governmental censorship) but because, like the newspapers, their dependence on revenue from advertising exercised a subtly inhibiting effect on their policies. Or perhaps it was simply that they conceived of their function as the propagation of culture rather than the criticism of it. Some of them seemed more interested in boosting the notion that reading was a worthwhile activity than in reviewing books. Culture, like education, had become a commodity to be marketed like any other.

These developments had an effect on journalism, especially literary journalism, as disastrous as the effect on higher education of its involvement with the national defense; but they did nothing to diminish the social status of American intellectuals. Just the reverse, in fact: insofar as cultural life became an adjunct alike of advertising and of the "entertainment industry," the glamour of these other milieux tended to rub off on the intellectuals. The popular image of the intellectual came in many ways to coincide with the image of the ad-man. More important, ad-men and entertainers tried themselves to look like intellectuals. David Ogilvy, an Englishman who specialized in giving prestige products an Anglicized image, made a pitch for advertising as a "creative" enterprise.[8] Likewise certain movie stars, notably Marilyn Monroe, have hankered after intellectual status—a development, well publicized by Miss Monroe's marriage to Arthur Miller, which could not have failed to alert people to the fact that intellectuals in America were no longer to be considered as abstracted academics. An intellectual, these days, might turn out to be a beautiful young woman with "problems."

The convergence of the world of culture with the world of advertising and entertainment was only incidentally a function of the rise of mass communications. It was primarily a function of the concentration of cultural life in the city of New York, a development, in fact, which was indispensable to the creation of an intellectual class in the first place. In the nineteenth century the United States was a country without a cultural capital, the best example of such a country in the world. The years between the Civil War and the First World War, however, saw the steady dissolution of provincial culture and the concentration of intellectual life in Chicago and New York, and by the time of the Second World War the isolated pre-eminence of New York had long been assured. Neither the newspaper business nor the publishing of books and periodicals nor, indeed, any form of cultural activity escaped the centralizing pull that governed the economy as a whole. The economic advantages of large-scale production gave rise to the popular press and the national magazine, both of them geared to an urban readership. Publishing, accordingly, gravitated to the cities. In publishing as in every other industry, moreover, a fierce competition tended to eliminate the smaller producers and to concentrate the control of the market in the hands of a few firms strategically located at the financial heart of the

8. David Ogilvy: *Confessions of an Advertising Man* (New York: Atheneum; 1963), *passim.*

nation. By the turn of the century most of the major magazines and all but a handful of the publishers of books had taken up residence in New York. Journalists, writers, artists, intellectuals of all kinds had no choice but to follow. The demands of this process again and again gave a new shape to men's careers. William Dean Howells moved from Ohio to Boston to New York. A whole group of intellectuals—Floyd Dell, Susan Glaspell, Carl Van Vechten, and others—migrated from Iowa to New York by way of Chicago. The "renaissance" in Chicago at the turn of the century was short-lived because by the time of the First World War most of its leading figures had gone on to New York. From then on, New York was unmistakably the spiritual home of the American intellectual. *The New York Times* and *The New Yorker* became national institutions because they provided, for the exiled multitudes, a tenuous link to the Mecca of the East.

The effect of this process was to create in New York not so much a community of intellectuals as a series of overlapping communities bound together by a common interest—the intensity of which, however, varied from one circle to another—in the current concerns of the capital city (much as the overlapping circles of Washington society shared a common interest in the general gossip of the bureaucracy), and beyond that, by a common devotion to the metropolis itself and to the intangible glamour it stood for. The "entertainment industry" —not only the mass media but the Broadway stage—furnished a particularly good example of this collective narcissism, this continual self-scrutiny. Transferred with much acclaim to the glamorous new setting of Lincoln Center in 1964, Broadway's fascination with itself showed up more clearly than ever before: of the three plays staged by the new Repertory Theatre, two of them, as Robert Brustein has observed, had "less to do with reality than with the personal lives of those represented at

Lincoln Center." S. N. Behrman's *But for Whom Charlie*, the third offering of the season, was based in part on the life of Eugene O'Neill, whose *Marco Millions* had preceded it, while the first production, Arthur Miller's *After the Fall*, concerned itself with the author's marriage to Marilyn Monroe and his relations with Elia Kazan, the producing director of the Repertory Theatre and thus the director of Miller's own play. "It is too bad, for the sake of symmetry," Brustein wrote, "that O'Neill did not write a play about S. N. Behrman and Arthur Miller."[9]

Something of the same parochialism infected other areas of intellectual life as well. Yet New Yorkers on the whole were probably more resistant to the idea of New York than most outsiders. The collapse of provincial culture left a vacuum which was filled by influences emanating from New York. In culture as in clothes, New York set the styles, and the greater the emotional distance from New York, the more faithfully were they followed. In view of all these things, the intensity with which American intellectuals identified themselves with the Kennedy administration was not surprising. The cultural tone of the New Frontier was the tone of Broadway sophistication, with an admixture of Hollywood. The nerves of the administration reached in one direction through the President's brother-in-law to Frank Sinatra's Hollywood "clan" and to Hollywood liberalism in general, and in the other, via the first lady, to the world of fashion (she herself had once worked as a photographer for *Vogue*) and of the fashionable arts. On the political side, the influence of the Cambridge academic and technological community—that other center, not so much of the intellectual life, as of the new educational bureaucracy—was everywhere to be seen. The New Frontier caught up the two dominant strands of the intellectual class and wove them

9. Robert Brustein: "Subsidized Rubbish," *NR*, CL (April 11, 1964), p. 36.

together. It synthesized Broadway and Route 128. The result, if it was not an intellectual "establishment," was something very much like it—almost indistinguishable, in fact.[1] The intellectuals, as a class, had achieved official recognition, affluence, prestige, and power, and something of the mentality that goes with them. If liberalism more and more resembled conservatism ("responsible conservatism"), it was because the intellectuals, for the first time in their history, had something material to conserve.

[IV]

The radicals, meanwhile—those who survived the disappointments of the thirties and forties—led a harrowing existence. Quite apart from the more obvious difficulties which confronted them—the difficulty, for instance, of opposing capitalism without endorsing Communism—they were subject to some of the same pressures as the liberals. Like the liberals, the radicals clustered together in little self-contained communities, living on their own myths and gossip; like the liberals, they fell easy prey to fashion. Isolation—"alienation"—did not necessarily lead to introspection.

Two writers, Dwight Macdonald and Norman Mailer, illustrate some of the difficulties that beset American radicalism in the forties, fifties, and sixties. Neither is "typical," but both illuminate, in different ways, the general conditions, political

---

1. Richard Rovere, in the title essay of his collection *The American Establishment* (New York: Harcourt, Brace & World; 1962), pp. 3–21, tried to satirize the idea of an establishment; but the satire was so uncertainly sustained that many readers found it difficult to tell which side of the dispute Rovere was upholding. The tone of the piece suggests that Rovere was half convinced by the proposition he was seeking to discredit.

and cultural, under which radicalism, in these years, was obliged to operate.

Dwight Macdonald's career falls into two parts. Until about 1950 he wrote chiefly on political subjects; thereafter he devoted himself mainly to "social-cultural reportage," in particular to the critique of "mass culture."[2] The first half of his career coincides with his editorship of *Politics*, a monthly that he founded in 1944 and ran single-handed until its collapse in 1949. Since then Macdonald has written for other people's magazines, especially *The New Yorker*, which, he has said, in spite of its large circulation "permits the writer to express himself without regard for the conventions of American journalism."[3] Some would argue that *The New Yorker's* own conventions—its air of aristocratic detachment, the inverse snobbery that reigns in its reviews (which in their eagerness to expose the pretensions of the avant-garde often end up by celebrating mediocrity)— are as stifling as the conventions from which it allows its contributors to escape. In 1946 Macdonald himself objected to *The New Yorker's* "suave, tone-downed, underplayed kind of naturalism (it might be called 'denatured naturalism')," which he compared unfavorably with the "cruder" naturalism of Theodore Dreiser and James T. Farrell.[4] When he later involved himself with the magazine, to be sure, Macdonald gave up neither his unconventional opinions nor his own way of expressing them; nor did he cease to be effective as an advocate of social change. It is possible, in fact, that he was more effective as a writer for a magazine with 300,000 readers than he had been as editor of *Politics*, which at its peak had a circulation of

2. Dwight Macdonald: "Politics Past," in *Memoirs of a Revolutionist* (New York: Meridian Books; 1958), p. 31.
3. "Amateur Journalism," in *The Responsibility of Peoples* (London: Victor Gollancz; 1957), p. 149.
4. Ibid., p. 114.

little more than 5,000.[5] Nevertheless, the latter part of Macdonald's career has about it something of the air of a strategic retreat. By 1950, Macdonald had tired, understandably, both of *Politics* and of politics. The state of the world appeared to him so hopeless that he no longer took pleasure in writing about it. In switching from political to cultural criticism, Macdonald saved his spirits, but he sacrificed some of the hardness and bite of his prose. Mass culture was a menace, but not so great a menace as the general dehumanization of modern life; it was a symptom, not the source, of the sickness of American society. Also it was an easier target. Practically everybody deplored mass culture, at least in theory. Macdonald's voice, accordingly, was no longer as disturbing as it had been in the days when *Politics*, almost alone among radical magazines, stood out against the cruelties and idiocies alike of Communism and "democracy."

Originally an admirer of the Soviet Union, Macdonald had abandoned Stalinism after the Moscow trials. For some time thereafter he was a leading member of the Trotskyite party. In the forties he gradually abandoned Marxism altogether. Thus although he opposed the Second World War, at its outset, on Marxist grounds, his Marxism, as the war continued, began to give way to pacifism, and by the end of the war Macdonald's indictment of American society was not so much that it was capitalist as that it was totalitarian. By the end of the war, he was arguing that the effect of the war itself, of total war in general, had been to brutalize all participants, thus breeding in America the disease that Americans were ostensibly fighting.

5. Macdonald himself, however, has the impression that "I'm better known for *Politics* than for my articles in *The New Yorker*." "A 'little magazine,' " he notes, "is often more intensively read (and circulated) than the big commercial magazines, being a more individual expression and so appealing with special force to other individuals of like minds." (*Memoirs of a Revolutionist*, p. 27.)

What Macdonald gradually realized, in short, was that the Allied war effort had emptied itself of political content. One could not even say, with Marx, that the war was a capitalist war. Rather, the war had become "unconscious" (irrational), an end in itself. "Everything possible is done by our leaders to *de-politicalize* this war. As it grinds automatically on, as it spreads and becomes more violent, the conflict becomes less and less meaningful, a vast nightmare in which we are all involved and from which whatever hopes and illusions we may have had have by now leaked out." The Office of War Information in a directive to its propagandists characterized the enemy as "a bully, a murderer, a thief, a gangster, etc., but only once in the lengthy document as a *fascist*."[6] Likewise General Patton urged his troops to kill the "German bastards" and the "purple pissing Japs" so that "thirty years from now, when you are sitting at the fire with your grandson on your knee and he asks you what you did in the Great World War II, you won't have to say: 'I shovelled shit in Louisiana.'" Patton's speech seemed to Macdonald to express the essential quality of the war. "At once flat and theatrical, brutal and hysterical, coarse and affected, violent and empty—in these fatal antinomies the nature of World War II reveals itself: the maximum of physical devastation accompanied by the minimum of human meaning."[7]

The atomic bombing of Hiroshima swept away whatever suspicions of benevolence still clung to the Allied cause. Even before Hiroshima, Macdonald had written: "To say that civilization cannot survive another such war is a truism; the question is whether it can survive this one."[8] The advent of the bomb drove him to the further reflection that the survival of civilization depended on the defeat, not of capitalism, but of the

---

6. "The Unconscious War," *Memoirs of a Revolutionist*, p. 110.
7. "My Favorite General," *Memoirs of a Revolutionist*, pp. 95–6.
8. "Horrors—Ours or Theirs?" *Memoirs of a Revolutionist*, p. 159.

national state itself. The bomb was not a historic anomaly, it was "the natural product of the kind of society we have created."

> It is as easy, normal, and unforced an expression of the American Way of Life as electric ice-boxes, banana splits, and hydromatic-drive automobiles. We do not dream of a world in which atomic fission will be "harnessed to constructive ends." The new energy will be at the service of the rulers; it will change their strength but not their aims. The underlying populations should regard this new source of energy with lively interest—the interest of victims.[9]

Under the new conditions of warfare, "every individual who wants to save his humanity—and indeed his skin—had better begin thinking 'dangerous thoughts' about sabotage, resistance, rebellion, and the fraternity of all men everywhere. The mental attitude known as 'negativism' is a good start."[1] It is hardly necessary to add that Macdonald never got much beyond the mental attitude known as negativism. The most telling comment on the situation of the American radical in the middle of the twentieth century is that although sabotage, resistance, and rebellion never seemed more appropriate, they were at the same time out of the question, if only because of the incalculable power of the nation-states the overthrow of which seemed to have become the precondition of survival. Revolution, as always, remained the remotest of political possibilities. A man who believed that revolution was the only solution to the problems of American society could only conclude that the problems were utterly insoluble.

That was exactly the conclusion at which Macdonald very soon arrived. "A revolutionary change," he wrote in September, 1945, " . . . never seemed farther away. What, then, can a man

9. "The Bomb," *Memoirs of a Revolutionist*, pp. 169-70.
1. Ibid., p. 170.

do *now*? How can he escape playing his part in the ghastly process?" He could escape it, Macdonald thought for a while, "quite simply by not playing it." The atomic scientists, if they had acted as whole men instead of specialists, might simply have refused to work on the bomb. But earlier in the same essay Macdonald had pointed out that "the social order is an impersonal mechanism, the war is an impersonal process, and they grind along automatically; if some of the human parts rebel at their function, they will be replaced by more amenable ones; and their rebellion will mean that they are simply thrust aside, without changing anything."[2] What, then, would the rebellion of the scientists have accomplished? Rebellion, to be effective, would have had to go beyond isolated acts of individual protest. But such a rebellion "never seemed farther away."

The cold war completed the destruction of what hopes had survived the war. When the Russians blockaded Berlin in 1948, Macdonald reasoned that the Western powers could neither withdraw their troops from Berlin nor leave them there without risking a third world war. "Both violence and non-violence, for different reasons, seem impractical today"—such was "the pacifist dilemma."[3] The Korean War likewise represented a choice of evils. On the one hand, it was necessary to resist Communist aggression; on the other hand, "the results of the Korean war have been disastrous, especially for the Korean people." "Perhaps there is no solution any longer to these agonizing problems."[4] In 1952, in a debate with Norman Mailer at Mount Holyoke College, Macdonald "chose" the West, but he did so without enthusiasm. "The choice," he remarked, "is not very stimulating."[5] Equally dispiriting was the reassessment of his earlier position in regard to the Second World War,

2. Ibid., p. 178.
3. "The Pacifist Dilemma," *Memoirs of a Revolutionist*, p. 197.
4. "I Choose the West," *Memoirs of a Revolutionist*, p. 201.
5. "Politics Past," *Memoirs of a Revolutionist*, p. 5.

to which he was driven by the course of recent events. He realized in retrospect that "the only historically real alternatives in 1939 were to back Hitler's armies, to back the Allies' armies, or to do nothing. But none of these alternatives promised any great benefit for mankind, and the one that finally triumphed has led simply to the replacing of the Nazi threat by the Communist threat, with the whole ghastly newsreel flickering through once more in a second showing." "This is one reason," Macdonald said, "I am less interested in politics than I used to be."[6]

Macdonald's choice of the West thus coincided with his withdrawal from politics. Given his statement of the problem, such a withdrawal was inevitable. Many others took the same course, without being able to state their reasons with comparable precision. The demoralization of radical intellectuals, in these darkest years of the postwar period, was very great. Nor have the succeeding years disposed of the central question Macdonald raised. If rebellion is futile and revolution unlikely, what can a man do *now*?

It is possible, however, that the question should not have been asked in the first place. It is possible that it was premature—as was the choice of the West. It is possible that Macdonald exaggerated the "automatic" character of American society, its resistance to change; just as he exaggerated that of the Soviet Union. One reason for Macdonald's despair was that he saw both the Soviet Union and the United States as totalitarian societies, obedient to a fatal dynamic of totalitarianism. True, he referred to the West, in the debate with Mailer, as an "open society," but he also declared that "we are becoming to some extent like the totalitarian enemy we are fighting."[7] Ten years earlier he had put it more strongly: "Far from decreasing

6. "I Choose the West." *Memoirs of a Revolutionist*, p. 201.
7. Ibid., p. 199.

in power, as all progressive thinkers from Jefferson to Marx and Lenin hoped and believed it would, the State is becoming an end in itself, subjugating the human being as the Church did in the Middle Ages. In the new religion of the State, which has reached full growth in Germany and Russia and which is steadily growing here, the individual is once more frozen into the hierarchical, irrational pattern of a society based on status."[8] In formulating this view of the state Macdonald was much influenced by Hannah Arendt's researches into Nazi Germany. Macdonald refers to Miss Arendt as early as 1945, in support of the proposition that totalitarian regimes make the concept of individual responsibility meaningless, indeed that that is their objective. Later he read with admiration her *Origins of Totalitarianism*, in which she argued that the essence of totalitarianism is its indifference to the utilitarian logic of everyday life. Totalitarian regimes, she contended, obey a logic of their own, the ultimate aim of which is a condition of total terror. Thus the destruction of the Jews was at once anti-utilitarian, since it impeded the war effort, and necessary, as a step toward total terror.

The only trouble with this theory was that Miss Arendt and her admirers fell in love with it. The effect of this attachment was to blind them to the differences between Stalin's Russia and Hitler's Germany. Khrushchev's de-Stalinization campaign, launched in 1956, revealed the weakness of the theory that totalitarian regimes were historically destined to pursue their insane logic to the bitter end. The objections to this theory were nowhere better stated than by Dwight Macdonald himself, in the aftermath of Khrushchev's speech to the Twentieth Party Congress. As he observed, Miss Arendt was "an enthusiastic generalizer, a system builder, and she, too [like Marx], believes in an inherent logic, a big basic pattern which cannot

8. "The Unconscious War," *Memoirs of a Revolutionist*, p. 112.

be violated." The question was, however, whether Stalin was "a normal expression of the Soviet system" or whether he was "a peculiar individual who cast his morbid shadow over a whole period of Russian history." Unless de-Stalinization was merely a temporary retreat, and Macdonald thought it was something more than that, it now appeared that Stalin was a "peculiar individual" and that the Soviet system was far more flexible than the prophets of totalitarianism had imagined.[9]

Macdonald's choice of the West and his general political despair rested in part on a theory of the nature of totalitarianism which events later showed to have been too rigid. In this sense his despair, like that of so many others, was premature. The world of the twentieth century—the Soviet Union in particular—has not turned out to be quite so grim as it looked in the late forties and early fifties. Nazi Germany itself, which looked then like the prototype to which all modern civilizations must eventually conform, more and more looks like a unique episode in human history, nonetheless appalling for that, but not so terrifying as an omen of the future. As Macdonald wrote in 1956: "Totalitarianism bends human nature, puts a terrible strain on the normal, mediocre man. When the pressure is removed, when Robespierre, Hitler, Stalin die, then human nature springs back to its normal shape, which is perhaps not very inspiring but is certainly preferable to the nightmare form given it by the totalitarians."[1]

On the strength of these observations, one might have expected Macdonald to return to political writing. If the Soviet Union was not quite hopeless, how much less hopeless was the United States! In fact, however, Macdonald did not return to political subjects. On the contrary, he announced in 1960 that he could not even bring himself to vote in the coming election.

9. "The Great Thaw," *Memoirs of a Revolutionist*, pp. 315–16.
1. Ibid., p. 317.

Thus he appeared to repeat, in milder form, the same error he had made in 1939, which he himself had later repudiated: the error of holding out for alternatives that "existed only on the ethical and ideological plane."[2] A "negativism," moreover, which could see no significant difference between Nixon and Kennedy was surely a negativism badly misplaced. It is the curious eccentricity of Macdonald's political abstention in 1960 that leads one to suspect that there was more to his negativism, all along, than a fear of an all-encompassing totalitarianism. The suspicion is strengthened by a close reading of the crucial essay, "I Choose the West," which shows that Macdonald in the very act of withdrawing from urgent political commitments was investing politics with an importance that it could no longer sustain. Like so many other intellectuals, Macdonald chose the West on the assumption that the cold war was a conflict of cultures, and on the further assumption that it was necessary to choose, in some absolute and final sense, between them. "I choose the West because I see the present conflict not as another struggle between basically similar imperialisms as was World War I but as a fight to the death between radically different cultures."[3] Having gone that far, it was easy to go the rest of the way and to define the choice (just as Sidney Hook had defined it) as a choice between "an imperfectly living, open society" and "a *perfectly* dead, closed society [my italics]."[4] The terrible demands of the cold war led Macdonald, like so many others, to confront the choice as if it were a matter of ultimate allegiance. It led him, moreover, to assume that conflict between Russian and Western cultures— "a fight to the death"—was inevitable. Not that there was noth-

2. Postscript to "I Choose the West," *Memoirs of a Revolutionist*, p. 201. I hasten to add that I myself, following Macdonald's example, took the same position with regard to the election of 1960.

3. "I Choose the West," *Memoirs of a Revolutionist*, p. 198.

4. Ibid., p. 200.

ing to choose between. The Soviet Union was a despotism; the West retained at least the vestiges of political freedom. But that did not mean that the differences could only lead to conflict. To "choose" between the two, however, was to assume that conflict between Russia and the West could not be avoided. If one assumed such a conflict, one had to choose—as most people had felt obliged to choose between Hitler and the West. But in the case of the Soviet Union and the United States, conflict was not only not inevitable but—if carried to the point of nuclear war—unthinkable. The obvious differences between the two societies did not alter the fact that the overriding issue was the avoidance of nuclear war, the search for a common ground, common interests, short of war.

As a practical matter, most intellectuals, even those who "chose" the West, tended to support both sides in whatever steps either took to diminish the possibility of armed conflict. Except for those like Sidney Hook, who defined the Soviet Union as a system of absolute depravity, the "choice" was a matter not of political action but of analysis and observation; yet most intellectuals insisted on talking as if it were a matter of political action as well, as if it reflected the available political choices. In fact, the respective nature of the two systems was quite irrelevant to the practical political choice confronting people in the 1950's—the choice between policies (whether Russian or American) which assumed that even nuclear war was preferable to "surrender" and policies which assumed that nuclear war made the concepts of victory and surrender obsolete. One could argue that American society was the most brilliant and virtuous in recorded history and Soviet Russia the most perfect tyranny, and still choose accommodation over "victory" or even "containment."

The actual differences between the two societies, in any

case, were hardly so clear-cut; but the act of "choosing" encouraged people to exaggerate them, and in particular to exaggerate Russia's resistance to change. Thus Macdonald spoke of the Soviet Union as "a perfectly dead, closed society." Macdonald, like Hook, promised to support the West "critically," but it would have been better to have taken an equally critical attitude toward Russia—that is, to have been as skeptical of sweeping generalizations about Russia, in any form, as Macdonald was skeptical of generalizations about the West. And indeed Macdonald (unlike Hook) did, later, take a critical attitude toward Russia. When it became clear that the Soviet Union was not by any means a "perfectly" closed society, Macdonald was one of the first to say so. What is important, however, is that saying so gave him so little pleasure. His sense of proportion returned, but his political passion did not revive. Having exhausted Marxism and then pacifism, he had arrived at his "end of ideology," as Daniel Bell called it, speaking for his generation as a whole.[5] Bell and others insisted that the end of ideology ought to be the beginning of something better; but even the "pragmatists," as we have seen, proceeded to make an ideology out of their lack of an ideology.

The fact is that politics without ideology, whatever else it may be, tends to become somewhat boring; and it was necessary for most people to put the ideology back into politics, whether it belonged there or not. Without ideology, politics lost its intellectual excitement. So too had religion, in Jane Addams's generation, lost its appeal as a field of argument and speculation when piety parted company with theology. For Dwight Macdonald's generation, political argument had once had the excitement of theology. Marxism, like a Jesuit school, repre-

5. See Daniel Bell: *The End of Ideology* (Glencoe: The Free Press; 1960), especially chapter 14 and epilogue.

sented among other things an exacting form of intellectual discipline.[6] For people raised in the school of Marxist polemics, the politics of the 1950's were singularly lacking in interest, because they had ceased to be a form of intellectual play. And it was not only the Marxists who suffered in this way, although they may have suffered more acutely. All intellectuals, simply by virtue of being intellectuals, approached politics with something of the same expectations; which, under the circumstances of the cold war, were bound to be disappointed unless the old fervor, the old blend of culture and politics, could somehow be recaptured.

[V]

Norman Mailer, Macdonald's adversary in the debate at Mount Holyoke in 1952, does not seem to have preserved a record of his own remarks—an uncharacteristic omission—but nobody need be in any doubt about what, in general, he said, because he has been talking for fifteen years, volubly, loudly, uproariously, on the subject of "I cannot choose"—the position he defended against Macdonald. The reasons for his inability to choose are no secret. Like Macdonald, Mailer sees American society as totalitarian, but it is suggestive of the difference between them that whereas the concept of totalitarianism always had for Macdonald a precise and definite meaning, Mailer has steadily enlarged it—as he has enlarged so many things, the length of his sentences, the heat of his indignation, the scope of his literary ambitions—until it includes everything he finds in the slightest degree distasteful: pacifists, liberals, modern architecture, Hollywood, experimental theater, homosexuals, masturbation, David Riesman,

6. Macdonald: "Politics Past," *Memoirs of a Revolutionist*, pp. 21–2.

beatniks, psychoanalysis, "minor" writers, book reviewers, fallout shelters, "the Establishment's defense of life," organized labor, mental health, motels, science, people who refuse to admit that bombs can be beautiful, people who drop bombs on other people, television, and cancer.

In order to understand Norman Mailer, it is first necessary to understand the sociology of literary success in America. English readers find Mailer baffling and outrageous partly because they do not understand the problem an American writer faces when he becomes a celebrity, the problem, apparently, being peculiar to America.[7] Many Americans are equally puzzled to find that literary success should be considered a problem. Consequently they dismiss the fear of it as an expression of the fashionable cult of "alienation." Sidney Hook, for example, cannot contain his impatience with writers who complain that success in America is worse than failure.

The hypothesis that mass culture and the popular arts—the Hollywood trap!—threaten the emergence of a significant culture of vitality and integrity because they constitute a perpetual invitation to a sell-out seems very far-fetched. Unless one is an in-

7. Beyond this, it is difficult for Englishmen to understand or sympathize with the desperation which underlies American radicalism—the sense of futility, in a gigantic country in which political debate is dominated by the organs of mass communication and in which public opinion, misinformed and even deliberately misled, seems at once powerless, when it is a question of persuading government to pursue more liberal policies, and omnipotent, when it is a question of compelling it to pursue policies even more illiberal than the ones it wants to pursue (as in the case of Cuba)—the sense of sheer futility, in such a country, which afflicts those who seek to check the suicidal impulse the American people seem bent on pursuing.

For a particularly clear illustration of this paradoxical contrast between European optimism and American despair, see George Lichtheim's review of Herbert Marcuse's *One-Dimensional Man* (*New York Review of Books*, II [Feb. 20, 1964], pp. 16–19) and the correspondence which followed between Lichtheim and some American students who took him to task for not understanding why it was necessary for any serious American scholar to think "negatively" about contemporary politics.

curable snob (I am old enough to remember intense discussions by otherwise intelligent people as to whether the cinema is an art), the forms of mass culture and the popular arts should serve as a challenge to do something with them. There are "sell-outs" of course but there are two parties to every "sell-out." The writer who "sells out" to Hollywood or the slicks cannot absolve himself of responsibility on the ground that he wouldn't be able to live as plushily as if he did. Why should he? I shall be accused of saying that I am sentencing artists and writers to starvation. But if scholars can live Renan's life of "genteel poverty" and do important work so can those who don't go to Hollywood.[8]

The problem, however, is not that writers are tempted to sell out, although it must be admitted that many people talk as if it were. The problem is only incidentally one of money; much more important is the impact of success, even an unsought success, on the writer's view of himself and his work. Success tempts him to become a public "personality," and if he gives in to the temptation, he soon discovers that it is easier to sell his personality than his ideas. His eccentricities, his foibles, his "image," in short, constitute an invaluable asset in the literary marketplace; he can trade off his "name" much as movie stars and baseball players make a profitable business of publicly endorsing other people's products. His name, moreover—at a somewhat higher level of aspiration—guarantees him a hearing; whatever he says or does, as long as the magic lasts, is automatically news. But the price, if he chooses to play this game, is that the writer has to stay in character, has to play the part that he has made for himself; for if he deviates from it, his public is no longer interested. In the same way Hollywood actors, under the "star system," are expected to play the same part over and over, their marketability depending on their predictability. But whereas the star is largely the creation of his press agents, the writer creates his part for himself and then

8. Hook: "From Alienation to Critical Integrity," *The Intellectuals*, p. 530.

proceeds not only to act it but, worse, to believe in it. At length he loses his real self and takes on a synthetic self, which he then proceeds to write about as if it were his real one. Ernest Hemingway is a notable example of the lengths to which this process of re-identification can lead. Lillian Ross's famous profile of Hemingway shows him acting out, down to the last detail of his private life, the public image of himself. Even his conversation, a mixture of sporting-world slang, assorted unintelligible grunts, and Indian language, had become a parody of the famous Hemingway style.[9] Nature imitates art; but when the art is the art of public relations, the results, for a serious writer, are likely to be disastrous.

Norman Mailer had the bad luck to achieve success with his very first book. *The Naked and the Dead* was an immediate best-seller. Mailer was twenty-five, living in Paris.

Naturally, I was blasted a considerable distance away from dead center by the size of its success, and I spent the next few years trying to gobble up the experiences of a victorious man when I was still no man at all, and had no real gift for enjoying life. Such a gift usually comes from a series of small victories artfully achieved; my experience had consisted of many small defeats, a few victories, and one explosion. So success furnished me great energy, but I wasted most of it in the gears of old habit, and had experience which was overheated, brilliant, anxious, gauche, grim—even, I suspect—killing. My farewell to an average man's experience was too abrupt; never again would I know, in the dreary way one usually knows such things, what it was like to work at a dull job, or take orders from a man one hated. If I had had a career of that in the army, it now was done—there was nothing left in the first twenty-four years of my life to write about; one way or another, my life seemed to have been mined and melted into the long reaches of the book. And so I was prominent and empty, and I had to begin life again; from now

9. Lillian Ross: *Profile of Hemingway* (New York: Simon and Schuster; 1961).

on, people who knew me would never be able to react to me as a person whom they liked or disliked in small ways, *for myself alone* (the inevitable phrase of all tear-filled confessions); no, I was a node in a new electronic landscape of celebrity, personality and status.[1]

Among other things, Mailer's unexpected triumph, at the very outset of his career, rendered him cruelly dependent on the opinion of reviewers, whose praise had assured the success of *The Naked and the Dead*. The result was that when the reviewers with one voice consigned his next work, *Barbary Shore*, to the ash-heap of literary reputation—Anthony West in *The New Yorker* said it was a book of "monolithic flawless badness"—Mailer was oppressed with a sense of failure out of all proportion to the actual defects of the book.[2] He not only read the reviews, he compulsively returned to them again and again, and when he compiled *Advertisements for Myself*, in 1959, he printed long excerpts from them, as he printed all the other derogatory comments on himself that, over the years, he had carefully saved. Already obsessed with the dream of becoming a "major writer," he was driven more and more to define his goal in terms of popular and critical acclaim; in terms, that is, of celebrity itself.[3] Unable to wrench himself out of the self-contained community, the endless convolutions of the literary circuit, into which his early success had cast him, he suffered even social snubs as if they were artistic disasters, brooding over them intently. He began his third book, *The Deer Park*, with the deliberate intention of writing another best-seller. "Six or seven years of breathing that literary air" had taught him that "a writer stayed alive in the circuits of

1. Norman Mailer: *Advertisements for Myself* (New York: G. P. Putnam's Sons; 1959), p. 92.
2. Ibid., p. 105.
3. "Before I was seventeen I had formed the desire to be a major writer." (Ibid., p. 27.)

such hatred only if he were unappreciated enough to be adored by a clique, or was so overbought by the public that he excited some defenseless nerve in the snob."

I knew if *The Deer Park* was a powerful best seller (the magical figure had become one hundred thousand copies for me) that I would then have won. I would be the first serious writer of my generation to have a best seller twice, and so it would not matter what was said about the book. Half of publishing might call it cheap, dirty, sensational, second-rate, and so forth and so forth, but it would be weak rage and could not hurt, for the literary world suffers a spot of the national taint—a serious writer is certain to be considered major if he is also a best seller; in fact, most readers are never convinced of his value until his books do well.[4]

The Deer Park "did well," but it did not sell 100,000 copies. It sold half that many. "Poised for an enormous sale or a failure," Mailer found that "a middling success was cruel to take." "Like a starved revolutionary in a garret, I had compounded out of need and fever and vision and fear nothing less than a madman's confidence in the identity of my being and the wants of all others, and it was a new dull load to lift and to bear, this knowledge that I had no magic so great as to hasten the time of the apocalypse, but that instead I would be open like all others to the attritions of half-success and small failure."[5] But instead of profiting from this self-knowledge—a self-knowledge which characterizes so much of the autobiographical writing in *Advertisements* but which exerts so little influence on Mailer's progress as a writer—he turned to a new undertaking more grandiose than ever, an undertaking destined to fail, it would seem, before it was fairly begun. He now proposed to write a long novel, a major novel on which his claims as a major

4. Ibid., p. 241.
5. Ibid., p. 247.

writer would rest once and for all, a novel so big, so shocking, so outrageously true to life, that it would not even be printable in America but would have to circulate, like *Tropic of Cancer* and *Ulysses*, as "an outlaw of the underground." It would take ten years to write and would have, when it appeared, "a deep explosion of effect."[6] But the magnitude of this enterprise, together with the advance publicity which Mailer lavished upon it, was self-defeating. Instead of writing "the long novel," Mailer wrote *The Presidential Papers* and then, with the excuse that he needed money, turned to another potboiler, *The American Dream*, which he sold as a serial to *Esquire* as "proof against the advertisements I had devoted to myself, against the enemies I had made, and even against the expectations of those who were ready to like my work most." In a recent interview, Mailer claims to have given up his ambition to be a "great writer" in favor of the more modest ambition to be "a professional writer—and one of the best professional writers in the country." Yet he still talks of "that big novel." He says it will be 3,000 pages long.[7]

Meanwhile Mailer had acquired a public personality which he proceeded to exploit in the most obvious imaginable way by writing a series of advertisements for himself, the first of which were published under that title and the rest of which made up *The Presidential Papers* of 1963. In freely admitting his wish to promote his reputation, Mailer may actually have avoided some of the psychic dangers of that kind of publicity. It is yet not clear how fully Mailer himself believes in the myth of Mailer. It is reassuring to find that the best writing in *Advertisements* is the purely autobiographical writing. On the other hand, all that one learns of his private life—if it is any longer possible to distinguish between his private and his public

6. Ibid., p. 477.
7. *Observer* [London], April 26, 1964.

life—suggests that Mailer increasingly acts as he believes his public expects him to act. *The Presidential Papers* consists of set pieces, of which Mailer is at once the reporter and the central character, and they show him to be acting very much *in* character as well: instructing Kennedy in his role as a charismatic leader, instructing Mrs. Kennedy in her role as a leader of the national taste, crashing the press conference after the Patterson-Liston fight. "I'm pulling this caper for a reason," Mailer tells Liston. "I know a way to build the next fight from a $200,000 dog in Miami to a $2,000,000 gate in New York."[8] His terms of reference confirm one's impression that Mailer's values have become indistinguishable from those of the entertainment world which he hates but from the embrace of which he seems unable to free himself. Success, for the American writer, is a carnival mirror in which he sees not himself but a cruel distortion of himself, without, however, being able any longer to tell them apart.

But there is another side to the matter. Mailer is not only a writer, he is a political and cultural radical bent on bringing about "a revolution in the consciousness of our time."[9] As such he is recognizably descended, for all his seeming eccentricity, from the line of Randolph Bourne and Lincoln Steffens. Like them, he has conducted his life as if it were an experiment. He has tried to plot the course of his career very deliberately, in order to achieve a certain end: the promotion of his own reputation, but also the promotion, in a somewhat old-fashioned sense, of the public happiness. His personal and his political ambitions run together, and it is hard to sort them out. His determination to write best-sellers, for instance, reflects his mis-

---

8. Norman Mailer: *The Presidential Papers* (New York: G. P. Putnam's Sons; 1963), p. 265.

9. *Advertisements*, p. 17. Cf. Steffens: "Before I die, I believe I can help to bring about an essential change in the American mind." (Above, p. 272.)

directed ambition to be a "major" writer, but it also reflects a
legitimate unwillingness to settle for a limited readership of
avant-garde intellectuals. Likewise his ambition to put himself
at the center of the political stage expresses more than unre-
strained egotism; it also expresses a desire to avoid the typical
fate of radical intellectuals, that of political irrelevance. Mailer
had a taste of that in 1948, when he worked for Henry Wallace's Progressive Party, and his revulsion was intensified by a
personal humiliation which attended the occasion of his leaving the party in 1949. Invited to speak at a "peace conference"
at the Waldorf-Astoria, Mailer disappointed his audience by
saying (as he remembered afterward) that "only socialism
could save the world, and America was not close to that, and
Russia was not close, and people should not believe in countries and patriotism anyway, and peace conferences like this
gave the idea that one could, and so were wrong." The feeling
that he was "betraying" those who had come to hear him drove
him close to tears, "and to avoid that disaster, I screwed up my
face into a snarl, feeling like a miserable and undeserving rat,
and then some flash bulbs went off," and the picture of his embarrassment and degradation became a matter of public record.[1]

After the Wallace campaign, Mailer made no further ventures into political sectarianism. Instead he attempted, as Lincoln Steffens had attempted, to play the part of a devil's advocate, "court wit," or "jester"; that is, he attempted to speak
for the "underground" in the very citadel of the "establishment."[2] Like Steffens, Mailer regards himself as an "outlaw,"
and he shares Steffens's suspicion that successful men are also
outlaws in disguise. Thus he describes Kennedy as "an outlaw's sheriff . . . one sheriff who could have been an outlaw
himself," and in directing a series of open letters to Kennedy,

1. *Advertisements*, p. 410.
2. *Papers*, pp. 1, 8.

Mailer was consciously addressing him, as Steffens had addressed the "big bad men" of his time, as "one crook to another."[3] The difference between them is that Mailer is far more deeply involved in the world of the establishment than Steffens was ever involved in the world of the big bad men. Not that Mailer has had any more influence over national policy. He claims to have assured Kennedy's election by writing of him as an "existential hero," but Kennedy did not show his gratitude, once in office, by following Mailer's advice. Mailer had no discernible influence on the Kennedy administration; but he nevertheless came much closer to sharing its values than Steffens came to sharing the values of the "good people" of his day. To be sure, Steffens, like Mailer, worshipped success, but he was sufficiently critical of his own motives not to pursue it for himself; the proof of which is that he survived twenty years of literary neglect and capped them by writing, not a gigantic monument to his own ambition such as Mailer has planned for himself, but the *Autobiography*, a work that owes its charm in large part to its being so utterly unpretentious. Mailer, on the other hand, is far too committed to the culture he claims to despise to be an effective critic of it, either from without or from within. He is not so much a devil's advocate as a man who has found it convenient to play the part of a devil's advocate, precisely because that is the part which his public expects him to play. "In America," he has written, "few people will trust you unless you are irreverent"; but the truth is that people trust you most when you merely *seem* to be irreverent.[4]

The fact is that Mailer's brand of cultural radicalism, a compound of Marx and Freud, has long since lost its capacity to shock. It is not that Marx and Freud themselves are no

3. *The Presidential Papers* (London: André Deutsch; 1964), n.p. [first page of unpaginated introduction written for English edition].
4. Ibid.

longer shocking or that a radical critique of American society cannot be fashioned out of their ideas. Herbert Marcuse, a radical thinker who makes no great show of his radicalism, has done that, and what is even more unusual, he has added some ideas of his own.[5] In some circles, however, Marxism and psychoanalysis have become clichés just because they have been associated for so long with the kind of self-conscious and mannered rebellion typified by Norman Mailer; and as clichés, they are so little shocking that it is necessary for Mailer himself constantly to try to go beyond them, to make more and more strident assertions of his nonconformity, and finally to throw his own person, in attitudes of rude and outrageous defiance, into the struggle, in the hope of making some ultimate proof of his revolutionary sincerity. But the deeper his involvement in the game of shocking for the sake of shock, the more innocuous is the impact of Mailer's rebellion. The wider the net of his indignation, the more his strictures come to resemble those interminable attacks on American "conformity" that were so popular in the 1950's. The deeper he digs in his probing for the sexual roots of social disorder, the shallower his observations become. He can write in all seriousness, and not only write but admiringly quote the sentence in another context: "The orgasm is anathema to the liberal mind because it is the inescapable existential moment."[6] *The White Negro*, which Mailer regards as the most daring of his writings and which the editors of *Dissent* published with great fanfare, is a rehearsal of old clichés about Negro sexuality; a reassertion, James Baldwin called it, of "the myth of the sexuality of Negroes which Norman Mailer, like so many others, refuses to

5. See Herbert Marcuse: *Eros and Civilization* (Boston: Beacon Press; 1955); and *One-Dimensional Man* (London: Routledge & Kegan Paul; 1964).
6. *Papers* (Putnam's), p. 198.

give up."[7] In his more reflective moods, Mailer can still talk effectively, as when, confronted with Baldwin's observation, he amended his thesis by saying that "*any* submerged class is going to be more accustomed to sexuality than a leisure class."[8] But reflective moods, on the whole, are missing from Mailer's latest work. In the same breath he goes on to say that Negroes are more sexual than whites because they "come from Africa" and "tropical people are usually more sexual," and that in any case Baldwin in attacking *The White Negro* is "being totalitarian."[9] Mailer's increasingly indiscriminate use of the word "totalitarianism" indicates what has gone wrong with his social and political analysis. Reaching for terms of ultimate condemnation, his voice becomes indistinguishable from the voice of those cultural critics for whom the quality of television or the design of the latest automobiles is a burning political issue. Mailer himself says of television: "Every time one sees a bad television show, one is watching the nation get ready for the day when a Hitler will come."[1]

It is not surprising that so much of Mailer's radicalism approximates the liberalism of the New Frontier. Take away the talk of "existentialism" and Mailer's praise of Kennedy sounds a great deal like Richard Rovere's. If Kennedy eventually disappointed him, it was because Mailer, like the liberals, expected

7. Ibid., p. 146.
8. Ibid. It must be admitted, moreover, that Baldwin himself comes close to endorsing the myth of superior Negro sexuality. In *The Fire Next Time* (New York: Dial Press; 1963), pp. 56–7, he accused white Americans of being "terrified of sensuality," adding somewhat defensively: "The word 'sensual' is not intended to bring to mind quivering dusky maidens or priapic studs." I understand that in Baldwin's new play, *Blues for Mister Charlie*, the same idea is asserted in a much cruder form, without qualifications.
9. *Papers*, pp. 146–7.
1. Ibid., p. 134.

Kennedy and his wife to set in motion the long-awaited "revolution in the consciousness of our time." The fact that Kennedy "was young, that he was physically handsome, and that his wife was attractive," convinced Mailer in 1960 that his accession to the Presidency would be "an existential event."[2] Under Eisenhower, "the best minds and bravest impulses" had been "alienated" from "the faltering history which was made"; under Kennedy they might return to the seat of power.[3] Kennedy as President might be "capable of giving direction to the time, able to encourage a nation," as other existential heroes had done, "to discover the deepest colors of its character."[4] Naturally Mailer was disappointed; the nature of his expectations left him very little choice.

A hopeless undertaking from the start, Mailer's ambition to make of himself "some sort of center about which all that had been lost must now rally" was flawed by the terms in which the ambition was conceived, flawed by the old confusion of politics and culture.[5] The political results of his efforts were negligible, and the literary consequences, judging from his recent writing, were disastrous. His attempts to enrich the cultural life of the nation ended by impoverishing his own art. All that remained was the receding vision of "the big book," but "when I sit down," Mailer confessed at the end of *Advertisements*, "when I sit down, soon after this book is done, to pick up again on my novel, I do not know if I can do it, for

2. Ibid., p. 26.
3. Ibid., p. 43.
4. Ibid., p. 42.
5. Ibid., p. 81. "He is asking from politics . . . what it cannot give," writes Richard Gilman; "we may speak of the art of politics but political procedures and truth are not the procedures and truth of art. A president is not 'supposed to enrich the real life of his people,' he is supposed to protect and preserve it, enrichment being precisely the function of the artist." ("Why Mailer Wants to Be President," *NR*, CL [Feb. 8, 1964], p. 23.)

if the first sixty pages are not at all bad, I may still have wasted too much of myself, and if I have—what a loss." Still a young man—he was thirty-six—Mailer, like Randolph Bourne, mourned the loss of youth. "How poor to go to death with no more than the notes of good intention."[6]

[VI]

With Norman Mailer, the body of ideas and assumptions which I have called the new radicalism achieved some kind of final and definitive statement. The confusion of power and art, the effort to liberate the social and psychological "underground" by means of political action, the fevered pursuit of experience, the conception of life as an experiment, the intellectual's identification of himself with the outcasts of society —these things could be carried no further without carrying them to absurdity. Perhaps Mailer had carried them past that point already.

Mailer was not, of course, a representative man of his time in the strictest sense of the term. Even in New York literary circles, he was an eccentric; men such as Irving Howe, the editor of *Dissent*, and Norman Podhoretz, the editor of *Commentary*, were probably more typical products of that milieu. Yet these men, more modest than Mailer in their ambitions and more restrained in their manner of expression, nevertheless shared many of Mailer's opinions, and their writings showed also the effects, on the one hand, of the "sense of comradeship and solidarity," and on the other, of the "feeling of beleaguered hostility" toward the rest of society, that have accompanied

6. *Advertisements*, p. 477.

the emergence of the intellectuals as a social class.[7] But in any case I have not attempted, in any of the studies in this book, to deal with representative or typical people. Dwight Macdonald was no more typical than Mailer; neither was Mabel Luhan or Randolph Bourne or Lincoln Steffens. Their lives express, not some sort of norm, but certain possibilities in a certain line of thought or action, which in many cases these men and women set out quite deliberately to explore to their furthest limits.

Therein lies the fascination of such careers. The idiosyncratic is sometimes more revealing than the normal (which in any case, where the history of ideas is concerned, is exceedingly hard to define), the extremes are sometimes more revealing than the middle-of-the-road—providing, of course, that one remembers precisely that they are extremes. As Richard Gilman said of Mailer, in reviewing *The Presidential Papers*, "Mailer was engaged in defining the President's existence by his own, as in some case, we all were. But we were at a much lower and more innocent level of the game, we had not institutionalized ourselves into an alternative to the President or into his counterpart, and we lacked a mystique and a vehicle for imposing it."[8] If it is important to understand that "we were at a much lower and more innocent level of the game," it is also important to recognize, in the first place, that we were playing it at all—to recognize, that is, that the megalomanic fantasies of omnipotence which stand forth so sharply in the careers of men like Norman Mailer and Colonel House exist, in more muted form, in all of us, as the ambitions of Colonel House, for instance, were mirrored, in colors more subdued, in Lincoln Colcord.

7. Renata Adler: "Polemic and the New Reviewers," *New Yorker*, XL (July 4, 1964), p. 64 (a review of Howe's *A World More Attractive* and Podhoretz's *Doings and Undoings*).

8. "Why Mailer Wants to Be President," p. 19.

I have argued that these fantasies of omnipotence, together with their concomitant fears of hostility and persecution, spring from the isolation of American intellectuals, as a class, from the main currents of American life. I have argued further that it was their sense of isolation which drove intellectuals to identify themselves with what Benjamin Ginzburg called the "practical sweep of American life." William James once compared the "tough-minded" to the hard-bitten men of the mining frontier, the "tender-minded" to the "tenderfoot" New Englanders, overrefined and effete. "Their mutual reaction," he said, "is very much like that that takes place when Bostonian tourists mingle with a population like that of Cripple Creek."[9] A Bostonian himself, who nevertheless strove to be "tough-minded" in his philosophy, James captured, in this image, the anxiety, the secret self-contempt, which runs through so much of the history of the twentieth-century intellectual. From James to Norman Mailer, different as they are in so many obvious respects, there is a curious line of descent. Half a century after James delivered his first lecture on pragmatism, Norman Mailer forced himself into the thick of the Patterson-Liston fight—another Bostonian tourist in the guise of a "Rocky Mountain tough."

9. William James: *Pragmatism and Four Essays from The Meaning of Truth* (Cleveland: Meridian Books; 1961), pp. 22–3.

INDEX

CHRISTOPHER LASCH was born in Omaha, Nebraska, in 1932. He attended Harvard (B.A., 1954) and Columbia University (M.A., 1955; Ph.D., 1961) and has taught history at Williams College (1957–9), at Roosevelt University (1960–1), and at the State University of Iowa (1961–6); he is now professor of history at Northwestern University. Winner of the Bowdoin Prize of Harvard in 1954, he has held both the Erb Fellowship, 1955–6, and the Gilder Fellowship, 1956–7, at Columbia University. Mr. Lasch is the author of one previous book, *The American Liberals and the Russian Revolution* (1962); he has edited *The Social Thought of Jane Addams* and has contributed articles to *The Journal of Southern History, The Political Science Quarterly, The Nation, The New York Review of Books,* and other periodicals. He lives in Evanston, Illinois, with his wife, the former Nell Commager, and their four children.

VINTAGE POLITICAL SCIENCE
AND SOCIAL CRITICISM